WINNERS DREAM

A Journey from Corner Store to Corner Office

BILL McDERMOTT

with Joanne Gordon

SIMON & SCHUSTER

New York • London • Toronto • Sydney • New Delhi

Simon & Schuster
1230 Avenue of the Americas
New York, NY 10020

First Simon & Schuster hardcover edition October 2014

SIMON & SCHUSTER and colophon are registered trademarks of Simon & Schuster, Inc.

"Ithaca" is excerpted from *C. P. Cavafy: Collected Poems* by C. P. Cavafy, introduction,
notes and commentary, and translation copyright © 2009 by Daniel Mendelsohn.
Used by permission of Alfred A. Knopf, an imprint of Knopf Doubleday Publishing
Group, a division of Random House LLC. All rights reserved.

For information about special discounts for bulk purchases, please contact
Simon & Schuster Special Sales at 1-866-506-1949 or business@simonandschuster.com

The Simon & Schuster Speakers Bureau can bring authors to your live event.
For more information or to book an event, contact the Simon & Schuster Speakers Bureau
at 1-866-248-3049 or visit our website at www.simonspeakers.com.

Interior design by Dana Sloan
Jacket design by Jackie Seow
Jacket photograph by Blake Little

Manufactured in the United States of America

10 9

Library of Congress Cataloging-in-Publication Data

McDermott, Bill.
    Winners dream : a journey from corner store to corner office / Bill McDermott with
Joanne Gordon.
      pages cm
1. McDermott, Bill. 2. Chief executive officers—United States—Biography. 3. Businesspeople—United States—Biography. 4. Entrepreneurship—United States. 5. Success in
business—United States. I. Title.
    HC102.5.A2M345 2014
    338.7'61005092—dc23
[B]
                                                                        2014016609

ISBN 978-1-4767-6108-4
ISBN 978-1-4767-6110-7 (ebook)

To my mother, Kathy McDermott.
For everything I was, am, and ever will be,
I owe it all to you.

Some people see things as they are and say, why?
I dream things that never were and say, why not?

— ROBERT F. KENNEDY
quoting George Bernard Shaw,
University of Kansas, 1968

CONTENTS

PART 1

HUNGRY

1

OPTIMISM

Nothing splendid has ever been achieved except by those who dared believe that something inside them was superior to circumstance.

—BRUCE BARTON

HEAR MY LITTLE brother yell, so I whip my head around and see smoke coming down our short staircase. Kevin is upstairs getting ready for bed. Our baby sister, Gennifer, is sleeping in the adjacent room at the back of our small house. Mom and I are in the kitchen washing dishes, and my father is working the night shift at Con Edison.

I race after my mom to the top of the stairs, where we see the flames.

This is real, I think. I am twelve years old, and our house is on fire. *We gotta move.*

I grab Kevin's hand as Mom runs through the thickening smoke to pluck Gennifer from her crib. We bolt down the stairs and out the front door, and make it to the street, where we wait for fire trucks.

More than the screams of sirens getting closer, the sound that resonates is the calm voice of my mother, and the words she speaks as we stand by the curb, our second story ablaze.

"It's okay, it's okay," she keeps saying, holding Gennifer in one arm and wrapping the other around Kevin and me. "This isn't a sad moment. It's a great moment. We've all gotten out safely. We've been through worse, and we will get through this." Again and again she repeats this pledge, like a lullaby. I believe her because she believes it. And because Mom was right; we had gotten through worse.

HOME BASE

I was born in Flushing, New York, in the borough of Queens, in 1961. During my first ten years, my parents, my two brothers, my sister, and I lived in a succession of working-class neighborhoods on New York State's Long Island: places such as College Point, Hicksville, Babylon, Brentwood—all blue-collar towns where my parents moved us from one rental apartment to another. Eventually we landed in a small, foreclosed house on Meadow Lane in the waterside town of Amityville, New York. The year we moved in, Amityville had yet to become known for its *other* house: that large Dutch Colonial on Ocean Avenue made infamous by the *Amityville Horror* movie posters. People in Amityville would call it the "the horror house," and tourists drove into our town just to see it.

My family's home was a quarter the size of the horror house but roomier than any of the apartments we had lived in previously. Located on the working-class side of town, our house had been so neglected by its previous inhabitants that when we moved in, as renters with an option to buy, we found dead squirrels and rats in its walls once we started to fix it up. We rebuilt the house while living in it, which felt like changing a fan belt while driving sixty miles per hour. But we had no choice. We were lucky to have found a house we could afford, and fixing it up felt like a privilege, and a family affair.

On weekends, relatives and friends descended upon our narrow slice of property with hammers and ladders, kindness, and maybe my favorite jelly doughnuts that my grandparents brought in from Stork's, a German bakery in Whitestone, Queens. Everyone worked together, reinforcing wood girders, replacing Sheetrock, reskinning the exterior with aluminum siding, all in a flurry of camaraderie that would one day remind me of that Amish community barn-raising scene from the 1985 movie *Witness*. My father would write checks for the materials as he got the money, and thanks to the generosity of friends and family, most of the labor was free. For more complicated stuff, my papa, a general contractor and construction foreman for the high-rises going up along the nearby Rockaway Peninsula, called in an expert electrician or plumber to handle a job on the cheap.

The renovation brought our house up in value, and my parents were finally able to pull together enough money for a down payment on an $18,000, thirty-year fixed-rate mortgage. For my parents, homeownership was a step up and a great source of pride. For me, it was home, and the happiest place in the world, despite its imperfections.

Even spruced up, ours was still the kind of house you could drive by hundreds of times and not notice. And because of the flooding, it was in a constant state of repair. The structure sat on an uneven slab of concrete next to the canal that ran behind the house, which meant that when big storms hit, water poured into our first floor. The canal overflowed into our house with such predictability that with every warning of heavy rains my mother began placing a two-foot-tall statue of Saint Jude—the patron saint of hopeless causes—in front of the house. If anyone could hold the flood back, it would be Saint Jude! Eventually the statue itself would also be underwater.

All that flooding formed stress cracks in the walls and the house's foundation, so as time passed, it no longer required an overflowing canal for water to find its way inside. Even after a light rainfall, one of us would have to hike to the hardware store to rent a wet vac. Sucking up puddles in our living room became as routine as shoveling snow.

LOSS

When the doctors first told my parents that their newborn son, my little brother, James Michael, might live for only a few days, my mom had insisted on taking Jamie home from the hospital and learning to care for him. For the next five years, the poor little guy went through major surgeries, including a colostomy. Despite all his medical complications, Jamie brought amazing joy into our family's life. We were so full of love for little Jamie, with his head of wavy, light brown hair and bright brown eyes. I swear, he just kept smiling through it all. In our eyes, he was an angel.

I was seven when Jamie passed away in his sleep. He was five. The day he was carried out of our Babylon apartment on a stretcher under a blanket, my mother channeled her energy into lifting the rest of us up and out of our grief, telling us that the death of her son was God's will because Jamie had so much good work to do as an angel in heaven. Over and over she said this, a refrain that came to nest in my head and my heart, becoming truth.

My mother, Kathy McDermott, had an ability to feel blessed instead of cursed during times of grave sadness or instability. She could separate life's difficulties from the gifts those difficulties brought. Even after caring for and praying and loving Jamie for all those years, she rallied enough strength the day we lost him to stave off her family's heartache by giving the rest of us the gift of a powerful idea: *our sweet angel Jamie was in a better place, and so are we for having known him.* Now it was his turn to watch over us.

. . .

Five years after Jamie's passing, with our house on fire, my mother's bobbing optimism once again pops to the surface, unsinkable. "We'll fix it up. We've done it before, and we'll do it again," she tells us. Standing next to her on the street, I know that she isn't just trying to make us feel better. She is working her magic by refusing to dwell on the tragedy of the moment, and, instead, she is moving on by telling us what she believes: there is nothing in that house more important than what is standing outside of it.

Even on a dark, smoke-filled night, my mom has the power to convince me that the sky is blue and limitless.

SACRIFICE

My brother, Kevin, and I were in the backseat of our green Chevy Impala. It was a few years before we moved to Amityville, and my parents were driving us to Bay Shore, Long Island. Dad turned onto a pretty street and slowed down the car in front of a single-floor ranch house, the kind that was a dime a dozen on Long Island, for people who had a dime. My mother, she loved this house, but Dad couldn't get the loan, even though he was moonlighting as a security guard and driving a cab in addition to his main employment. Their disappointment was palpable, even to a nine-year-old in the backseat. Driving by at five miles per hour, I sensed a rare sadness in my mom, a woman who always insisted "Money is only as good as the happiness it can buy you and those you love." My heart hurt because my parents couldn't get that house. Years later, when I had my own car, I'd take my kid sister to the wealthy parts of Long Island and do my own slow drive down the tony streets. "We're going to live in one of those houses one day," I'd tell her. The appeal of a grand house did not diminish the joy I got from our modest home, which made me as happy as living in the Taj Mahal. I gave my dad all the credit he deserved for being able to buy it and keep us in it.

My father, Bill McDermott, was a hard worker. His definition of success was punching the clock every day and showing up for work when he was needed. As a high-voltage troubleshooter for Con Edison, New York City's electric company, he descended into the dark tunnels that snaked beneath Queens and Manhattan, sometimes lowering himself into manholes that were still on fire after underground explosions. His job, as he explained to me, was to service the city's huge electric feeders by using a blowtorch to melt copper so it formed a bond on a feeder to keep water and other materials from penetrating the electrical system. His work buddies called him "the Spider" not only because he was so good at navigating the web of underground cables that powered New York City, but also because he could weave hot liquid copper around thick power lines with the dexterity of Spider-Man shooting webs from his wrists to wrap around criminals. My dad took great pride in the craft of soldering and cable splicing. In my mind, he was a real-life superhero.

His schedule, however, was as predictable as a power outage. Sometimes our house phone would ring at one in the morning, and Dad would climb out of bed, put on jeans, a T-shirt, and industrial overalls, and then go scrape ice off the car windshield so he could drive into lower Manhattan to figure out how to get the power back on before Wall Street's opening bell. His was hard, physical, dangerous labor. Once, he was rushed to the hospital after a drunk driver plowed through safety cones and crashed into an aboveground transformer that he was repairing. By the time we got to the hospital, he had sixty-five stitches.

"Dad, how you doing?"

"Never been better," he replied, as if he had just returned home from a regular day at work. "How was your trip here?" Like Mom, Dad didn't dwell.

Yet for as hard as he worked, financial stability was elusive. Trying to support a family with four kids, dogs, while making every house and car payment, plus shouldering years of unexpected expenses, all on a cable-splicer's salary, was the epitome of the working-class treadmill. And for thirty-seven years at Con Edison, he never dialed it back, earning promotions that led him to a top-paying union job. Still, expenses just kept flowing.

My folks were not poor. We weren't impoverished. We had it much better than other families who had to go on food stamps or welfare, in many cases despite their best efforts. But the money from each paycheck went fast. Some months there just wasn't enough cash to pay for everything.

I understood all this because I had courtside seats to the pressures that come with living paycheck to paycheck, and the challenges of a young marriage. My parents had me when my mom was eighteen years old and my dad was twenty-two, so in a sense, the three of us sort of grew up together, which made it easier for me to relate to them, and was possibly why, as they gazed at their dream house through the Impala's windows, their own longing washed over me. Man, how I wanted them to have that house.

That money was tight was no secret. In our small homes and apartments, I was privy to life's real problems, hearing things that most kids don't, and always taking internal notes. I think I was a lot more curious and mature than most kids my age, listening more than I talked. And although my mom and dad did not grouse about their problems and blame anyone or anything for their money troubles, they didn't go out of their way to shelter their oldest child from reality. Instead of being sent outside or plopped in front of the TV, I'd stay at our round kitchen table listening to my parents figure out how to pay the bills and get through the cycles of daily life.

The unfiltered exposure to my family's circumstances taught me that hard work did not always pay off. I also understood that anything earned or given could be taken away: a house, a job, a brother. I developed a bias for truth, especially news no one wanted to hear, because the more I knew, the more quickly I could find a solution instead of dwelling on a problem.

JOY

Every year, my dad saved enough money to get our family to the New Jersey Shore for a week or two during the summer. We'd rent a beach bungalow in the seaside town of Stone Harbor and spend our days on the beach. Dad loved to show me the paycheck that included his vacation pay added to his regular weekly salary. The number on the check seemed so big! Even if we barely had enough gas in the car to make it back to Amityville, we cheered that Dad got his family to the shore.

Year round, good memories outweighed the rough ones: Friday nights, my dad arriving home for the weekend and turning up Ray Charles's "Busted" on the record player as my mom cooked dinner. Me, watching *The Honeymooners* reruns with my parents, having no clue what was so funny but laughing hysterically because they were. My dad, Kevin, and me sitting in our empty living room after the house had been ravaged by another flood, the three of us cheering as the New York Jets football game played on a TV that we'd propped up on a picnic table because the living room furniture was piled up on the front lawn to dry out. The whole family eating the filleted fluke I'd caught from my twelve-foot-long Sears Gamefisher, with its 7.5-horsepower Ted Williams engine that barely powered me from the canal to the Great South Bay and back. Playing hoops with Kevin next to our house, where Dad had perched a net. Treating my sister, Gennifer, to the movies the first the time I watched Rocky Balboa scale those seventy-two steps in front of the Philadelphia Museum of Art. My mom, tucking me in and insisting, "Bill, the best part of you is you."

We laughed a lot. For years, at family get-togethers, my nana loved to retell the story of the night she was visiting us and sharing Gennifer's bed in Amityville when a scurrying sound from within the walls woke them up.

"What's that?" Nana asked.

"Don't worry, Nana, it's just the rats," replied her barely stirring granddaughter. "You can go back to sleep."

Amityville had its fair share of rats—big ones—especially near the water. And when rats have a history with a certain location, such as an abandoned house, you can bet they'll come back, even once the house is inhabited. We weren't stepping over rats, but a few did play in our walls, so my family put up with the uninvited guests. My sister especially did not like them, but in an act of heroism that night in bed, she masked her fear with nonchalance to help our nana feel safe. Nana just assumed that she had a brave little soldier lying next to her. "Don't worry, Nana, it's just the rats" was a punch line Nana would repeat for years.

If there was a reason to celebrate, we milked it. On New Year's, the whole family would stay out until the early morning hours, often dancing and eating at the home of a family we knew that owned the famous Italian restaurant Angelo's of Mulberry Street in New York City; they threw unbelievable parties at their home about a mile from our house. For big occasions, my family went all out. On Christmas Eves, after we were in bed, Dad would sneak outside and throw pebbles on the roof to simulate Santa's reindeer landing. He had us convinced that if we got up and walked around, Santa would split because he didn't like being discovered. Then, on Christmas mornings, if the present I wanted didn't appear under the tree, Dad would continue the momentum he'd started the night before.

"Come with me, Bill," he'd say and walk me to a corner of the house where a new fishing rod or bike was waiting. The holidays had to mean more debt for my parents, but they never let that dampen the Christmas spirit. For us kids, it was a magical time.

BETTER

Even my brother, Kevin, who was tougher around the edges than I was, agreed that my family generated enough love to fill a mansion. So instead of feeling angry that my parents were putting me in Skips sneakers from the dollar store instead of cooler Pumas, I put myself in their shoes. I believed that they deserved better. Not better in terms of material possessions—although they wanted to get me Pumas even more than I wanted those shoes for myself—but better stability. After seeing how much my parents gave and how little they got, I could not let that go on for another generation.

Maybe I could empathize with my parents because I was their oldest child, or because of how I was hardwired, or maybe because my mother repeatedly told me, often in the same breath, that "anything worthwhile in life does not come easy" and that "you have the potential to do anything you set your mind to." Whatever the reasons, I wanted to come through for my family, to protect them when they got clobbered with crisis. What's more, I'd been given, and was maybe even born with, enough confidence to believe I could do it. And even though I wasn't starving and my parents weren't asking for money, I saw money as a way to give myself financial independence and to give my parents the security that they gave me with their love. I wanted to be their Saint Jude.

2

UNDERDOG

It is a rough road that leads to the heights of greatness.
—LUCIUS ANNAEUS SENECA

WHEN I WAS in first grade at St. Ignatius elementary school, Sister Jean Agnes, a teacher who never hesitated to smack my fingers with a ruler to punish me for my poor handwriting, walked up to my mom and dad on parents' night. I was standing next to my father when he asked the Sister how I was doing in school.

"Well, Mr. McDermott," she said, all but ignoring my six-year-old ears, "Bill's a good boy and behaves well, but just don't expect too much of him. He'll probably be a mechanic, or maybe a truck driver." My parents had nothing against mechanics or truck drivers, but a few weeks later, they pulled me out of St. Ignatius.

It was too late. I had overheard the bleak forecast, and despite my parents' obvious disagreement with the nun's assessment of me, her words stung, and then they stuck.

STREET FIGHTER

I remember the date: March 8, 1971. It was the day that Muhammad Ali and Joe Frazier fought at Madison Square Garden for the world heavyweight championship. The bout was called the Fight of the Century. Everyone in my neighborhood was talking about it. The fight had also captured the imaginations of people around the world. In America, the boxing match became a sort of release valve for a slew of tensions that gripped the country at the beginning of the 1970s: Vietnam. Intense racial divides. Women's lib. These and other conflicts that swirled around society didn't penetrate my life— my parents didn't argue about the war or debate President Richard Nixon's policies—nor did the outside world take up a huge piece of the real estate in my ten-year-old mind.

On the afternoon of the Ali-Frazier duel, I was riding the school bus home to our second-story apartment in Brentwood. My family had just moved into one of the identical, two-story brick structures built as part of a new housing development. The block I lived on was so fresh from construction that there was no grass, only gravel mixed with chunks of cement. I didn't know many kids yet, but we'd relocated so many times that I'd honed my senses, and could walk into a school yard and figure out who was in charge. That afternoon on the bus, the kid in charge was an eleven-year-old boy named Angelo.

I was looking forward to listening to the fight on the radio with my dad, and everyone on the bus was talking about the night's big event. Ali was seeking to regain the title that had been stripped from him in 1967 when he refused to obey his draft notice to join the US Army. He'd fought only two times since coming back to boxing in 1970. Like the country, the bus was slanted heavily toward Ali. Secretly, I also liked Ali, who was physically much bigger and a more compelling figure than Frazier. But my dad, he was rooting for Smokin' Joe, the current heavyweight champ. So I was, too.

"Who you for?" Angelo asked me as we got off the bus. I told him I was for Joe Frazier. Wrong answer.

"I'm for Ali. Let's fight." He punctuated the statement with a right hook to my chin.

Even though my dad, a former US Marine, had taught me how to fight, I had never been in a real match. I didn't even like to get angry or raise my voice. I was competitive, sure, but never a troublemaker.

Unlike me, though, this kid Angelo was a street fighter—the kind of boy who probably spent more time outside than in. He also was older and bigger, and while I was a decent size for my age, good at sports, and no lightweight, I was no Joe Frazier. The school bus rumbled off, leaving Angelo and me standing face-to-face in the unfinished gravel lot. We began to pummel each other, as kids and even adults formed a circle around us; a main event before the main event. Angelo was relentless. He kept coming after me with his fists. I was holding my own, but he had the edge. He also had the crowd on his side. They knew him and started chanting "Angelo! Angelo!"

He backed away for a moment, just long enough to reach down to the ground and pick up one of the cement chunks left over from the construction. He jumped on top of me and started pounding me with it. I tasted blood on my lip. But no one shouted for him to stop. Their hoots and chants only got louder, encouraging him to keep going. I knew I was on my own and risked a lot more than a bloody lip. No way was I going to lose an eye, or die, in some cockfight over Joe Frazier. My fear turned to resolve. By being the first to draw blood, Angelo had, according to street-fighter rules, given me the right to defend myself in any way I could.

The jagged chunk of concrete came at my face, and my survival instincts kicked in. In an act of self-defense, I reached into my pocket and pulled out the first thing my fingers touched: a pencil. Just a regular lead pencil. Frantically, I thrust the sharpened end at Angelo, and it punctured the skin on the right side of his face, just below his eye and near his ear. When I yanked out the pencil, it created a two-inch gash down his cheek. The face bleeds heavily, and Angelo jumped up and off me, dropped the rock, and grabbed his cheek. I stepped back, relieved but also in shock from what I had done. But the kid had gone too far with the rock. He left me no choice.

I had to get out of there, but I didn't run right away. As in the movie *The Godfather*, where Michael Corleone shoots a mob rival and a corrupt police captain in Louie's Italian restaurant, and then calmly drops the gun on the floor and walks out the front entrance, I dropped my pencil, backed away without looking anyone in the eye, and walked to the street corner—where I stepped it up until I was safe at home behind the bolted door of our apartment. When my mom saw me, I was caked in sweat, dust, blood, and tears.

"Mom, I felt like it was me or him! I had no choice but to get him with the pencil, and I'm just telling you because I think they're going to come and try to kill us, and I don't know what to do!"

"Bill, don't you worry about it," she said as she walked me into the bathroom to clean me up. "You are safe now." She wasn't angry. She knew that if I hurt someone, it was because I had to defend myself, not to prove I was a tough guy. "If they dare come to our home, I'll take care of it." She wiped a wet washcloth across my face and kissed me on the head.

That night, Dad and I listened to the radio as Muhammad Ali dominated Joe Frazier for most of the first three rounds, before Joe delivered a head-snapping blow to Ali's jaw. Good ol' Joe held his own, attacking Ali's body for twelve more rounds. In a brutal battle that lived up to all the hype, Frazier won.

Walking to the bus stop the next morning was the second scariest thing I'd ever had to do on my own, after fighting off Angelo. *Would he and his friends come after me? Harder?* I had no interest in fighting him again. But when I saw Angelo, the side of his head plastered with gauze and tape, he didn't do or say a thing. I didn't say anything either. Maybe someone told him that I had every right to defend myself with the pencil, since he'd started with the rock, or maybe he and the other kids now knew that I could defend myself. Whatever the reason, it was over between us, and I was relieved, but I wasn't proud that I had to hurt someone to end it. I never had another problem with Angelo or anyone else in that neighborhood again. Plus, I had proof I could survive on my own. The underdog could win.

JOB ONE

My parents gave me permission to dream big and got me believing that I could do anything I set out to achieve. So when I decided to start earning my own money, I had very high aspirations—especially for a paperboy.

At eleven, I was young to be delivering newspapers, but still I answered an ad to be a paperboy for the largest newspaper on Long Island at the time. Each morning, a truck dropped off a few stacks of flat papers in front of my house. After stuffing any special inserts into each paper, I'd load as many as I could into the big metal basket on the front of my blue Schwinn bicycle and the two baskets on either side of the back wheel. I carried the rest of the papers in my backpack. School started at eight thirty, so to get through the roughly 150 houses on my route in time for the first bell, I was usually pedaling by six o'clock in the morning.

The more houses I had on my route, the more money I could make in tips, so soon I was going door-to-door to sign up new subscribers. I had my shtick down:

"Good morning. I'm Bill McDermott, the newspaper boy in the neighborhood, and I noticed you're not currently getting the paper home delivered, so I just want you to know about my services."

I had studied what good newspaper delivery looked like. Some delivery boys were sloppy: they just threw newspapers on lawns, rain or shine, but if there was even a drizzle, someone's paper lost its value. I made it clear to people that I took the job seriously and wanted to be conscientious about how I served my customers.

"I can be flexible in terms of how you'd like the paper delivered, ma'am. Inside your door. In the mailbox. In plastic, so it won't get wet. And I always put the coupons in the right place, so you never have to worry about that." Eventually I more than doubled the number of houses on my route.

The key to getting good tips was whether or not the newspaper showed up how people wanted it. Most people asked for it in the mailbox, but older folks preferred it between the screen and the door. Back then, a few people requested the paper in a plastic bag, so I always had some on me.

The job got trickier as the number of houses on my route increased, but my two-hour delivery window stayed the same. Delivering all the papers in one run became impossible, so I had to bike back home to replenish my supply. To make sure the papers arrived before people left for work and before my school started, I thought through my route. Speed alone would not solve the problem. I could pedal only so fast. I came up with a methodology to maximize the time by redesigning the route in a way that allowed me to cross town quickly, come home to reload, and finish in an hour and a half.

Collecting my money each week required another plan. Most folks left my weekly fee—and hopefully a generous tip—in a white envelope that I'd left for them; some scribbled "Thanks" or a smiley face on the front. I'd toss all the envelopes into a bag, and then go home and dump the bag on the kitchen table to count out who'd given me what. I was meticulous in tracking how each customer paid me, information I recorded in a little green book. I put circles around the names of the good tippers, and I treated those folks extra nice, maybe taking the time to put a special weekly flyer *on top* of their newspaper, with a note calling it out, so they'd be sure to see it.

The biggest problem was that some people ignored the envelope and didn't leave me any money, which became a cash-flow issue, since I paid the newspaper company for all the papers myself. To get the money I was due, I had to knock on my customers' doors and ask for it. I didn't like to do this, but I did it—usually on weekends when I had more time and people were more likely to be home. Still, some folks could go for weeks without answering their doors. It could have been easy for me to lose track of who owed me how much, but with my careful record keeping, I could always defend myself when someone who owed me $7.50 denied it.

"What are you talking about, kid? The paper is only a dollar fifty a week."

"I know, sir," I'd say, pulling out my little green book. "But my records show you haven't paid me for five weeks." I'd smile, and, invariably, because my notes were so good, I'd get my money with little hassle—and often with a substantially bigger tip, as those late payers got a little sheepish about stiffing the polite paperboy. "Keep the change, kid," they'd say and hand me a folded ten-dollar bill.

I became keenly aware of the connection between my money and my customers' happiness. If I gave my customers what they wanted in the way they wanted it, they would give me more money. And for a kid who wanted to make money, this was an important revelation. In addition to the cash, I considered it an accomplishment if people liked me. I felt good when I got a nice word out of a grouchy man who just wanted to get back to his football game, or when someone's mother thanked me for doing a good job and invited me inside for a glass of lemonade.

Over time, I expanded my business. "By the way," I'd say, "I also have holiday cards, if you'd be interested." Back then it was common to sell boxes of American Greetings cards to households, and I would bring a bunch of boxed cards with me on days when I went door-to-door. I figured that adding another product was a good way to make the most of the opportunity I already had, standing in front of my customers when they had money in their hands.

Later, when I sold cookies door-to-door, I loved the sense of anticipation whenever I rang a stranger's doorbell, and the more heated rush I felt when that stranger said yes. If we had a friendly conversation, all the better. A nasty no or a slammed door didn't faze me. I just walked faster to the next house, where the potential for another yes awaited.

I was enjoying *the process* of making money more than counting or even spending it. Pitching Christmas cards to newspaper subscribers. Tracking customers who didn't pay to keep my cash flowing. Chatting over lemonade about a housewife's new couch.

At the end of each week, I took my route money and wrapped rubber bands around the stack of worn bills, and then stashed the thick rolls in a hollowed-out cross of Jesus Christ that hung over my bed. While other kids were saving up only for baseball cards, I was after something more. Something bigger. Anything I could do to make my parents smile—buying a little piece of jewelry for my mom or picking up the dinner check at Howard Johnson for my dad—brought me incredible satisfaction. Having a steady job and money saved gave me a sense of control in my unpredictable world.

WEAR THE JACKET

Most people in our neighborhood knew that I was always trying to make a buck, so they often asked me to babysit their kids or do odd jobs.

Once, a young couple who lived down the street offered to pay me twenty dollars to move an enormous pile of dirt into their backyard and spread it out so they could reseed their grass. The couple was nice, and twenty dollars was another twenty dollars. Unfortunately, I misjudged the time it would take, as well as the intensity of the labor. I had no gloves, and the shovel's wood handle began cutting into my hands. This work was hard and physical, but even as the afternoon I planned to finish turned into a second afternoon and then a third, I didn't stop. There were moments I wanted to throw that shovel into the canal at the back of the house, but I didn't quit. I'd watched my dad get up in the middle of the night often enough to know that work is sometimes doing what we do not want to do, and I believed it was important to do the job I promised. I kept shoveling.

When I finished, it didn't feel right to ask the couple for more money. We had an agreement, and I didn't want to ruin my relationship with the husband and wife, because I liked them, even if they knew they were getting a sweet deal. Besides, asking for more money would come with a megadose of guilt—the kind that comes with a Catholic school education. If I gave anyone any reason to think I was cheating him or not delivering what I'd promised, guilt engulfed me.

My first chance for better-paying employment came when I was on the cusp of fifteen, and the Finast supermarket chain opened a store in our neighborhood. When I heard that Finast was hiring, I picked up a job application and filled it out at home. My mom signed it because I was a minor. On the appointed day, I stood outside Finast in a line of applicants that stretched two blocks from the store's front doors and bright red signage. Scanning the competition, I realized that I was clearly the youngest person in line, the least experienced, and thus a definite long shot for one of the few openings. *Why hire the kid?* they'd think.

I was edging closer to the front of the line, where a woman behind a card table was accepting applications. When I stepped forward and handed her mine, she placed it on a pile of indistinguishable white forms. That's when I noticed a man wearing a green sport jacket standing a few feet away. *Nice jacket*, I thought. *Must be the boss.* I thanked the woman behind the table after she told me the store's manager would review my application and be in touch, and then I walked straight over to the man in the green jacket. The name Jack Kelly was embroidered on it.

"Hi Mr. Kelly, I'm Bill McDermott," I said and put out my hand. "I just want you to know that I waited on line for the last hour to submit my application because I really want to work here." He shook my hand and looked down at me, an eyebrow raised.

"Sir, I guarantee that if you give me this job, I'll work very hard for you. I just need a chance." Jack Kelly looked over at a coworker who was within earshot, and they both thanked me for my interest. When I left the store, the applicant line was still down the block.

The new store was less than a mile from my house, and the second I shut our front door, my mom called to me. "Bill, there's a Mr. Kelly on the phone, and he wants to speak to you! A Mr. Finnegan is also on the line. They're with Finast." She smiled as I took the receiver.

"Hello, Mr. Kelly, Mr. Finnegan. How are you?"

"Bill, we think you have a lot of energy," I heard Mr. Kelly say. "You can start tomorrow." Just like that, very brusque. "Make sure you dress in nice pants and a collared shirt, and get here ten minutes before your shift at four o'clock. I'm a real stickler for being on time, you hear me, kid?"

"Yes sir, Mr. Kelly, I'll be there!" Me being me, I arrived a half hour early.

The work wasn't glamorous, but I was excited to have a real salary. I started out corralling shopping carts from the parking lot. I was careful never to ram them together and shove them against the store's walls. I treated those carts like china. In the parking lot, if I saw a customer struggling to get bags into her trunk, I'd run over to help but refuse to take the quarter tip if she offered. "No thank you, ma'am, just doing my job. Really, it's my pleasure." I wasn't lying; I loved that job.

I graduated from the parking lot to stocking shelves. The day I accidentally cut my hand with a box cutter as I sliced open a carton full of canned goods, a coworker drove me to the hospital and waited while they stitched me up. I was back at Finast within a few hours. The way I saw it, I owed Finast at least ninety minutes. Plus, I wanted to prove that my injury wouldn't stop me from completing my stocking duties, and get me demoted back to collecting carts.

I took every job seriously, and whether I was stacking cans in a supermarket smock, digging dirt in muddy shorts, or delivering papers

in my school clothes, I started to develop basic work habits. By maximizing my time, being polite and conscientious, staying true to my word, showing up on time, and holding myself accountable, I was acting like a professional before I had to look like one. I was "wearing the jacket" long before I could afford or need a real jacket of my own. I understood that whether someone's pay was hourly or salaried, his collar blue or white, professional work habits alone wouldn't get people promoted, but a lack of professionalism wouldn't get people anywhere. So even when my jobs were small, I acted big.

I don't think my boss, Mr. Kelly, who was a good man and wore his own green jacket well, employed a lot of kids like me. "He's going places," he told my dad one day, which was a much rosier outlook than Sister Jean Agnes's prediction about my future.

EVEN BETTER

I was fifteen, making minimum wage, about $2.30 an hour. But it was a union job, so, like my dad, I took every ounce of overtime I could get because it paid time and a half. Double time during holidays. As I'd stopped doing the paper route, I had hours that weren't being eaten up by Finast, school, or basketball, so I took two other jobs. One consisted of doing mundane tasks for the village of Amityville, like painting fences or picking up litter around town. The other job, I liked much better: I was a floating busboy at a white-glove Italian restaurant, Amato's, which was so high-end that it took American Express cards and even had its busboys wear tuxedos—a uniform that demanded more respect than the job itself. I loved the tux.

At Amato's, I made $10 for a five-hour shift plus any money the waiters shared with me for taking their customers' dirty dishes to the kitchen and pouring coffee. After every shift, as the waiters tallied their tips, I prayed they would take into account my efforts to treat their customers well and throw me several bucks. I always

asked diners if they enjoyed their meal, and suggested a cannoli or some spumoni for dessert.

By the time I was sixteen, if I wasn't at school, I was busy stocking, bagging, hauling, and busing. For a while, I even worked the midnight shift at the Merritt gas station, where just trying to stay awake was a chore. From midnight to eight in the morning, I'd service twenty cars at most. Not an ounce of skill was required. The boredom was torturous.

Still, I had more money than ever—too much to keep in the cross above my bed and enough to buy myself the occasional luxury. My favorite purchase was a hardy sheepskin coat, the kind with the faux fur trim, chic in the 1970s. I picked it up for about $200 at an outlet shop that sold clothes not quite as high-end as Macy's. The minute I saw that coat, I wanted it. Walking the streets of Amityville in what became my signature coat, I felt as cool as New York Knicks basketball guard Walt "Clyde" Frazier.

I was grateful for the work I got, and to men like Mr. Kelly, who took a chance on me. And while I loved the work and the money, I suspected a hodgepodge of minimum-wage jobs wasn't making me as much cash as my time and effort deserved.

One afternoon, walking home from Amato's in my waiter's tuxedo and black velvet tie, I noticed a Help Wanted sign in the window of Amityville Country Delicatessen on the corner of Bayview Avenue and Merrick Road. I walked in. It was a small box of a place, nothing fancy. A pay phone. Racks of chips. Beer, soda, household goods, and a deli counter.

"What are you looking for?" I asked the man standing behind the cash register.

"I'm looking for someone who wants to work hard and is willing to put in a lot of hours." I smiled, partially at him, partially to myself. Work hard? Please, this guy had no idea who he was talking to.

3

THE GREATEST COACH

Be more concerned with your character than your
reputation. Your character is what you really are, while
your reputation is merely what others think you are.

—JOHN WOODEN

"BILL, I KNOW you like to score," my father said to me before one of our biggest basketball games, "but tonight I need you not to shoot and focus only on defense." I was surprised because I could sometimes score up to twenty points a game, and we were playing for the basketball league's championship. "The only thing I need you to do tonight is stop that kid Chase," Dad explained.

I was in fifth grade, and this kid Chase was the top scorer in the Catholic Youth Organization (CYO) league, plus a good six inches taller than me—just huge. "If he doesn't score a single point, we win the game. Better yet, if he scores fewer than ten, we win the game. But if you try to outscore him, Bill, we will lose. So your mission tonight is to sacrifice your own scoring. Just make sure Chase doesn't make any baskets." I didn't argue.

For as hard as he worked, my father always made time to coach his sons' teams. On the hardwood under the bright fluorescent lights of any gymnasium, the man was in his flow, his mind focused on two things: winning and teamwork. Without the latter, he would teach me, the former was either impossible or worthless.

My dad inherited his fierce will to win from his father, pro basketball player and Hall of Famer Bobby McDermott. My grandfather was a gifted player who left his Queens, New York, high school after just one year to play pro ball in 1929. He made only four bucks his first game, but he was soon setting records and advancing to better teams before signing with the Original Celtics from New York, which were part of the American Basketball League. "Mac," or "Mr. Basketball," was a leading scorer known for making consecutive, at times game-winning, two-handed set shots from midcourt—sometimes from behind the center court line. His impossibly beautiful arches were art. During one game on record, the five-foot-eleven guard hit fourteen shots in a row from near center court, and eleven straight from the foul line. Incredible! When he played for the Fort Wayne (Zollner) Pistons of the National Basketball League, he was named Most Valuable Player four seasons in a row, from 1942–43 to 1945–46, after which the league's coaches, players, and sports editors voted my grandfather the greatest basketball player of all time.

Just as impressive, Bobby McDermott was also a great player-coach: the rare athlete who both plays ball on the floor and coaches the team from the sidelines. Earlier in his coaching career, he led the Pistons to two consecutive championships.

When he retired from pro basketball in 1950, Bobby McDermott was thirty-six and considered by many to be the greatest basketball player of his generation. He spent the rest of his too-short life having a lot of fun off the court while selling life insurance for a living.

Tragically, at forty-nine, he died on his wife's birthday of injuries suffered from a car crash. I never knew my grandfather, but how I would have loved to see him play.

My father displayed a similar intensity on the court, so much so that my brother would say our dad coached as if every game were the NBA finals. It's true that he took it seriously. For special games, Dad wore a suit and tie. He dressed out of respect for his players and for the game—my dad, *he* wore the jacket—and when I helped him coach my brother's teams, I wore my Easter suit and tie. Dressing well broadcast to everyone that we'd come to win, not just to play.

TEAM OVER EGO

Dad taught me that winning required knowing my opponents' strengths and weaknesses. "It's not about you," he said, "it's about understanding them." Beating someone like Chase was less about exercising my skills than about shutting down his skills. During that final game, I put my ego on hold and followed my dad's advice. In the end, Chase and I scored only four points each, and my team took home the trophy.

My father's second obsession was teamwork. He loved to win, yes, but he also understood that teams, not star players, won games.

"Winning is not about how many points one player scores, but about *the team* winning." This was my father's mantra, and why he had us practice passing the ball more than dribbling or shooting. Dad preached selflessness for the good of the group, and that none of us was as talented as all of us.

Our youth basketball teams were made up of players from north and south of Amityville's railroad tracks, which separated the middle- and working-class communities from poorer neighborhoods. But Dad wasn't concerned about anyone's address. He just wanted great players, wherever they came from. His role was to help us play to our strengths—whether you could shoot, rebound, or defend—and get us to work together as a team.

For me, the feeling of being part of a winning team was a rush, similar to how I felt when I signed up new customers on my paper route, landed a new job, earned a big tip, or saw my mom's face when I did something good. Team sports, with their we're-in-this-together high fives, energized me. On the contrary, solo sports often sapped me. I played golf with my dad as we got older, but mostly to hang out with him and my brother, Kevin, and enjoy being outside in the sun. But golf had no passing, no huddle, no camaraderie. The esprit de corps that I inhaled as a kid became addicting.

FUNDAMENTALS OF PLAY

I was helping my dad coach my brother's fifth-grade team the night we came up against the Huntington Super Sonics. Officially, we were the St. Martin of Tours, but we called ourselves the Green Machine because of our uniforms. Not only was every player on the Super Sonics bigger and slightly older than almost everyone on our team, but one of the Sonics' players was the son of New York Nets pro basketball coach Kevin Loughery, who was in the stands during the game. By halftime, the Green Machine was down twenty-one points.

"Dad, how long are we gonna wait to make our run at these guys?" I asked my father in the locker room. It was time to employ our team's biggest advantage.

"Okay, Bill, let's go into the full-court man-to-man press," he said. "Let's see if we can exhaust and distract them, really throw them off with a high-pressure defense." I nodded. I knew Dad's press had a twist: speed.

My father, as coach, probably taught me more basics about how to be successful in business than any teacher or boss ever did. It's ironic, considering that he never worked in an office. Among his lessons, my dad stressed the importance of the fundamentals of play. At the end of each practice, he had every player take fifteen foul shots. My dad also convinced me that as long as there was time on the clock, we had a chance of overcoming any crisis on the court, no matter how far behind we were. Especially if we had the fundamentals down, we could come up with a new play, get back the ball, or keep the other team from scoring.

That's what happened during the second half of the Super Sonics game, when we surprised the other team with my dad's version of a full-court press. We never guarded the man taking the ball out of bounds. Instead, we put two players on the Super Sonics' best dribbler. With our five guys on four of theirs, we had a power advantage, and the Sonics didn't know what to do or who should get the ball. It was chaos. By the time the Sonics figured out what we were doing, we had made three or four steals and cut their lead in half. The momentum hit, and we just kept coming.

What the other team had in size and might, we made up for with quickness, an unexpected strategy, and a well-drilled team that knew what to do. We had prepped for the situation. We just ran and ran and ran until we ran them right out of the gym and won the game.

Dad never punished his players for lousy performance, as long as we put in the effort. He never took a guy out of a game for having a bad night shooting, as Dad believed that doing so would only increase the pressure the kid put on himself to be perfect. If one of us was wide open, Dad urged us to take the shot. "Go for it!" he hollered from the sidelines. He'd rather we miss than not try at all, a freedom that gave us incredible courage. Plus, Dad's theory was that even if we missed, we had a chance to get the rebound or get a foul shot. He was playing the odds. If we didn't shoot at all, we had zero chance of scoring.

Sometimes I'd sit in the bleachers and watch my dad play ball. Once, he and some Con Edison buddies went up against a team of local college students, and I watched as my father cleaned up the court with those cocky kids. At forty, he could still make the long shot from midcourt.

4

FIND A WAY

The dictionary is the only place where success comes before work.

—VINCE LOMBARDI

THE DELI'S OWNER stared back at the tall teenage kid in the tuxedo as I assured him that if he wanted to hire a hard worker, I was his man.

"I can also bring an understanding of how to serve food to your constituents," I said, trying to be businesslike as I explained how, at the Italian restaurant where I currently worked, we wore white gloves. Most teenagers around town weren't tossing out words like *constituents*, so Bob realized I was serious.

"How many hours can you give me?" he asked.

"I can give you as many hours as you can handle." I told him what I was making from my three jobs combined. He looked at me. Good help was hard to find, and he probably figured that a kid in a penguin suit couldn't do much harm.

"I'll pay you more," he said. "But you gotta come in on holidays, work a few night shifts—especially on Friday nights, because we're open till one in the morning. And . . ." He hesitated, raising an eyebrow. "You gotta learn how to wax the floor."

"No problem."

Bob hired me on the spot.

A NEW MISSION

Whenever I had to make a big decision, my mother would tell me that as long as I could put my name and photo next to my actions if they appeared on the front page of the *New York Times*, I shouldn't hesitate to go for what I wanted. I felt guilty about quitting my jobs at Finast and Amato's, but I knew the deli was a much better deal for me than balancing multiple jobs, and not just because of the money. I wanted one purpose to pour myself into versus multiple missions. Just looking around that deli, I sensed a mission.

The first thing I had to learn about was the meat slicer, so that I could make sandwiches. The machine was easy enough to use, as long as I didn't rush. I lost a few fingertips, but they grow back as long as you don't slice the bone. I also learned how to run the register, stock the deli's shelves, and fill the refrigerator when suppliers delivered new shipments. Staples like potato and egg salad arrived in big plastic buckets a few times a week.

I worked hard, as slacking off was not part of my genetic code, but I didn't aspire to be the deli manager or anything.

After about a year, Bob wanted out. He coleased the deli and the adjacent Sunoco gas station with his business partner: a man named Eddie, who drove an Eldorado convertible. Once, Eddie took me to the "21" Club in Manhattan. I remember wearing my only suit and tie. When we entered the dark nook of the historic restaurant, everyone we saw seemed to know him. I was next to a man who could handle himself, and it made an impression on me. I wanted to be just like Eddie—but when Bob wanted to sell, so did he.

The deli and the gas station were not easy businesses to unload. Sunoco's parent company, Sunmark Industries, owned the land under both the station and the store. Bob and Eddie only leased the land and the right to operate each facility on a year-to-year basis. Any new owner was buying only those rights, knowing that Sunmark could take back the lease, or repurpose the land, after any twelve-month period—which left whoever owned the lease little if any security. Eventually a local entrepreneur named Ernie stepped up and offered Bob and Eddie $50,000, cash. They accepted. But Ernie was interested only in the gas station. For him, the convenience store was just an inconvenience, so he kept me on to oversee operations. I got to keep my job and take on more responsibility.

This was the first time I was in charge of a business, and I loved being able to think of an idea and, *pow*, make it happen. I spruced up the place a bit, made a few changes, and our business started to improve. As I balanced high school and work, I began to feel as if I was coming into my own—until summer.

Before I left town for my family's annual vacation to the Jersey Shore, Ernie panicked. He needed someone to man the deli while I was gone, so he placed an ad in the newspaper for short-term help, but the guy he hired robbed us. He and some buddies came to the deli one night and stole almost everything. All the stock, the equipment. Even the slicer. The place was wiped out. When I returned from vacation, the cinderblock building looked like a bomb shelter. I was upset when I saw what had happened. Even before Ernie put me in charge of the deli, I'd invested a lot of time and effort into working there, making it better, and I had come to feel a sense of ownership. Worse, with nothing to sell, we had no customers, so I was out of a job.

Ernie's solution was to try to unload the deli's lease for half of what he originally paid, but people thought it was overpriced because the real value was in the gas station, and nobody wanted to risk $25,000 to lease a shell from a big corporation that could cut him loose on a whim. The building sat idle into the fall, until Ernie caved.

It wasn't as if I hadn't thought about buying it. In theory, it made no sense: I didn't have the money. I was in high school full-time. But embedded in my upbringing was a philosophy I was about to test: never let the circumstances of a moment supersede the size of your dreams. Rules, assumptions, and doubts were no match for my will, creativity, and hard work. If I wanted something, I would find a way.

I did the math, figuring out how much I could make every month after paying for products and employees. When I talked to my parents about buying the deli, they didn't think I was crazy. They trusted me, they knew I was driven, and they thought I was smart, so they believed that, yes, I would find a way to make it work. And because they believed in me, I believed in myself even more. Plus, they offered to help. Mom said she would oversee the deli when I was at school, and my father, brother, and sister would also pitch in.

So when Ernie asked me to have dinner with him at Amato's, I'd done my homework. Sitting across from him in one of the dark leather booths, being served by a waiter in a tux like I used to wear, I listened to Ernie tell me I could have the deli for $12,500. We both knew I didn't have that kind of cash, but with my plan and my family's support, I had the confidence of someone twice my age, and with much more experience.

"Ernie, it's not going to happen, but"—I had my pitch ready—"give me a fifty-five-hundred-dollar loan, and make it seven thousand with interest, with payments due monthly. I'll pay it all off in a year. If I don't pay you back in twelve months, whatever improvements I made, whatever stock I have, whatever I put into the place, it's yours. You get it all." I paused for a second. I was holding myself accountable for my own success. If I failed, I lost. But if I succeeded and paid Ernie back the money on time, I would own everything, including the lease for the deli, and have nothing to lose. He looked at me. I'd presented Ernie with an idea that he hadn't considered. But Ernie was a street-savvy businessman.

"All right, kid, you got a deal." We shook hands in the dimly lit restaurant.

I knew that I was going to do a lot more than just pay Ernie back. I saw a little store without limits and was determined to build that deli into the best place in the neighborhood.

TRUST IS THE ULTIMATE CURRENCY

For customers, the deli was just a small, forgettable stop in their day; a place they popped into on their way home from work or as they headed to the beach on a hot weekend. My store might not have been a destination, but that didn't stop me from wanting to make the experience a fantastic part of their journey.

First, I needed products to sell. The shelves were empty, and I had no cash for inventory. Just as I had done with the paper route, and just as my dad and I did on the basketball court, I came up with a plan. I already knew all of our suppliers, and they knew me as the nice, hardworking kid who always helped them unload their trucks and took care of their accounts, making sure that they got paid once Bob left the business. So I reached out to almost all of them, from the beer guy, to the milk guy, to the cigarette guy. I was honest about my situation. Then I made a proposition:

"Look, I can't afford to pay you now, but I need this break to give me a start."

I asked them to give me my first order on consignment. If they did, I promised to pay them back as soon as I got ahead. And if that day never came, if the deli failed, I said I would always owe them in arrears for the initial shipment. I offered to put the terms in writing, signing any document they wanted that said I would always owe them the first order.

I also vowed never to trade them for another vendor. "I won't shop you," I said, "and you can even jack up the price on the first order to improve your margin." I wasn't looking for an accommodation, just a fair business arrangement.

The vendors were part of my business's ecosystem, as important to me as my customers, and they deserved the same respect. If my suppliers weren't happy with the arrangement, I didn't want to be in business together. If you weren't all-in, I didn't want you in at all.

Every single vendor made the deal with me on a handshake. Not one had me sign something. I think they believed in me, but we also had a level of trust based on our past work relationships. So, together, we filled the shelves with stock, which put me in business. I'd never forget what they did for me, and they knew it.

WHO IS MY CUSTOMER?

The shelves were full. The refrigerator was humming. The floors were waxed. But I had some serious competition. On one side of the deli, an arm's length away, was the 7-Eleven. Another block down the street was my former employer, Finast. I had to figure out ways to get people into my store.

I tried lowering my prices and marking down staples, advertising milk for ninety-nine cents. People came in, but I watched as they grabbed up my milk and left without buying anything else. I soon realized that competing with larger stores on price was a losing strategy. I could never afford to buy big enough quantities to benefit from economies of scale. Even if I could, I had nowhere to store excess inventory. I also realized that I could not beat my competitors on selection, offering customers twenty different cereals because, again, I didn't have my competitors' money or the space.

I was David amid Goliaths. What, I thought, did I have that the Goliaths did not? What could my little deli give people that 7-Eleven and Finast could not? I thought back to how I delivered those newspapers, and I asked myself a simple but critical question: *Who are my customers?* What did they want other than cheap milk and choices, which my competitors offered? Where could my store add unique value? Similar to basketball, winning at business was not going to be about me, it was going to be about them. Everything I did had to strengthen my customers' ties with the deli so that they kept coming back and spending money. If my interests were aligned with their desires, we'd both win.

To *do* things differently, I had to *see* things differently. I became a one-man market research department, and discovered that my customers were a reservoir of information and ideas, if I paid attention. Always curious about what people had to say, I was now even more obsessed with watching and listening.

Who, I asked myself, *is my base?*

I identified three key types of customers. The first was easy to figure out even though they didn't come into the store that much. A block and a half away was a senior citizens' complex. I had observed that many senior citizens, including my own grandmother, preferred not to leave the comfort of home. And, of course, there were some who could not get up every day and walk down the street to buy stuff like cold cuts and orange juice. *Bam!* I knew what to do: none of my competitors had delivery services, so the deli would deliver to your door. Done. I had my first customer base.

Next, I paid close attention to the guys in jeans, T-shirts, and work boots who streamed into the deli on Friday afternoons. These blue-collar workers would roll in after a long week and toss me twenty-dollar bills like they were singles—but they'd show up again on Sunday mornings, scraping quarters out of their pockets to pay for another pack of cigarettes. Watching them, I realized a few things. First, they weren't price sensitive; they just wanted their favorite brand of cigarettes and something good to eat. They were also willing to pay whatever I charged for a good product like a delicious sandwich that filled them up—at least on Fridays.

They also wanted, and they deserved, to be treated with the same dignity as an executive just off the train from the city. People in suits and ties were good customers, but there weren't enough of them to keep a little business like mine growing. It was the working-class men like my dad to whom I needed to cater. Extending myself to them was easy because I had so much respect for how hard they labored.

"Hey, how you doing? Are you gonna catch the game on Sunday? How's the new baby?" I remembered what they said so that the next time they came in, I could pick up from our last conversation: "Is your arm still giving your trouble? Can you believe the Jets' streak? How's your daughter's cold?" Making an effort to remember their stories not only made them more loyal to my store but also established a relationship between us.

The problem, however, was that the workers were rich on Friday night and broke by Sunday morning. It hit me: I would extend them credit. I bought a little black-and-white notebook to track names and purchases. Every time someone took something on credit, he initialed the entry. Then, on the following Friday, he paid off the balance, and the cycle would start again. Sure, sometimes one customer would fall a little behind, and I'd roll him into a second or a third week, but they always made it up. Not one person ever cheated me. Again, win-win.

My third market was high school students, which I identified by happenstance. I watched day after day as kids, some of whom I knew from school, lined up outside the adjacent 7- Eleven. It was killing me. How could I get those kids to walk past the 7-Eleven, which was right next to their school, and walk a little farther to my deli?

One day I walked down to the 7-Eleven to ask the kids why they liked it so much. Immediately I noticed something odd. A bunch of kids were hanging out in front of the store, waiting. The manager was letting only four into the store at one time. I turned to one of the kids.

"Hey, why are you lined up out here when there's plenty of room inside? What's up with that?" The kid shrugged, but I got it. The manager thought that if he let too many kids into the store, it would be easier for them to steal stuff. And he assumed they would. The 7-Eleven didn't trust its teenage customers, so instead, here was this kid with money in his pocket, waiting in the cold. Okay, I knew what to do. I told the kids they would never have to wait outside my deli. I'd let them in forty at a time if necessary. I treated them with the same trust and respect that I treated adults, and it didn't take long before the deli was bustling after three o'clock on weekdays. I had to buy more soda, candy bars, and other stuff to keep the shelves stocked, which, of course, made my vendors happy.

One day a kid came up to me. "You know, Bill, it's really great that you welcome us, because when we want to be treated with re-spect, have good food, and a good time, we come here. When we want to steal stuff, we go to 7-Eleven."

The high school kids. Senior citizens. Blue-collar workers. This was my base, and my strategy for the delicatessen became so simple, so clear. Once I knew my customers, what they wanted, and what I was good at, I focused on it relentlessly.

QUALITY

No one was going to keep coming into the deli just because I gave them credit and respect. I needed high-quality products.

I served only the best possible cold cuts, and no rolls from out of a bag. My breads were baked fresh and delivered daily. Plus, my beans, my potato salad, my macaroni salad, my tuna salad were all homemade. Nothing came from a can or tasted like it had been sitting around in one of those big plastic bins, because it wasn't. The salads tasted fresh because they were made by my mom, an amazing cook. Every other day, she prepared a fresh roast beef in an oven in the back of the deli. People would pay anything for her hero sandwiches. I might have been the entrepreneur, but Mom's cooking was the honey that drew the bees.

Together my mom and I went out of our way to make everyone feel that our business was not just one-sided. Local policemen could walk in and get a free cup of coffee and a doughnut; in turn, I felt safe knowing that my little store was always on their radar. And we gave our regular customers small but meaningful things. You're a mother juggling groceries and two kids? Please, let me carry the bags to your car. Here, take some of my extra tuna salad home to your family for dinner, no charge. If I had extra ice and knew I wasn't going to move it, I gave a free bag of it to a customer who was headed to the beach. It cost me little—maybe ten cents for the bag—but it built loyalties, and they'd come back to shop.

The store was also immaculate. I not only washed the floor every night but also waxed it so that the next morning you could almost see your image in its dark glossy sheen. My employees and I wore white shirts, black ties, and black pants, and we put on white gloves when we handled the meat.

Did we need to do all of that? No. But we did.

MANAGING MY PLAYERS

At the deli, my mom practiced what she always preached to me: be yourself. Every day that she came in, Mom was herself: sparkling, happy, kind. My mother loved people, and people loved her. That was her magic. Our neighborhood was full of characters. Ralph the mailman. Andy from the car dealership. For every person who walked through the door, Mom had a warm smile. She treated customers like her own family, making all sorts of wonderful side conversations as she bagged goods or poured a cup of coffee. Maybe she offered some advice to a girl having problems at home, or an empathetic ear to a foreman after a hard week at work. I have no doubt that some people came into the deli just to talk to my mom.

Even though Mom was the superstar, I still needed other players. No way could I have succeeded without the help of a few people—mainly my dad, my siblings, friends—even a few girlfriends. My sister, Gennifer, couldn't wait to get behind the counter. And when she did, customers loved her. I built a wall of trust around a small team to avoid what, in small-business lingo, is known as "silent partner" syndrome. Because it's so easy to steal from a small business, by pocketing cash instead of putting it in the register, I had to be careful about whom I hired. If I let just anyone work in the store, I'd have people sharing in my profits without my even knowing about it.

A BIG IDEA

By the summer of 1979, I was eighteen and attending Dowling College, a small liberal arts school in Oakdale, Long Island, about a half hour from Amityville. Dowling attracted middle-class kids from the area. About half lived at home and balanced school with jobs. It was an ambitious student body. One older student, John McGowan, was a clam digger by profession, and everyone called him "Mudrake"—after the long, spiked tools used to find clams in mucky waters. John knew a lot about spreadsheets and computer programming, and he tutored me through more than one course. Had he not taken the time, I would have been lost. I was grateful for his generosity, and we became good friends.

Besides being a good college and an easy commute, Dowling's other attraction for me was its campus. The school was housed in a stunning mansion built at the turn of the century by a member of the wealthy Vanderbilt family. The L-shaped building's façade was handsome red brick and stone. Its ornate interior had been restored, and some of the classrooms overlooked the manicured lawns that separated the mansion from the Connetquot River. It was glorious.

As much as I loved being there, I had no time to hang around campus. I scheduled my classes on Tuesdays and Thursdays so that I could spend as much time as possible at the deli. I'd do my homework behind the counter, either after we closed or between customers' visits. I was always careful to hide my textbooks behind the meat slicer so no one knew I was studying. I never wanted customers to worry that they were interrupting my homework.

School was going well, and so was the business. I had enough continuous profit to share money with my family, pay for my education, and buy myself a brand-new 1980 metallic gray Firebird, which I waxed and polished like a trophy. Sometimes I just gazed at the beautiful vehicle.

I also felt good that I was able to pay back Ernie his loan ahead of our agreed-upon schedule.

Despite the deli's success, I never felt financially safe. There were plenty of weeks when we had thin margins, and I had to work more hours because I couldn't afford to pay anyone else. I realized that I could be up by $15,000 one week, but then the air-conditioning would go on the fritz, and overnight the business was barely making a profit. Watching my friends and other families head to the beach on summer weekends while I stayed inside working the store could be a bummer, yet somehow I knew my day at the beach would come. And even with the success, there was no one moment when I knew we'd made it. No finish line.

So, because I never felt safe, and because I was driven to improve,

I knew we had to do more than just sell more of what we had. My eyes were open for new ideas to keep the store growing.

Mimicking the competition was a losing strategy. I no longer wasted time thinking about what other convenience and grocery stores were doing, like whether they put paper towels on sale or what beer they advertised. Instead, I was open to the unexpected. My favorite idea came to me because I never stopped looking around corners for what was next.

One afternoon, I was walking through a mall, and I noticed a bunch of kids huddled around a video game machine, plunking their parents' quarters into the slot, one after the other. I stood mesmerized at the long line of kids jangling all that change in their pockets. *Bam!* It hit me. *Gotta get me one of those games for the deli.* I found the name of the owner on the back of the video game, wrote down the phone number, went straight home, and called the guy.

"I want one of those games," I told him. "How much?"

"Five thousand dollars." I didn't have that kind of money and said so straight out. "Okay, four thousand," he countered. The second he undersold himself, I knew I had him. "I don't have that either," I answered.

"So why am I bothering with you?"

"Because I do have an idea." I told him about my deli, and how I was going to build a little game room off the side of the building. I had the perfect spot: a small area where the gas station attendants sometimes went to rest. "Look, I see how many quarters kids put into these games," I explained. "Give me a few boxes at no cost. You'll still own them, and I'll split the quarters with you fifty-fifty for as long as I have the machines in my store. If at any time you don't like the arrangement, take back the games. They're your property." I even offered to sign a note to that effect. "C'mon," I urged him. "Let's give it a shot. I know it's gonna pan out."

He was in. Just like my vendors, and just like Ernie, he liked an idea he never expected to hear—even if it sounded a little risky. I had painted my own vision of what success could look like, and because I believed it, someone else did, too.

Back at the deli, my brother, Kevin, who had always been much better than I was at construction, built a game room big enough to house three machines, including Asteroids and PAC-MAN. I had diversified by extending my core business, almost at no cost. The kids loved it, and I loved the sound of recurring revenue as kids popped twenty-five cents into my machines, and maybe bought a Coke or some candy to eat while they watched their friends play. Rock 'n' roll.

MOVIN' OUT, MOVIN' ON

Sometimes after a late shift at the deli on a Friday or Saturday night, I would join friends at a nearby bar or restaurant to hang out and relax after another long week. Places throughout Long Island loved to play tracks from a local hero, Billy Joel. The singer-songwriter had grown up nearby, in Hicksville, where my family had also lived for a bit. The guy was slightly more than a decade older than me, yet for a lot of us throughout the working-class stretches of Long Island, Billy Joel represented something momentous: it was possible to move beyond the world we knew and do something unexpected and amazing, like writing hit songs.

Every time I listened to the words of Billy's first big hit, "Piano Man," I felt like he was singing about some of the people I knew. People on my street, or customers who came into the deli, or people who maybe worked around town. The song was populated with men and women who imagined better lives for themselves: a waitress who practiced politics, a real estate novelist, a bartender who wanted to be a movie star, if only he could "get out of this place," according to Billy's lyrics.

GET OUT OF THIS PLACE

As much as I loved my family and my home, and for as much pride as I had in the neighborhoods where I grew up, I was going to move on. Like that piano player, I did not want be a deli owner in ten years, standing behind the same counter selling the same people the same cigarettes and trying to come up with a good answer when my customers asked me, "Man, what are you doin' here?"

It was never my goal to build the deli into some big store or a big franchise. I knew it would always be a small business. I was okay with that. The deli had always been my means to an end: a way to pay for my education. I was proud of what I had built, but once I finished college and paid off all my college bills, I was ready to move on.

So I sold the deli, which for the buyer was most valuable for the land that it sat on.

I used the sale's profits to help my mom and dad buy a vacation house in a beautiful community near Myrtle Beach, South Carolina. It was not the single-floor ranch house they once dreamed of owning. But that was fine, because their dream had changed. Seeing their joy brought me tremendous peace.

The time had come to do something for me. I was hungry, ready for more. Ready to be a person of significance beyond Amityville, even though I was not entirely sure what that meant. But I did have a hunch what it would look like.

5

WANT IT MORE

The thing always happens that you really believe in;
and the belief in a thing makes it happen.

—FRANK LLOYD WRIGHT

THE MORNING OF my interview in New York City, I go to my closet to pick one of two $99 suits that I'd bought at the mall. I choose a navy pinstripe and pair it with my white shirt and burgundy tie. The night before, a nor'easter storm that hit Long Island flooded the entire first floor of our house. So I won't stain the suit, Kevin carries me down from upstairs and through four feet of water to the car, where my dad is waiting to drive me to the train.

At the train station, my dad wishes me luck as I get out of the car. I look back at him.

"Dad, I appreciate it, and thank you for getting me here and everything, but I just want you to know I'm coming home with my employee badge in my pocket. I guarantee it." My father shakes his head and says with a smile, "Bill, you don't need to worry about all that. Just do the best you can. I couldn't possibly be prouder of you."

"Dad, I love you. I'm coming home with a badge in my pocket." I close the door and ride up the escalator to the train platform.

For as much as I loved running my own business, becoming an entrepreneur was not my desire. From my vantage point, successful individuals—people of distinction and significance—wore suits and rode trains into New York City, where they poured into huge office buildings and worked for big companies. That's where I was headed that day. I was confident, yes, but I was not cocky. I saw myself as a business athlete who wanted to be trained by a corporation whose name I would be proud to have on a business card. And, man, was I excited about business cards.

Technology, I had come to believe from my college classes and from talking to my commuting customers who stopped in the deli, was the gateway to a big future. So in 1983, in search of my first professional job after college, I orchestrated my own direct mail campaign, sending out a résumé and cover letter to several technology companies with big offices in Manhattan. IBM and Xerox Corporation were my dream employers. I'd heard exciting things about Xerox from one customer in particular: a nice guy named Ken, who smoked Merit cigarettes and worked for Xerox in New York City. I liked Ken a lot, he was a good guy, and when we chatted over coffee on his way to work each morning, he told me about Xerox's sales training program. "The best in the world," he said, and I was sold. I just needed to get an interview. I didn't know anybody or have any connections, so I just got lucky when Xerox invited me to interview for an entry-level sales job at its Manhattan offices.

Sitting on the train after bidding good-bye to my father, my suit dry thanks to my brother, I take the company's literature out of my briefcase and read all about how Xerox's CEO, a Mr. David Kearns, was using something called "leadership through quality" to save

Xerox from losing more money to its overseas competitors, which were building cheaper and better-quality copy machines. I think about Mr. Kearns and his quest for quality as the train rolls into Manhattan's skyline.

From Penn Station, I take a subway train uptown toward 666 Fifth Avenue, where I join about two dozen other young applicants in a waiting room inside Xerox's hiring center. The others look so polished, like they came from families with fathers that were executives and mothers who took them shopping at Brooks Brothers. And here I am among them in my $99 suit.

I do a little math, and I realize that the chance of snagging one of the few spaces in the sales training class is slim. I have to figure this thing out, fast. Find a way to get it done and get one of these jobs. Instead of panicking, I start asking the other interviewees questions, making small talk.

"Hey, where are you from?" I hear names of affluent suburbs like Greenwich and Princeton.

"Where'd you go to school?" Yale, Notre Dame. It's like everyone around me is from another planet. Either they don't ask me where I went to school, or they haven't heard of Dowling.

Then I ask a few of the guys what they are here for; what they want to accomplish. One says he is "doing the rounds, talking to Xerox and maybe Merrill Lynch and Morgan Stanley." The others are also cool, telling me they are "considering their options," "surveying the situation," "interviewing here and there." *Okay, I get it.* We are different, but that's the secret. I want this job so much more than you and you and you. I know exactly why I am here: to land the best job of my life. At Xerox.

I'm done interviewing the competition. *I got this*, I think, and when I hear someone call my name, I walk in to meet the hiring manager, ready to sell myself.

Later, after half of the original candidate pool is asked to take a psychological test, I figure I must have done okay on that as well as in my interviews because I am invited to meet with several sales managers at Xerox's uptown office at 9 West Fifty-Seventh Street, the sexiest address on the planet. I arrive and take an elevator up to the thirty-eighth floor.

All told, I get through about eight interviews. *This is fun, a game I want to win.* With each conversation, my energy and desire heighten. *I can taste this.* Finally, my last meeting is with Xerox's local district manager, a senior sales executive named Emerson Fullwood, a person I suspect has the power to hire me.

I wait on a bench with one other applicant in the demo room, where Xerox showcases all of its machines. It's like a museum overlooking Central Park. I'm on top of the world, and if I want to stay here, I must nail this final interview. After about an hour, the wall clock ticks closer to five o'clock. I figure that Mr. Fullwood has either forgotten about us, or this wait is a test. I walk up to the receptionist. Her desk plate tells me her first name is Joanne.

"Joanne, I just want to introduce myself. I'm Bill McDermott, and I am waiting for an interview with Mr. Fullwood, and I'm not in any way impatient. I just want you to let Mr. Fullwood know that no matter how long I have to wait, I will be here when it is convenient for him. But please give him the message that I will not go anywhere; I will be here as long as he wants me to wait."

Joanne smiles as she gets up and goes into his office with a piece of paper. In a few minutes, she comes out and motions for me to follow her down a long hallway toward Mr. Fullwood's corner office. Standing in front of me is a handsome gentleman. He is beautifully groomed and impeccably dressed. I take a seat and a deep breath and hear my mom's voice: "Bill, there's no ceiling on you. There's nothing that you cannot do. Just remember, be yourself, that's the most important part of you. Just be you."

Mr. Fullwood apologizes for running late, and the interview begins. It is just an incredible exchange. I am so happy to be here, in this moment, and Mr. Fullwood is a delightful, honest, open man. He asks me about my college experience, the deli, my parents, what I believe in. Finally, he asks me what I want.

"Bill, what's your dream?" No one outside my family has ever asked me what I want, but it's a question I've waited years to be asked by someone who has power to grant it to me.

I tell him how I admire David Kearns's focus on quality, and how I am willing to do anything for Xerox. "Sir, one day I would hope to become the CEO."

Nothing in my upbringing informed me that such an ambitious answer for an entry-level job could be taken for hubris, or come off as insincere, let alone ridiculous. I am just being me, full-throttle Bill. While other applicants are "considering their options," and going for some sales job, I am going for a dream.

"Bill, it was very nice meeting you," he says at the end of the interview. "You obviously have tremendous passion. We have very rigorous processes here at Xerox to review candidates. The human resources department will get in touch with you in the next few weeks. Thank you very much for your time." *Oh, we are not done.*

"Mr. Fullwood, I don't think you completely understand the situation." I pause, and then explain. "I told my father as I left him at the train station today, that I guaranteed I would come home tonight with my employee badge in my pocket. In twenty-one years, I've never broken a promise to my dad, and I can't start now." Silence. I don't fill it. Mr. Fullwood looks at me with his head kind of tilted, like a puppy waiting to see what I'm going to do next, but I don't make the next move.

This man doesn't know my family history, and I don't want or need him to know about the floods or the fire or how often my dad works overtime. No one owes me anything because of my past. All I can do in the present is ask for a chance to be miraculous in the future. I look into Mr. Fullwood's eyes until he smiles.

"Bill McDermott, I am going to do something I have never done in all my years at Xerox and hire you today. As long as you haven't broken any laws, you can go home and tell your father that you will be working for Xerox." I have to be sure I am hearing what I think I am hearing, because this is big.

"Mr. Fullwood, when you do the background check on me, I'll check out just fine, but I do want to confirm that you're going to hire me at the Xerox Corporation and I'm going to work for this company, yes? You've given me the job, is that right?" He nods as if even he can't believe it, and as I shake his hand, he holds it.

"Mr. McDermott, that's right." I gotta hug this man, so I do.

"Mr. Fullwood, I won't let you down. Thank you. Thank you very much." I pump his hand a few more times before leaving his office. I high-five Joanne on my way to the elevator and wave to the other applicant, still sitting on the bench.

Thirty-eight floors down, I charge out of the front of the building, onto Fifty-Seventh Street, and into the rush-hour flow of men with loosened ties and women in their business suits and sneakers. I run west toward Sixth Avenue, and on the corner I see a restaurant called the Bun n' Burger. I walk inside, find a pay phone, and take a quarter out of my suit pocket. I dial my house and get my mom and dad on the phone.

"Break out the Korbel," I declare. "I got the job! We're gonna celebrate tonight!"

PART 2

EMPATHY

6

LISTEN AND LEARN

*No one cares how much you know, until they know
how much you care.*

—THEODORE ROOSEVELT

T'S AUGUST 1983, it's hot, and I am a sales trainee hauling a small
but surprisingly heavy copy machine up four narrow flights of
stairs of a New York City brownstone. Behind me, Bob is carrying a
smaller but equally weighty electronic typewriter. Bob is a marketing rep about ten years older than I am, one of the experienced sales-
men that I've been traveling with for the past few days as part of my
training. Bob is supposed to be teaching me how to sell.

That morning, Bob got a lead, and because the faster we chase
leads the better chance we can close a deal—"C'mon, Bill! Let's go,
kid! Grab that box!"—we had just walked uptown at a decent clip
in the ninety-degree heat with the two machines. When we arrived
at the Upper East Side address, no elevator. *Man,* I had thought, *you
gotta be kidding me.*

We had been buzzed into the building. Now, balancing the machines on our backs, we are taking one stair at a time until we reach the fourth floor. When we summit, there's no time to catch our breath because the staircase empties us into what must be a home office. And a nice one. There's a large wooden desk and some filing cabinets in the middle of an elegant living space. A professionally dressed woman in a suit and heels walks out from a back room. I'm about to say hello when a cat—*a cat!*—leaps off an embroidered couch and flies at me and lands on my chest. I feel its claws sink through my suit and into my skin. *This cannot be!* The lady is staring at me. Bob is staring at me. I am sure his lips mouth a four-letter word, and even though an instinct urges me to save the suit and remove the cat, I don't. The second the animal hits my chest, a stronger instinct tells me that this is it, we have the deal. In that moment, I understand something Bob does not: *this cat is the boss.*

Bob is sweating. He just wants to unpack the machines from their cases and start the demo already. But I know what to do next, and it has nothing to do with those machines.

Even at twenty-two, as a nascent marketing rep in training, I was consumed with what people wanted and how I could give it to them. The intent in sales was making sure I found out what their desires were, and making the connection between that and what I had to offer, fast. If I drew it out, I'd lose it all. This was the art I lived to master.

The cat is clinging to me like a tree, but I smile at the woman and say, "Garfield's got nothing on this cat!" I'm not angry. I just want those claws out of my skin, so I peel the animal off my body. But I do not let it go. I hold on to it. I pet it. The lady walks over to where I am standing. The expression on her face, and the fact that she lets her pet wander around her office, tells me she loves this animal. "Beautiful kitty," I say. "What breed is it?"

The two of us start talking about her cat, and then about pets, and then dogs. I tell her about the German shepherd named Leo that showed up at the back door of Amato's restaurant every night. "In Amityville, where I grew up, ma'am, and worked as a busboy during high school." I tell her that the dog's owner was a good-hearted homeless man named Ray, and both he and the dog came looking for leftovers. "The three of us had a little routine. I'd sneak Ray food that hadn't been touched and give Leo scraps from diners' plates." In this small but intimate conversation, this woman with whom I probably have nothing in common and I are chatting like we met at a friend's rooftop cocktail party.

Bob starts twitching, like he can't believe his sale is about to go down the toilet because this rookie kid is screwing around with some stupid cat and telling stories about some homeless dude. Bob still doesn't realize that Garfield is the president of this company.

Eventually I hand the cat to its owner, and we move to her desk, where I unfold an eleven-inch-by-twenty-five-inch diagram of the copy machine's control panel that I'd pulled from my briefcase, and also carried up those stairs. Leaning over, I begin to explain how she can operate the copier once we take it out of its canvas case and plug it in. She interrupts me.

"Hon, do I really need to see a demo?" And it's done. She orders one copier and one typewriter. Boom. Bob says nothing, not sure of what has just happened. We never even unwrap the machines.

Back on the street in the relentless city heat, Bob looks at me and shakes his head. "Bill McDermott," he says, "you're either going to be the next CEO of Xerox, or you're going to jail."

From day one, I knew that sales was about people, not just products. A lot of other salespeople either didn't realize that, or they didn't care. I would walk into an office and try to figure out people's moods, their needs, their desires. Did I have my own agenda? Absolutely. But I had an interest in others' agendas, too. I wanted to know what mattered to someone standing in front of me; once I connected with people on a more personal level, anything became possible. A laugh. A lesson. A friendship. Even unloading thousands of dollars' worth of hardware without a demo. More than the machines Bob and I hauled up the stairs of the brownstone that day, and more than her business, what mattered most to the woman was her cat. Garfield was in charge. Over and over, in cold call after cold call, I tried to sense what mattered to people—and do something about it.

IMPROVISE

Still a trainee, I got paired with another more experienced marketing representative named Richard Reid. Richard was a good man, but our styles were different. He was reserved and was more process oriented than me. When Richard first met me, he saw a small-town kid in the big city—a "country bumpkin," he told his wife the night after we met. According to Richard, I talked too much.

One day Richard suggests that we head to a synagogue on Madison Avenue, where he's been unsuccessful at upgrading a disgruntled Xerox customer's machine. We walk into the temple's administrative office, and an older man, but not, I gather, a rabbi, recognizes Richard. The man puts up a hand. "You know what, you've been here before, and we really don't have a need."

It's clear to me that this guy doesn't want us to be here. Like most New Yorkers, he's quick to say no even at the whiff of a sales pitch. But in the McDermott dictionary, the word "no" means "maybe," and my objective is not to sell him anything but to give him what he wants. My mind races as I ask myself, *Who is this man? What is he trying to get done here? Why is he so resistant to us?* I figure that Xerox probably sold him a machine that didn't perform, and nobody had followed up in a way that made him happy.

This conclusion was not difficult for a Xerox salesperson to come to in the early 1980s. The Xerox Corporation was at a precarious point. Here was a company that had invented an industry—the mass copy-making market—with a revolutionary technology called xerography. Some even hailed xerography, which translated to "dry writing" in Greek, as revolutionary as the invention of the wheel. That comparison seemed ridiculous even back in the eighties, when faxing was considered high-tech. But before xerography went mainstream, making a copy of anything—a recipe, a Bible passage, a tax filing—was a messy, expensive proposition. Not something the average person even considered doing before the 1960s. But after Xerox introduced its first single-page, dry-copy machine in 1959, copying's utility went viral. People started to make copies of everything from invoices and employee memos to comic strips. Xerox monopolized the industry throughout the sixties. It hit $1 billion in sales in just eight years, faster than any company ever had. Xerox's was a legendary run.

But Xerox stumbled into the 1970s. Drunk on its success, the one-time "little engine that could" got fat and bureaucratic and let product quality and customer service slip. As a young go-getter who had pinned his dreams on Xerox, I was only slightly aware of—and maybe a bit blind to—my employers' shortcomings. I believed so much in Xerox, and in our CEO's recent promise to turn us around by improving quality and customer service, that on sales calls I stood behind the Xerox brand. I believed we had the best company, the best people, the best training, and a great vision for our future. Despite our problems, the company was still revered in the marketplace. So whenever I met prospective customers, I saw myself as selling them a brand, not just a box.

When I come up against disgruntled customers, similar to the gentleman who wanted to kick Richard and me out of his temple, I know that launching into a scripted pitch will kill any chance we have. Instead, I try to imagine how the person is feeling. Ignored, maybe. Even unloved. The office manager probably believes that he was sold a piece of junk, and regardless of how many Xerox people had visited him in the past, he is rightfully sore that no one took care of his needs and solved his problems.

"Sir, we aren't here just to sell you something," I say, then deviate to a topic that interests both of us. "The synagogue is such an historic building, and every time Richie and I walk by, we're just amazed at the architecture, its beauty. Since I'm Catholic, and Richard here is a Catholic, can you tell us a little bit about it?" He smiles. The next thing we know, the gentleman is offering us iced tea, inviting us to sit down so he can tell us the history of the congregation. The temple and his heritage matter to this man—and, I assume, so does making the Xerox Corporation pay for its past transgressions.

In that moment, I tell myself that I cannot talk to this man about his future with Xerox until I remedy our company's original sin. "Sir, if I may. We've obviously let you down. We need to make that right." He looks at me, willing to hear me out. I assure him that we will take care of him, and then ask if he will allow us to fix the broken relationship, as well as the faulty copier.

If empathy is about figuring out what matters to other people, improvisation is about answering that question in the moment, and then acting on it. Improvising under stress requires courage, which was why, as a newly trained salesman, I often compared myself to a marine just out of boot camp. When we were under fire, the tendency for both soldier and salesman was to stick to the tactics we were taught, because doing so felt safe, especially in unpredictable situations.

Xerox armed its salespeople with various strategies. The S.P.I.N. sales training technique, for one, called for assessing a customer's "Situation" and "Problem," and then articulating the "Implications" and, finally, a "Needs Payoff." This tactic wasn't a bad way to sell, and I leaned on S.P.I.N. during my first months. But I also learned what soldiers discover on the field of battle: even a great strategy rarely survives first contact with the enemy. I didn't see my customers as my adversaries, but since my earliest days on the front lines of selling, I would go into meetings prepared to follow a plan such as S.P.I.N., yet also prepared for something to throw me off—like a cat or an angry customer. Only by improvising through imperfect situations could I create more perfect outcomes.

One hour after Richard and I were almost ushered out of the synagogue, we had scheduled a time to come back and demo Xerox's newest machine. The deal was as good as done.

FREEDOM

During my first year at Xerox, I reported to two different managers. Ron was a seasoned sales manager who smoked cigarettes in his office and ate tomato soup with a tuna fish sandwich for lunch at his desk almost every day. We worked well together because I was young and spry and liked to run, and Ron was happy to let me be young and spry and run. On the rare day that Ron felt it was his duty to travel with me, I ran extra hard. I did not like feeling managed, or babysat, and after a day of trying to keep pace, Ron was all too happy to let me go back to selling solo.

My next manager, Mark, was sharp. He trusted me to do my thing, as I regularly exceeded my sales goals. I appreciated the freedom he gave me. Even though I worked for a big corporation, I felt like an entrepreneur, in charge of my own piece of real estate.

I came to respect my first two managers for giving me space. Effective leaders, I was realizing, didn't spend their time supervising highfliers but rather investing time with people who asked for and required support. If I needed my bosses to break through Xerox's bureaucracy to get my customer's credit approved or deal with a complex shipping issue, I asked Ron or Mark to make some internal calls, and they always did. But mostly they let me run loose.

HONOR THE ECOSYSTEM

Because I graduated at the top of my sales training class, I was assigned the sales territory I wanted. Fifty-Seventh to Fifty-Ninth Streets between Fifth Avenue and Park Avenue was a dense strip of activity, and its adrenaline hit me every time I walked out of Xerox's uptown headquarters. Our building's sloped glass façade, with its huge ruby-red "9" statue perched on the sidewalk, was located in one of the hottest neighborhoods on the planet. Midtown Manhattan. Center of my universe. I fell in love with Central Park, Trump Tower, the Plaza Hotel, even the hot dog vendors who sold me lunch for a buck. Like a baseball pitcher from a farm team called up to play for the New York Yankees, I could not have been more fired up.

I was determined to be Xerox's number one new-business salesperson in the country. That was my goal my first year. Number one out of about eight hundred.

Bounding through midtown each morning, I'd gaze up at the skyscrapers that lined the avenues and see floor after floor after floor of potential customers. All I had to do was get past the buildings' lobbies. In the 1980s, Manhattan's office buildings had light security. What they did have were doormen, and these guys were the gatekeepers. I admired these men who stood on their feet all day monitoring the hundreds of expressionless faces that flowed in and out of their jurisdiction. Doormen weren't second-class citizens, and I showed them the same respect I showed my business prospects—the same respect I'd shown teenagers at my deli; the customers that the 7-Eleven ignored.

I became friends with doormen up and down the avenues. We didn't go out for beers, but I knew their favorite teams and their kids' names. And they knew that I was from Amityville, still lived there with my parents, and rode the Long Island Rail Road into Manhattan every day. Sometimes I brought them a Styrofoam cup of coffee or a bagel, and we chatted for a few minutes about sports, the weather, family.

What they did for a living was important to them, and it was important to what I did for a living. We all knew it. Eventually whenever something wiggled in any one of the buildings on my beat—a new corporate tenant moved in, for instance, or a company expanded onto another floor—I heard about it through the doormen. Some left messages for me at work, and they all had my business card: Bill McDermott, Marketing Representative, The Xerox Corporation. They passed my card to new tenants. "Call Bill. He'll take care of you."

I was able to scale my sales because many doormen let me stage product demonstrations in their lobbies. Together we'd get the building manager's permission, and I'd put up some signs and pass out flyers announcing the upcoming demo, trying to create a little buzz throughout the building. Maybe I'd provide refreshments next to the machines, so that people walking in and out of the lobby would be inclined to stop. "How's your day going, ma'am? Please, enjoy a few cookies; take some back to your office for your coworkers." They'd linger, and we'd visit. If I could get a secretary to try Xerox's electronic typewriter, which Xerox called the Memorywriter, suddenly her manual typewriter back at the office wasn't looking too impressive. And when someone saw me demo how a Xerox machine could enlarge and reduce documents, run two-sided copies, and beautifully reproduce photos, the tasks appeared effortless—almost fun. In my training class, I had won the demo-rama, where salespeople showed off their ability to demonstrate Xerox's products. I danced with these machines.

After each lobby demo session, I swapped business cards with dozens of people, following up the next day to schedule appointments. In a typical office building with forty-five floors and five companies per floor, I could reach fifty companies in one afternoon, a huge base from which I sourced new leads.

I showed receptionists and administrative assistants just as much respect. They knew I was there to sell something, and I never hid that fact. But I also wanted them to know that they weren't mere obstacles to my prize. Having a real conversation with a secretary took only a few extra minutes—"What's cookin' in your world? Here's what's cookin' in mine"—and made everyone feel good.

Secretaries and doormen were part of my territory's ecosystem; important people that other sales reps often ignored. But being kind to everyone was not just the right thing to do, it was key to selling more machines. I also got to know some fantastic people while getting easier access to decision makers.

Engaging with people on a personal level definitely helped strangers feel like friends, but if I was going to be the best marketing rep in the country, I needed to be more than just a nice young man.

7

OUT-HUSTLE

The harder you work, the luckier you get.
—GARY PLAYER

WALK INTO THE marble lobby of 745 Fifth Avenue, say hello to the doorman, go up the elevator, knock on an office door, have a quick conversation with the receptionist, and get invited in to see the office manager. She's a lovely lady. I introduce myself, and we make small talk for a few moments.

"Well, it's interesting you should stop by," she says. "Our copier is down again." This I already know because I had seen the broken copier in a corner when I walked in. Xerox salespeople were trained to identify equipment within ten seconds of entering a room, like a cop who walks into a bar and immediately knows what brand of cigarettes is in the bartender's shirt pocket. If a Xerox salesperson was lucky, there would be a piece of paper taped to the machine: Out of Order. If a Xerox salesperson was very lucky, it would not be a Xerox copier, but a competitor's. Today I am very lucky.

"Wow, what does that mean to you when the copier's down?" I ask her. She explains, and I listen. When she is done, I put my spin on Xerox's S.P.I.N., eventually sharing how a newer copier will increase her productivity.

"That all sounds about right," she says, "but I need to get authorization from my boss, and he's not in." Other salespeople, especially someone on his first day selling solo, as I am today, would take this as a no, say thanks, and leave. I say, "Not a problem. How about this: I know which copier you need, so I'll just have one delivered, no signature required, and when your boss comes back, it'll be up and running, you'll finish your job, and if it performs to your satisfaction, we can do the paperwork then, no big deal."

"Really, you can do that?"

"I can do anything. The copier will be here by noon tomorrow." She nods, and I almost jump out of my suit. The trust clock starts ticking. That copier has got to show up.

I run the few blocks back to my desk and spend the afternoon dealing with Xerox's back office, navigating a frustrating maze of paperwork and process to ensure that a Xerox 2350 arrives at 745 Fifth Avenue not a second past noon the next day. If it doesn't, I lose trust and my first sale. Even if the back office screws up the paperwork, or the delivery truck gets the wrong address, it's all on me. I take no chances.

My diligence pays off. The machine arrives. I am there to usher it into its new home, and I stand by as it's installed. Then I waltz through my demo. I leave the machine overnight, a happy puppy with its new owners well trained in its care. I can barely sleep. The next day, I'm back. The office manager has finished her project. Her boss is pleased, and he signs the prepared contract I'd brought with me, as well as the pickup order so that the old copier can be hauled away.

Back down in the building's lobby, I high-five the doorman and walk outside feeling like I own the city.

TACTICS

Months into my job as a solo marketing rep, my sales began coming in so high that my peers were asking for advice or to tag along with me on sales calls. I never refused. I got a lot of pleasure helping someone clinch a deal or better manage his or her time. Like basketball, we were a team. As we huddled around someone's desk, I felt like my grandfather on the court while I explained my techniques to my teammates.

I wasn't smarter than any of them, and my tactics weren't complicated. I just hustled.

For me, hustling began with a will to win backed by a strong work ethic and integrity. Although I hustled, I wasn't a hustler. Salespeople could be saddled with a shifty reputation, but I believed that most folks who chose the profession were givers, not takers. The best ones genuinely wanted to help other people find solutions to problems. That's still the job. If we are good at it, we can make a career out of it. And as long as I am selling to others in a way that aligns my desires with their interests, I never see selling as a win-lose proposition. I always want a win-win.

At Xerox, my hustle also was about speed and action, envisioning and managing desired outcomes. Everything I did had a purpose. I walked into a prospect's office determined to close a deal, and I beelined through the halls of Xerox with a destination in sight, whether it was my boss's office or the men's room. I always knew where I was going, and I wanted to get there and back to selling as quickly as possible. I never rambled, not in my walk or in my talk. Everything had a bull's-eye.

I also had fun along the way, sharing little stories about my day and making people smile, but I never stopped moving.

I was surprised by how much time other salespeople spent in the office, at their desks in the bullpen, instead of on the streets. They'd

be filling out their Franklin day planners with beautiful penman-
ship or organizing their business cards or talking on the phone when
I was whisking out of the building like a tornado.

Most of my tactics were behaviors I'd been prone to since childhood.

I worked a lot. By 5:50 a.m., I was on a train from Amityville,
willing the wheels to roll faster to speed my one-and-a-half-hour
commute. By 9:00 a.m., I was on the streets, prepared to pack fifty
sales calls into the day instead of the typical thirty; more chances for
yes. I blew past the long lunches my colleagues invited me to and just
kept jammin'. I was too poor to eat and too amped up to slow down.
There was no time, no reason, for even the smallest creature com-
forts to crawl into my world. At the end of a day, when my coworkers were headed to the subway or a bar, I was heading into the office
to tighten up for the next day.

When rejected, I persevered. Some salespeople, I noticed, ducked
into Bloomingdale's or grabbed a drink to kill time to avoid another
fruitless cold call. Even on a tough day, I resisted artificial pick-me-
ups. I'd gone into sales accepting that it could be disheartening—I'd
experienced rejection from the paper route, whenever someone
dissed my offer to buy a batch of greeting cards. So the issue for me
was not whether I'd hear a no after knocking on a door—that was
inevitable—but how many yeses I could accumulate.

My hustle was also about discipline. I became adept at organizing my work and managing my time, habits I picked up from my
other grandfather, Papa, the construction foreman. He was no superstar athlete like my dad's father, Bobby McDermott, who off the
court had a tendency to bulldoze through daily life. In contrast, my
mother's father managed his existence with an architect's precision.
As a kid, I'd walk into his garage in awe. Every tool had its place,
like in a museum. On Sunday mornings, I'd watch him polish his
dress shoes and select one of his ties, dressing to show respect as well

as earn it. My grandfather micromanaged the details of his life, creating a sense of peace and purpose that I found appealing, and which I adopted.

I also looked for hidden and bigger opportunities. Once I connected with someone, I looked beyond the sale in front of me. Was the office a subsidiary of a larger firm? Did the company have more locations at which I could replicate this sale many times over, and offer the overall organization an attractive price based on the size of the ultimate deal and exponential productivity gains? "Who are the buyers in other departments?" I might ask, or "Is there a national purchasing manager I may call to share what you've accomplished here?"

I also sought out any affiliation that had the potential to yield more sales. I wanted to meet anyone my customer could influence. "Are you familiar with the people down the hall who own the advertising agency? Wonderful, would you mind letting them know that I'll be coming by?" I was willing to talk to anyone and aimed for as high up in the company as I could get.

I was known for being extremely prepared. I studied and became as familiar with Xerox's history, technologies, and products as I was with my own family. Sometimes I would tell prospective customers how, in the 1930s, a poor physicist-turned-law-student named Chester Carlson toiled away in a small Astoria, Queens, apartment—not far from where I was born, by the way—inventing a new way to copy words onto paper. And then maybe I'd explain how a business owner named Joe Wilson used his resources and his company to perfect Chester's invention and bring it to market to create the Xerox Corporation. And how, now, Xerox's CEO, David Kearns, was dedicated to the highest-quality products and service.

"Please, will you tell me about your own company's history?" I loved to ask. Not only did I hear fascinating stories, but the more I learned about someone's business, the more I could cross-sell from

Xerox's portfolio of products, or upsell add-ons, in ways that were meaningful to that person's business.

I had all of Xerox pricing options and combinations memorized. Other salespeople might get a prospective customer's specifications and then scurry back to Xerox's offices to calculate a proposed payment plan, and then phone the prospect the next day with the numbers. I would run the numbers in my head, on the spot, and tell a potential buyer just how much the copier would be each month to lease or to buy outright. When it came to pricing deals, my accounting wasn't complicated. I had just entered the room prepared to close a deal that made sense for the customer and made money for Xerox.

After every sales call, I followed up within twenty-four hours. After a meeting, I immediately wrote a letter to people thanking them for their time and summarizing what we'd discussed and agreed to do next. My own memory was pretty sharp. But without something in writing, I risked being forgotten in the blur of the day and losing the sale. My twenty-four-hour rule also built my credibility. Manhattan was a tough town. If I wasn't buttoned up, people could forget—or rescind—what they had promised me. My twenty-four-hour rule ensured that they didn't.

I knew success was not an accident, so I was always hungry to learn from the pros.

One thing I learned was that for all the different selling styles, it was self-confidence that distinguished high performers from those who barely met their quotas. One of Xerox's best salespeople was a dignified, well-mannered man whom I greatly admired. He taught me how to earn customers' respect by playing the part of their equal. "Ask them to hang up your raincoat. And remember, Bill, never talk to an executive standing up. Get them to sit down with you, like a gentleman," Mike told me. "And if they offer you something to drink, accept it. Of course you're thirsty. Now you're dialed in, and ready to have a real conversation."

Once, I traveled with a marketing rep named Darrell, who, in contrast, was unprofessional and, by my standards, did everything wrong. He got to the office late. He phoned in sales forecasts from his bathtub. His suits needed pressing. But what Darrell did have was the self-confidence to close. His famous lines seemed so simple: "So, ma'am, how many machines would you like? Do you want them today? When would you like the copier delivered, sir?" As late and lazy as Darrell was, the man asked for an order, which many salespeople hesitated to do. I was similar to Darrell. I loved to close. But unlike Darrell, a respect and lust for the entire sales process fueled me, from dressing the part and walking the streets to the first hello and the final handshake.

At the end of each day, I arrived back at 9 West Fifty-Seventh Street, entered my sales team's bullpen, grabbed a Magic Marker, and walked up to the poster boards that listed every salesperson's name. Next to my name, I would write the number of units I'd sold that day and how much money I'd brought in. I didn't strut. I wasn't obnoxious about what I had accomplished. I cheered my teammates for their day's successes—and if someone had a lousy afternoon, I'd invite him to join me the next day to regain his energy. But I did not hide or apologize for my dream. Everyone knew that Bill McDermott wanted to be Xerox's number one salesperson.

In pursuit of that goal, few things slowed my pace. Among those that did, though, were family and friends. When I received a telephone message from my sales colleague Richard Reid that he wouldn't be at work because his wife was in labor, I hightailed it out of my office, bought some flowers at a corner bodega, and took a cab to Lenox Hill Hospital. I was the first non–family member to see Richard's newborn baby girl.

Another thing that hijacked my attention was the magnificent Steinway & Sons piano showroom on Fifty-Seventh Street. If I had five extra minutes, I'd stop on the sidewalk and stare at the small herd of glossy pianos on the other side of the glass. *One day,* I promised myself, *I'm going to get one of those.* If I had a few more minutes, I'd go inside and wander around, maybe run my hand along the curved lid of a baby grand like it was the hood of a Porsche. I'd always admired beautiful objects, yet I was not explicitly after a Steinway or even a Porsche. Objects were symbols of the future my mind focused on achieving. *I will get there. I will be there.* My dream was not about being rich, but about high achievement. It was about significance. For a young professional who grew up with very little money, the stuff money could buy was an easy way to measure progress. Ultimately, however, I knew that my life's value would never be measured by things acquired, but by heart, by will, and by honor.

That's why I had my limits as to how far I was willing to go for a win.

INTEGRITY

The very first time I talked to Xerox's CEO, David Kearns, I apologized.

The day started like any other. I was making cold calls in midtown, and after entering a building on Fifty-Seventh Street, I had taken an elevator up a few dozen floors to the office of an executive whose name was on my call sheet. I did not have an appointment. I walked up to the receptionist, we chatted, and I told her that I was from Xerox and wanted to introduce myself to her boss. She said okay with a tinge of reluctance and pointed to a glass-walled office where a man was sitting behind a desk. The door was open. When I walked in, I extended my hand.

"Hello, sir, I'm Bill McDermott from the Xerox Corporation. Very nice to—" My words lit a fuse.

"How dare you bother me with a sales call!" he yelled. "Do you know who I am? I'm David Kearns's neighbor!"

Apparently the man's company was already a Xerox customer. He had a right to be upset. I had come in uninformed, but his reaction was extreme. After trying to apologize, I turned around to leave the office. But the man followed me into the crowded waiting room and continued to berate me, insisting, loudly, that he was going to call David Kearns himself and get me fired. It was too much. I stopped and turned to face the irate individual.

"Sir, I understand what you're saying, but please understand something from my point of view."

"What's that?" he demanded, looking down at me. I felt the weight of brochures in my briefcase.

"I have been thrown out of four offices today that were twice as nice as yours. Have a good day." He was silent as I turned and exited the office. Standing alone in the mirrored elevator, I looked at my reflection and saw a tall, young man in a spiffy navy blue suit and red tie. "McDermott," I said out loud, "you totally screwed this up. They're gonna fire you."

As upset as I was, I also felt like a man because I had refused to sacrifice my self-respect, even if doing so meant losing the greatest job in the world. I did, however, cringe at the thought of the angry customer talking to Mr. Kearns about me. Since joining Xerox, I had developed a real admiration for our chief. He had a clear vision and was a strong leader, but not in an iron-fisted way. Easy to smile, David was someone I wanted to follow. "I will tolerate the skeptics, but not the cynics," I'd heard him say in a corporate video. His positive attitude won my loyalty.

By the time the elevator doors opened into the building's lobby, I had made a decision. I ran to the first pay phone I saw and poured a few coins into the slot. I dialed the Xerox Corporation's main number and asked the operator to please put me through to the office of the chief executive officer. "Yes, ma'am: Mr. Kearns." If I could get to him before his neighbor did, maybe I'd have a shot at keeping my job.

"Mr. Kearns," I said when I heard his voice, "my name is Bill McDermott." Into the pay phone's sticky receiver, I described what had just happened at his neighbor's office, including my final insult. "Sir, I apologize if I've offended the Xerox Corporation, but I had to be true to myself. I was only acting with the highest integrity trying to sell my stuff, and if I messed up, I accept the consequences completely."

"Bill," he said, "I want you to know that if that jackass calls me, I'll let him know you're my best guy out there. Keep doing what you're doing, kid."

From that point on, my enthusiasm and loyalty for Xerox doubled. More than ever, I wanted to be the next David Kearns.

By the end of 1984, I believed I was on my way. I had done it. My total sales that year were 1,004 percent of my assigned quota, outpacing hundreds of other new-business sales reps. I ranked as Xerox's top marketing representative in the United States. I had earned more than four times my base salary in commissions. I couldn't afford a baby grand, but I was saving to buy my first house in Amityville. For the second time in my Xerox career, my mom and dad broke out the Korbel.

After toasting my accomplishment with my parents, I went to sleep and woke up at five o'clock the next morning, ready to do it all again.

8

REGISTER AMBITION

Control your own destiny or someone else will.
—JACK WELCH

ARLY ONE WEEKDAY morning, I leave my parents' house in the dark and instead of catching my train, I drive my Firebird over the New York State border toward Xerox's offices in Stamford, Connecticut, where the top regional executives work. When I park in the empty lot, at about seven o'clock, the lights in the building still haven't been lit.

I have no appointment, and my surprise visit has the potential to scorch my career. I'm just a low-level marketing rep showing up unannounced to see Roy Haythorn, a vice president and general manager of Xerox's eastern region, for one reason: I'd been passed up for a promotion to an account representative position.

I know Roy from last year's President's Club trip, the annual celebration for Xerox's top sales performers. He's one of the most dynamic leaders I've seen at Xerox. Relentlessly upbeat, the man believes that everyone should win on merit. Roy's also a bit of a gun-slinger. He holds monthly instead of quarterly meetings so that his teams know exactly what to do to hit their sales targets, and when his people succeed, Roy throws spontaneous, often lavish celebrations. I like Roy.

My intent here is not to reverse the decision and get the job I'd lost. I am here to understand why and to make sure that Xerox's leadership understands my ambitions. If I was passed over for performance, I need to know how I can improve. But if I was overlooked for reasons that had nothing to do with my skills, I want to register with Roy just how serious I am about excelling—and working for a company that makes that happen for people who show results.

Sitting in my car, waiting for a parade of Mercedes-Benzes and BMWs to arrive, I contemplate other outcomes. If Roy refuses to see me, I'll assume that Xerox does not stand by its open-door policy, and I'll consider quitting. If, after our meeting, I don't believe Roy supports me, I'll assume that Xerox isn't sincere about nurturing top talent, and I'll send my résumé to a company that is—like one of the financial firms that are always trying to poach people from our sales force. A third scenario, I know, is that I'll leave Stamford satisfied, but because I broke the coveted chain of command, people below Roy will retaliate and sabotage my career. It's a risk, but I cannot hesitate to ask for what I want.

As a kid, when I delivered newspapers, I walked up to strangers' front doors and asked for unpaid route money. As a salesperson, when I make cold calls, I almost always ask for the order. Now, to ensure that I do not fall through corporate cracks, I have to ask for the job I want. *Here we go.*

Inside the lobby, I ask the receptionist for Mr. Haythorn's floor, flash my business card, and am waved through. I exit the elevator and walk past offices lining the perimeter. The quiet, stark décor has the hushed aura of power, which pumps me up even more than New

York City's bustle. I approach Roy's assistant with a smile. He has just arrived. One moment. Yes, he will see me.

In his office, I thank Roy for his time and explain that I was passed up for an account representative job. Roy has no idea I was not promoted. The account job is three levels below this man's radar.

"Mr. Haythorn, I did not come here to get anyone in trouble or to ask for the assignment," I say. "The decision has been made; I understand that. I am here to understand why I was not selected, given that my sales were three times higher than the sales of the person who got the job, and to understand how I can do better so I can keep moving up, because that's why I came to work for Xerox." I am not asking Roy for a guarantee that I'll get any gig I want. I'm asking to be heard, to be mentored, to be seen as a contender for top jobs.

"Bill, I'm glad you came and brought this to my attention." I'm relieved. Roy doesn't sound annoyed. "Today is important, Bill, but the long haul is more important. Nine times out of ten, things will go right for you, but maybe one time out of ten, they won't. Don't let that stand in the way of your ambition." Roy was telling me to be patient. Then he said, "As long as you perform, and as long as I'm around, things will be good for you at Xerox." I believe him. *Take care of your top performers, and they will take care of you.* When I get up to leave, we shake hands. "Thank you, Roy. Thank you for your support."

On the way out of the building, I see Emerson Fullwood, polished as ever but shocked to see me walking Stamford's hallowed halls.

"Bill, what's going on?"

"Emerson, I was passed up for a job, and I needed to understand why. So I came to see Mr. Haythorn." Emerson thinks I've gone too far. He, too, urges me to have patience. He assures me my time will come.

Was I being too bold? To me, approaching Roy was no different from approaching the top manager at the Finast supermarket to state my case instead of hoping my application got noticed in the pile. I respected protocol. But in truth, I didn't have the patience to let it thwart my career. I had to speak to someone who believed that performance deserved to be rewarded. That was Roy.

Driving back into Manhattan, I feel as if I've accomplished something much greater than if I had actually gotten the promotion: I had stood up for myself. No one would ever care about my career as much as I did. Careers had to be nurtured and protected, and that was how I would go after my dreams. As long as I acted with integrity—I wouldn't badmouth or offend others—I felt comfortable, and unapologetic, being my bold self.

A few months later, when an account representative position opens up, I am chosen to fill it.

PREMEDITATED MOVES

The man in charge of Xerox's New York operations, Tom Dolan, squints at me over a slice of pizza as if trying to figure out a puzzle. Tom is several months into his new job supervising three branch managers, twelve sales managers, and 168 sales reps, of which I am one. Someone in management had suggested to Tom that he spend time with me. Tom saw no reason to hang out with a rookie sales rep, but I'd been the top-selling US salesperson in my category for the past two years. Tom asks to go to lunch.

This lunch is a big deal. In my quest to make it into Xerox management, I want management to know who I am. So over pizza and the clamor of midtown's lunch hour, I don't even consider curbing my energy. Tom is two levels above me, so I talk about my past few years at Xerox with my usual spray of enthusiasm. I even admit my desire to be the next David Kearns. I see no need to hide my aspirations.

I ask Tom, "What do you think about Mr. Kearns's quality initiatives? Are they working? Getting more traction? Is Xerox's newest line of copiers, the 10-series, still selling well?"

He answers my questions, but all the while looks at me from the other side of our booth as if I've downed the entire pitcher of Xerox's Kool-Aid. Tom is as loyal to Xerox as anyone, he is no cynic, but still his head tilts, like Emerson's did the day of my interview. I will come to know the thought behind this look: *Is this guy for real?* Because he's not sure, Tom schedules another lunch.

This time Tom asks more questions. I tell him more about my family, about the corner deli and how I used its profits to pay for college. It feels, even to me, like a more meaningful conversation. This time Tom doesn't tilt his head. I walk away hoping he likes me. I would enjoy his friendship, and soon I will need his support.

In the months since I'd sprinted up to Stamford, I'd spent my nights completing Xerox's management readiness program, a series of training classes and procedure manuals for potential leaders. At the end of the program, people who wanted to interview for management positions were grilled by a panel of senior executives. The panel assessed whether they were ready to apply for a management role, and doled out one of three statuses to each candidate: you were either deemed ready to interview for management positions within one year or in one to three years; or, according to the panel, you were not management material and never would be ready. The last was not uncommon.

I took all the classes, read all the books, I knew all Xerox's processes and was prepared for the inquisition. The verdict? I was young, and labeled ready in one to three years. For me, a lifetime. So when a position managing a sales team in Xerox's uptown territory opened up, I called Tom.

PASSION AND PLANNING TRUMP AGE AND EXPERIENCE

I want that job. The sales manager for Team F—Xerox's sales teams were named by letters—will oversee sixteen marketing reps cold-calling on small and midsized businesses. We would go after new accounts, not existing clients. The territory is huge, running north of

Fifty-Seventh Street to 155th Street, passing through Harlem and to the Bronx, and spanning west from the East River all the way to the Hudson River.

The territory also includes Manhattan's Upper East and Upper West Sides, which are probably the most expensive places to live in the city. Their respective blocks of posh residential high-rises book-end Central Park. From a salesman's perspective, the neighborhoods are rich with firms that cater to the wealthy—and these small shops need the newest copiers, typewriters, and fax machines. Plus, who wouldn't want to spend his days on these beautiful streets? River to river, Fifty-Seventh Street to Eightieth Street is the most beautiful piece of Manhattan.

Farther north, Harlem and the Bronx are more diverse and even more interesting. Their streets have their own splendor. They also have more crime. This year the Bronx is being depicted in Tom Wolfe's best-selling novel *The Bonfire of the Vanities* as the last place a corporate guy in a suit and tie wants to get lost. But the book paints an exaggerated picture. Many Bronx neighborhoods are on the rebound, full of small to midsized retailers, manufacturers, independent law offices, insurance brokers. As I see it, all of uptown is rich in opportunity, with thousands of companies that need Xerox products to help them grow.

I want to lead this team more than anything, but according to Xerox's human resources rules, I am not eligible to interview. That's why I reach out to Tom.

"Tom, this is my job. I know it, and I'm right for it. I want to go for it with everything in my heart and my soul. If I get it, I will make Team F number one. Please, I am asking you, Tom, can I have your support?"

If this had been the first time Tom had met me, he might not have agreed. He urges me to go for it. But to make it happen, he has to get his boss's approval so that I can bypass the HR rules. His boss permits me to apply. Tom, however, is not the ultimate decision maker. A district manager named Kathy Mullally will make the final call. It's up to me to convince Kathy I am the best person for the job.

Just one problem: Kathy was one of the executives I'd bypassed when I'd gone to Stamford to talk to Roy. Even though that was a while back, corporate feathers can stay ruffled a long time. It's possible Kathy is upset about my trip up to Connecticut.

The day of our interview, Kathy's office feels lucky. She works in Emerson's former space, the place where I'd asked him to help me keep my promise to my dad. Two years later, this office feels familiar, but the job candidate looks a little different.

I am no longer wearing $99 mall attire. I really did like that suit, but when I looked around at Xerox executives that I admired, the ones that stood out in the sea of brown and gray Brooks Brothers wore gorgeous blue suits from Giorgio Armani, with beautiful, crisp white shirts and bright blue or red ties. Men like Barry Rand, the president of Xerox's US operations, always looked sharp. I kept my eye on Barry, and as my bank account increased, I took my newly acquired American Express card into Saks Fifth Avenue and pulled an Armani off the rack. That's what I'm wearing for my interview today, with a handkerchief peeking from my breast pocket. Dressed beyond my present pay grade, I am wearing the jacket. Kathy's eyebrows go up when I enter her office.

If I get this job, I will be one of the youngest sales managers in Xerox's history. For now, I am the least experienced candidate. When I found out that some of the other contenders were in their thirties, I knew I had real competition. I had to prove that my passion and performance trumped their age and experience. So I had done a little reconnaissance, approaching the other candidates after their interviews.

"How'd the conversations go?" I asked.

"Oh, pretty good. I'm considering the job." Their faces were blasé. *Okay*, I think, *same old story: they don't want this job as much as I do*. I feel sure I can beat them on passion, but that will not be enough.

"How's your marketing plan?" I asked my competition. "Did they like your plan?"

"Well, we didn't review a plan in detail. It was more like a Q&A." *So, not only do I want it more, but I also have a plan.* I had thought a lot about how newly elected presidents make it a point to distinguish themselves during their first hundred days in office, so I asked myself: *How would I handle my first hundred days as a sales manager?* I typed up my strategy on several sheets of paper, which I wrapped in a clear report jacket and have carried with me into Kathy's office.

At first, I let Kathy ask all the questions. I respect her authority. I also don't need to waste her time seeking predictable answers to generic questions about salary and the sales turf. I did my homework. I know these answers. When I do ask a question, it will count.

Our conversation covers my knowledge of Xerox's products and procedures, topics I'd tackled with the management panel. My answers are thorough. Only after I have addressed all her questions am I ready to launch mine.

"Kathy, may I go off script a bit and tell you what makes me different?" Not better, I say, *different.*

"I'd appreciate that, Bill, because this is a very hard decision."

"You already know my record since I joined Xerox. My passion has only increased since then, and let me tell you why, Kathy. I have found my calling, and it's not being an individual contributor hitting big numbers. My dream is to help others hit big numbers. Ask anyone on my account team now. When they're down and out, whom do they travel with to get their confidence back? Whose desk do they stop by to ask for help with deals and handling executive meetings? I never cut corners when it comes to helping people, because that's when I fly. Kathy, helping people is what makes me happy! This is what I love to do, and this is what I promise you I will do for my team."

"Bill, if you were to take this job, you'd get a significant pay cut."

"Kathy, there were times in my life when I couldn't put two

bucks together. It's not about the money for me, although I know how to make it up, and I can explain that to you. This job is a step to my ultimate dream, which is someday to be the CEO of Xerox."

Kathy, I imagine, has her own dreams, and to reach them, the people she hires have to make her look good. So I tell her how, if I get the job, I will make us both look good. "Kathy, I have a plan. Would you like to see it?"

I hand her my report and walk through it page by page. First, I go over process. Xerox's senior executives are trained in the science of management, and I want to reassure Kathy that I, too, know the methods: I will have monthly planning reviews with each sales rep on my team; each week, I will evaluate everyone's forecasts and his or her pipeline to validate if the marketing representative and the team is on track; every day, we will measure individual as well as team performance; I will hold people accountable for results, and if they don't deliver, I will write a letter of concern, issuing a formal warning, in case we have to walk someone out the door. I tell Kathy how many phone calls Xerox wants its reps to make each day, but because my standards are higher, my reps will make more calls than the company requires. My people will also knock on more doors and send more letters.

I have proven that I know process and will exceed even Xerox's expectations. But what makes me different?

In the first hundred days, I tell Kathy, I will assess each of my team member's strengths and create four miniteams, each led by one of our strongest salespeople, who will rotate teams to spread their individual talents. I also will teach my team the same tactics that I used to reach number one as a salesman. I don't know if Kathy is a basketball fan, but I tell her I will be a player-coach.

"Kathy, you know that I can sell. And I know that I can get everyone on the team to sell. Give me this chance, and I will make this team number one in the country. I guarantee it. Number one."

"Well, Bill, that is very different from everyone else." She is smiling. "I appreciate everything you've done today." I'm usually good at reading people, but now I can't tell what she's thinking. *Thanks but no thanks?* I can't leave without knowing.

"Kathy, I respect you, and therefore I don't want to ask you tedious questions. I only want to ask you one more: Will you give me your trust and give me a shot at doing this job?"

"Bill, there's a process we have to go through . . ." I read her now. *Don't push.* The closer in me wants to know, but I must be patient.

"Kathy, my trust is in your hands, and I believe the right thing will happen. I'll be in the office early tomorrow if you'd like to talk some more." She doesn't make any promises, and I head for the train to Amityville. I believe I have done everything I can do to win this job.

To get what I want, I have to give others what they want: performance. Unless I consistently meet and exceed goals and deliver on promises, no one owes me a thing. Passion is important, I know. Passion propels me forward during tough sales days and gives me the courage to take risks. Passion drove me to Stamford. But even if I want something more, I will never get what I want unless I have results to show for all my effort.

Early the next morning, I leave home when it is still dark outside. At the office, I am the first one on the floor. Kathy is the second. She calls me into her office. "Bill, I am taking you into my confidence. I want someone willing to walk through fire to get this job. You're my choice. You got the job. Please just give me a chance to tell the other candidates."

"Thank you, Kathy. Thank you for believing in me. I will not let you down." I'd promised Kathy I would make the team number one. So although I'm ecstatic, there is no time to celebrate. It's already March, which means I have only eight months to live up to my promise.

9

PLAYER-COACH

If we take people as we find them, we may make them worse, but if we treat them as though they are what they should be, we help them to become what they are capable of becoming.

—JOHANN WOLFGANG VON GOETHE

NEVER BEFORE HAD I managed a team. Sure, I had managed my staff at the deli, but that was no basis for leading sixteen marketing reps to achieve the goal I'd promised to hit. The Xerox management classes had taught me some basic processes—how to track people's progress, when to review performance—that provided a little stability in an unpredictable profession. I believed routines had a place. If I found ones that worked, I repeated them. But procedures were not leadership.

My first two bosses at Xerox were good men, but because I was so self-motivated, they had left me alone. And while there were several senior people at Xerox I admired from a distance, leaders I wanted to learn from, I had not worked with them.

Two touchstones from my life gave me the tools and the confidence to do my new job. The first was basketball. Because I had coached alongside my dad, his overriding philosophy—put team over self—influenced how I worked with others. My grandfather's legacy was also powerful. Bobby McDermott was a player-coach who didn't bark orders from the sidelines but rather called plays as he ran up and down the court, sweating alongside his teammates. Mac shared his skills as he executed. That's how I wanted to lead: beside my team in the field, not from behind a desk.

My second touchstone for how I wanted to lead was my mom. With expectations for my team so high, I could not motivate people with fear or intimidation. Neither trait was in my upbringing or in my nature. So I would try to lead with the kindness, optimism, teamwork, and discipline that winning demanded.

Plotting my first hundred days on the job, I framed my intentions. To make Team F the top new-business sales team in the country, I would do everything I could to give my team a reason to strive for it, the confidence to go for it, and a map to get there.

HIGHER PURPOSE

Our sales numbers would determine whether Team F was the best. Did we bring in more revenue and sell more units than any other team? I had estimated the dollars we had to make and the amount of machines we needed to sell to ensure our success, and then I increased those numbers beyond even my own expectations. But numbers alone would not inspire—for some, they could actually intimidate. My team needed more meaningful targets.

"This year," I would tell Team F on day one, "every one of you who is eligible will make it to President's Club, the company's annual trip for top performers." To my knowledge, no team in the history of Xerox had ever sent all of its eligible salespeople to President's

Club in the same year, a grand trip that celebrated the past year and motivated people for the next. The audacity of that goal—every person had to outsell hundreds of other talented salespeople—would give the group something to strive for, together. The chance to make history would, I believed, become a purpose, a cause, more exhilarating than selling machines and making commissions.

To help propel us to number one, I would make the work personal by asking everyone to write down his or her own aspirations. "What do you want to achieve this year? In this lifetime?" Whatever their desires—to buy a new car or make a down payment on a house—I needed to know what mattered to them, and so did their coworkers. Their responses would get posted on what I called our "Wall of Goals" for all to see, so that the entire team would become obsessed with cheering on one another. Individual aspirations would be the girders that bolstered our success.

BUILD 'EM UP, DON'T BREAK 'EM DOWN

Life was full of naysayers whose loser talk dragged people down. As a team leader, I vowed never to be like that. My job, as I saw it, was to build people up. If I only told my people what to fix about themselves, they would lose confidence in what they did well. So I committed to touting, again and again, whatever traits made each team member shine. Building people up also meant that I would reassure folks that anything they had convinced themselves they could not do was, indeed, doable. *Don't let anyone else determine your fate*, I would try to teach them.

PROVIDE A PLAN

In addition to building miniteams, my plan would be specific about what people needed to do to sell well. What to say, how to say it, how to tackle a particular slice of territory. The tactics I would share worked for me as a solo salesperson, so I figured they were worth repeating. "These are the plays you will run. So incorporate your style, use your skills, but don't rewrite the plays."

Once I told people how to execute—how to initiate a conversation, how to demo, how to follow up, how to close—I would trust them to do it. When others put their trust in me, as Roy, Tom, and Kathy were doing, my own confidence heightened. Could I have the same effect on my team members? Yes, if I did not micromanage their every move. As a sales manager, I would try to find the balance between coaching and babysitting, and try to unleash talent by letting people run free, a lesson my first two bosses taught me, if inadvertently.

HIRE AMBITION

I inherited several marketing reps who already worked on Team F, plus there were a few sales slots to fill. I wanted the best performers, but the best new talent had choices because the midtown and downtown teams also had open spaces. I focused on recruiting ambitious, proactive personalities.

Sean McGee was just out of Xerox's training class when he called me to schedule a meeting, which showed me that he had chutzpah and a sense of urgency. When he came to see me, I pitched him: "Sean, midtown has the high-profile corporations and the marble lobbies, which I love. And downtown, with its traders and bankers, Masters of the Universe are making their dough. Sean, I understand that uptown is not as glossy. But that's why I love it and why you'll love it, too. It's real, and it's rich with opportunity. There's so much potential for smart talent like you, Sean."

Talented professionals like Sean wanted to work for people who would propel their careers. I assured him I would. "My job is to teach you to sell and to scale so you can achieve your own ambitions, Sean. As soon as you get the opportunity to advance your career, I'll be the one telling your story to the next level of management so you move up fast. You have my word. I won't hold you back." By the end of our meeting, Sean was in.

When necessary, I plowed through corporate procedures to draft someone. Tony Garcia was an experienced professional who spent five years selling huge shipping containers to steamship companies before applying to Xerox and interviewing with me. He could cut big deals in an unglamorous industry. Plus, he understood how to sell to a variety of people, not just corporate executives. But what sold me on Tony was that he had the confidence to ask for what he wanted.

"I don't mean to put any pressure on you, Mr. McDermott," he said as our interview came to a close. "But I have two offers from other companies, and I need to decide on one by midnight. Can you make a decision today?" I loved it. Tony was closing me! I wanted him, so I pulled an Emerson. When Tony left my office to pick up his wife at her workplace, I picked up my phone and made a few calls to expedite a job offer. The last call I placed that day was to Tony's wife—from my conversation with him, I knew where she worked, and I tracked her down.

"Mrs. Garcia? Hello. I'm Bill McDermott. When your husband arrives to pick you up, please tell him he has a job waiting for him at Xerox."

In the spring of 1987, sixteen marketing representatives made up Team F.

"You do not work for me, I work for you!" I declare as I walk around our team's cluster of desks each morning and inhale another can of Diet Coke. Breakfast.

"Tony, you're on your way to leading the region in revenue; tell me how I can help you get there. Sean, you're almost up to a hundred units; what do you need from me to break into triple digits? Michelle, you want that vacation in France; how can we work together to make that happen?"

CROSS-POLLINATE TALENT

As planned, I divide my sales force into four miniteams led by our most talented reps. But neither the miniteam leaders nor I are held up as stars. Everyone is asked to showcase his or her favorite techniques. You're a consummate closer? Please demonstrate to all of us how you do it. If you're a sweet talker on the phone, let's hear the pitch. Our best writers pass out copies of their proposals and follow-up letters. No one keeps secrets. The transfer of knowledge is swift. One person's tactics become everyone's habit. As each indulges his or her own skills and learns new ones, the most effective methods are being adopted by all of us.

ROLE-PLAY, REHEARSE, REVIEW

The team spends hours in Xerox's showrooms demonstrating our machines to one another. I simulate sales calls and fire questions at each one of my reps: "What do you know about my business?" "How can you make me more money?" "Why Xerox and not that cheaper copier from Canon, or from Minolta, or Sharp?" I push people into corners, forcing them to rethink a play under pressure, to improvise, before they must do it on game day. In the safe environment of our home office, I am teaching people to compete.

We also rehearse how to talk about competitors. "Don't try to hide their advantages," I say. "State them up front, get them out of the way, and then move on to our strengths." Transparency builds trust, I promise them. We practice how to solve an office manager's problem. "You're a doctor," I remind them. "Search for their pain, then make it better."

Every morning, I bring the team together and state our goals and our plan for that week or for that day. And at the beginning of each month, each salesperson sits down with me, and together we revise his (or her) revenue and unit sales goals based on what he has, or has not, achieved. We also agree on how he will work his territory— Which companies will he target? Which aren't worth it?—so he knows what he is supposed to do to build toward his goals. I keep the support spigot flowing, breaking down our big goals into weekly and daily objectives.

ROLE-MODEL AND DEMYSTIFY

Five days a week, I am in the field. If someone doesn't feel confident presenting or wants backup support, I hop a cab or the subway to be wherever I am needed. "Just ask," I tell my people. My job is to provide air cover for the troops.

I can't be everywhere at once, so I am teaching everyone what I do and how I do it. But lectures and memos are not as effective as showing people the art of the deal, live, in front of customers. At least once a month, I travel with each rep for a day. "Don't schedule the no-brainer accounts," I insist. "Schedule the ones you can't get done." Swooping in to close is never my main intent. I'll do it, but no one benefits if I always do their job for them. My objective is to demystify my behavior so that my reps can watch, learn, and work on their own.

I share whatever tactic can give someone an edge. We racewalk to meetings instead of taking cabs. The physical rush stirs the adrenaline, I tell them. As we walk, I talk. "Remember, imagination begets the event. So right now, imagine what you want to accomplish in detail." As we wait to be buzzed into a building, I whisper a reminder: "Find the decision maker and shake his hand, but be the last one to let go." If a twenty-two-year-old woman can hold on to the hand of a man twice her age, it unlocks her confidence.

One afternoon, Tony Garcia and I are on our way to meet with a small manufacturer in the South Bronx, a business owned by a cranky elderly man and run by his two sons.

"They never buy anything," Tony cautions me as we drive there in his 1975 Chevy Caprice, a huge box of a car that makes Tony feel safe in certain neighborhoods because it looks like an unmarked police vehicle. We park and walk inside. There Tony begins pouring his attention into the owner's sons. *Wrong move.* I jump into the conversation and redirect everyone's attention to the older gentleman. Dad. I ask him about his business, its history. Owning a business is hard. Never ends.

"I get it," I offer. "May I have a seat?" I pull out a chair and recall the challenges of owning the deli, "much smaller than your business, of course," I say, and then talk about competing with bigger stores and trying to prevent my employees from stealing cash from the register. The man begins nodding, and we commiserate as if we'd known each other far longer than five minutes. Soon I am not some sales guy. I know his pain.

After we leave, I explain to Tony why I focused on Dad.

"Tony, he built that business himself and deserves our respect. Second, he's alert. Those kids may be running daily operations, but, have no doubt, Dad is still in charge. So ask yourself," I say to Tony, "why is this man so grumpy? Maybe he's fed up with hot shots like us coming onto his turf and telling him what to do. He should be. Maybe he's sad that his sons stopped asking for his advice." Tony nods, taking mental notes. "If we listen, we can put ourselves in that man's shoes, and allow him to be heard and make him feel better than he's felt all week. Then we've earned the right to tell him what we're about and why we're here. Tony, that's why we left with a new customer."

TURN LEMONS INTO LESSONS

Although a lot of Xerox's sales reps have attended some of the best colleges in the country, there are some fundamentals that can be learned only on the street. On the sales trail, I play professor.

One frigid winter morning, I am headed to a meeting at a high-end actuarial firm with one of my youngest salespeople, Greg Mc-Stravick. Fresh from graduating Villanova University, Greg is also one of the best on my team, combining incredible intellect with ambition. In him I see high potential.

It's cold outside, so instead of walking to our meeting on the Upper East Side, Greg and I, both of us well over six feet tall, fold into the backseat of a warm taxi. Rare for me, but, man, it's freezing. We are not the only people with this idea, and on Fifty-Seventh Street, the cab gets stuck in the glue of midtown gridlock. The clock is ticking. Time to bounce.

"Get out of the cab," I tell Greg as I pay the driver. "We're walking." He reaches into his jacket pockets. "And hold off on the gloves."

"Why?" His breath forms a wispy cloud in the frigid air.

"You'll see," I say. About a half dozen blocks later, we arrive at a building as glossy as its address. Five floors up, several pristinely dressed men greet us as the elevator doors open to their office. We shake hands. "You're freezing," one of them says as he grasps Greg's icy palm, adding, "Thank you for going through the trouble of coming here today." I look at Greg and wink. During the next hour, he does a fantastic job with the buttoned-up actuaries, answering their questions and presenting our products. Everything goes perfectly, until the end. They say they are ready to buy, which is good because I say our paperwork is ready to sign.

"Greg?" He is reaching into his briefcase for the contracts we prepared at the office. The room is quiet as he shuffles through papers. My best student looks up at me like a kid who forgot his homework. No one speaks.

"Gentlemen," I break in, "thank you for your business. Not a problem. We will have the order agreements to you by the end of the afternoon." Alone in the elevator, I download a lesson that the emotion of the moment has already seared into him. "Greg, a sales professional never leaves home without a pen and a contract." Enough said. My opinion of Greg is unchanged. I know what a sales call such as this one can do to a career: its lessons become lifetime habits.

WORDS CHANGE MINDS

Not everyone has a natural ability to build quick rapport with strangers. Some reps put me to sleep when they walk through a pitch. So I come up with ways to help them open up and sustain conversations. Feel-Felt-Found is my own twist on Xerox's S.P.I.N. technique. "I know how you *feel*, others have *felt* the same way, and they have *found* . . ." The conversation it sparks is the same premise as S.P.I.N.—listen to someone's problems, empathize, find a solution—but my Feel-Felt-Found is easier to recall in a tense moment. Plus, it's more authentic. The reps like it, and they use it.

With the success of Feel-Felt-Found, I see how creatively packaging an idea elevates the mundane. I've never shied from grand language, invoking analogies, and peppering my sentences with superlatives. I talk in exclamation marks! Now, as a manager, my brain is churning out pungent mantras that encapsulate my philosophies: *Teams have no secrets. None of us is as smart as all of us. There's nothing noble about mediocrity. Don't limit your dreams.* I indulge in any phrase that jolts people out of a funk or the humdrum mind-set of selling office machines. Words, I know firsthand, can change minds.

ACCENTUATE AND CELEBRATE THE GOOD

After joining reps on a call, I begin my debrief by praising at least three things they did extremely well. "Greg, you're one of the best when it comes to listening and quickly understanding a company's business. And you have the courage to ask for the order. Fantastic." Then I pick one thing—not five, just one—that can be improved.

"Just keep one other point in mind because it's going to make you a stellar performer: in your precall planning process, always have your contract ready." Because I speak without judgment, people listen without fear.

And every time someone returns to the office with another sale, he or she rings a small bell I installed. Everyone cheers, and high-fives sweep the bullpen.

GIVE DISCRETIONARY EFFORT

I am also trying to create a collective passion for generosity. Whenever people hit or exceed their sales goals, they must spend 10 percent of their time assisting teammates who are missing their targets. I learned this tactic from my dad, on the court, who stressed that no one player was as important as the entire team. "When we each give discretionary effort, we will all win," I tell Team F as they prep for the day. Such deliberate kindness is contagious.

Blitzing is a common practice throughout Xerox's sales force. On a designated "blitz" day, a sales manager sets a unique goal, and everyone on the team heads out to his or her individual sales territory to try to meet the goal, returning at the end of the day to report results to the group. Whoever wins earns applause, a prize, and free beers after work. Blitzing broke the monotony of sales, I got that, but I saw blitzing as counterproductive because it had the potential to pit teammates against one another. So I put my twist on the blitz. On a designated day, I pick my team member whose sales need the biggest boost, and we all pounce on his territory. The mass effort generates new leads and business, lifting the blitz recipient's sales as well as his spirits.

My blitz is not about creating a hero for a day or motivating people with free drinks.

Nor is it about singling out a poor performer. Everyone knows his or her blitz day will come.

TOUGH CONVERSATIONS

More than direct sales, I am discovering that motivating others to meet high standards is my passion. Ensuring that Team F does not harbor underperformers is my job.

For a lot of marketing reps, Xerox is their first job after college. I am young, too, and know all the distractions, especially in New York City. If someone begins blending too much partying with the job, rolling in late on Mondays after another weekend in the Hamptons, or if I notice inconsistent behaviors, or think that this person has checked out emotionally, I do not ignore it. "Time to talk," I say, and invite him or her into my office and shut the door. It's my responsibility to prevent people from flailing.

"Bill, why are you on my case?"

"Performance is the price of freedom, my friend, and I'm on your case because your low numbers mean we're going to be spending some time together." I am a coach, not a babysitter. Laziness is different from an inability to perform. For me, inability is not failure. "We can either fix it or talk about where else you can go to soar."

Threatening termination is never my intent. I want to give underperformers a choice. And success, I try to make clear, is their choice. "You're either going to choose to be a winner, or you're going to water it down because your interests supersede our team's success." Even when I am disappointed, I don't lose my temper or spew four-letter words. My people must feel safe, even when their jobs are on the line.

HOLD NOTHING BACK

Confidence, preparation, reading a room, building rapport, problem solving, improvising—I am passing on to my team everything I can. I hold nothing back. I give them my script, choreographing the sales calls down to the handshake. My miniteam leaders are spreading the gospel. I am pumping my people so full of self-assurance that they are ready to burst. When I let them loose on the streets of New York, packs of hungry, well-groomed sales reps, they are itching to sell and to win.

THE VIRTUOUS CYCLE: SELLING VALUE AT FULL PRICE

"Undersell your product, and you undersell yourself," I chant. "Discounting is the easy way out. The loser's escape hatch." I do not believe salespeople should lean on the crutch of discounts. Doing so chips away at the trust between a rep and a customer, as well as a salesperson's top line. Still, discounting is tempting, especially given Xerox's sales parameters at the time.

Xerox gave its reps permission to sell every copier model within a specified price range. But if salespeople quoted the high price first and then reduced it, the reduction cut revenue for Xerox as well as the salesperson's commission. Instead of discounting, I believed in selling products for what they were worth. That meant full price.

For some products, Xerox rewarded its salespeople for *the number* of units sold. Xerox's product portfolio included a line of electronic typewriters called Memorywriters, so named because the machines could store the last words a user typed, or even recall entire documents. Xerox wanted to increase its share in the growing electronic typewriter market, so getting its Memorywriters into customers' offices was a companywide priority. To stimulate Memorywriter sales, Xerox gave reps additional compensation for the number of machines they sold, in addition to the reps' overall sales revenues.

I took all these rules and developed a sales philosophy. One that would help meet Xerox's goals; help my sales reps exceed their goals; and give customers more of what they wanted: productivity. The key was to get my reps to think about their jobs differently. Not as salespeople trying to unload a box within a discount range, but as innovators who had various tools to achieve great outcomes for everyone. I told my salespeople that their job was to look at Xerox's entire portfolio of products for ideas that could help the customer perform better, and offer solutions beyond what the customer originally thought she needed. A customer who wanted a faster copier may not have realized the additional benefit of swapping twenty manual typewriters for electronic ones. So I taught my sales team to think in these terms—solution over price—and then bundle the appropriate amount of Memorywriters in with the number of copy machines a customer needed.

To make it easy, I designed a matrix of pricing options that built Memorywriters' prices into the full price of various copier models. The matrix also accounted for economies of scale: the more copiers a customer bought, the more electronic typewriters it could get, and the greater its productivity. Without selling copiers for less than they were worth, we were giving the customer more value. In turn, Team F and Xerox achieved their mutual ambitions: higher revenue and unit sales. Everyone won.

For customers, receiving dozens of typewriters with their copy machines, at no additional cost, was exciting. For my team, bundling multiple products into one sale was also a more efficient way to sell than trying to orchestrate two separate deals. To make it even simpler for the reps, I scripted the entire transaction, from the conversation to the administrative contracts, so there was no debate about how it should unfold. But much more than bundling boxes, Team F was broadening the conversation from a piece of technology to productivity. As a result, we brought in maximum revenue while increasing our unit sales. And Xerox gave us credit for both.

WHAT MATTERS

I am riding shotgun with Everton Harrison, a man about five years my senior, to the Bronx. We have a day of appointments, including one with a prickly buyer for a health care company who Everton tells me is unhappy with his Xerox service. He wants to deal only with "the boss."

It's raining as Everton merges his beat-up burgundy Volvo onto the Cross Bronx Expressway. Static pieces of Bon Jovi's "Livin' on a Prayer" fill the car, and the right windshield wiper is broken. I take out my handkerchief and roll down my passenger-side window to try to wipe the windshield clear.

"Ev, man, let me wipe this down for you." I succeed only in spreading around the water. No luck, and the right sleeve of my jacket is soaked.

"Bill, I'm so sorry about your suit."

"Ev, what are you worried about? It'll dry." Everton seems a bit self-conscious about the Volvo, with its lifeless wiper and bum radio. On the floor, by my feet, there is also a ragged hole. But I couldn't care less about the Volvo; I grew up riding in old cars. My brain is focused on amplifying Everton's confidence for the day's calls. Ev's former boss had told him that he wasn't cut out for "this type of sales." I disagree. Everton played soccer in college, and he still has the stamina and drive of a competitive athlete. When mixed with Ev's easygoing personality, it's magic.

"You start the conversation," I tell him as we head to the health care company. "If you lock horns, remember, the customer is not your adversary."

"He's really upset."

"Look, he went into the deal wanting it to work. Everyone goes into a deal wanting it to work. But Xerox failed him. We failed it. We gotta own it. Don't focus on selling, Ev. We're not here to chase the money, we're here to make that guy fall in love again. The money will come. Trust me on that, Ev. The money will follow."

"Got it."

"If something comes up, and you're stalled, pass the conversation to me. I'll run with it, then I'll pass it back to you to close it out, which you're so good at doing."

At the customer's office, I see that Ev is right. The buyer is mad. But we play it like we practiced—passing the conversation, owning our mistakes—and by the time we leave, the man has given us permission to replace his old copier with a newer model, plus deliver several Memorywriters.

Everton is on fire, and so am I.

By noon, we are hungry. Everton has been hounding me to try his favorite Jamaican joint. Rumor is that Ev and Hilvan Finch, another salesman who works the Bronx, took their former manager to eat there and ordered her something called a Jamaican meat patty. The sandwich is essentially bread laced with coconut milk folded around a ground-beef filling, and so loaded with fat and calories that it put their boss to sleep in the backseat of the Volvo. Now it's my turn to try it.

Everton parks, and we run into the restaurant, dodging raindrops. We order the food and run it back to the car in knotted takeout bags. I start to eat while Everton drives to our next appointment.

"The famous coco bread!" I say, lifting what looks like an empanada out of a Styrofoam box. Balancing the sandwich as the Volvo hits potholes is not easy, especially with my feet trying to prevent the bag with Everton's lunch from tipping over. We are quite the sight: Ev trying to navigate the Bronx through a water-coated windshield while I sit shotgun, navigating a steaming Jamaican meat patty so that its juice doesn't stain my pants.

I loved these uncalculated moments with my teammates. In the field. At the office. After work. Team F became a family. On winter weekends, we rented ski houses together in upstate New York. During the summer, we decamped to the Jersey Shore. After work, we'd meet for drinks on the forty-fourth floor of the Gulf + Western Building, and then go dancing at nightclubs like Studio 54 or the Silver Shadow. Like the most memorable scenes from my childhood, uncalculated moments were incredibly meaningful to me, from coco bread in the Bronx with Ev to cocktail hour at the Rainbow Room with everyone.

THE REAL WIN

By the end of 1987, Team F was Xerox's number one new-business team in the United States.

More significantly, every single person on the team that qualified for the trip earned a space at the President's Club, which to my knowledge was a first for the company. We celebrated by sunbathing on beaches and dancing on tables. Xerox's president of US operations, Barry Rand, a man I looked to as a role model, publicly recognized our accomplishment. When he walked over to congratulate my team during one of the dinners, I could not have been more proud.

"Bill, never change how you lead," Barry reassured me. It was Barry who instilled in me an idea that was becoming a cornerstone of my style. "Leadership," he liked to say, "is the art of developing followership."

After managing Team F for nine months, I knew for certain that winning through other people moved me more than doing it solo. Inspiring a team to go for something audacious by igniting its confidence, unleashing its talents, teaching new skills, and shaping all of our different strengths into a collaborative force was what I wanted to keep doing. So in 1988 I did it again. I had a few new players, but that year my team was number one again.

The real rewards, however, were not the vacations or what we bought with our money. Yes, members of my teams traveled to new places, bought houses, paid down loans, treated themselves to luxuries. I swapped my Firebird for a brand-new red Corvette. But if you asked me then, I could have predicted that in thirty years, everyone would forget how much cash he or she made or which island we visited. More likely, they'd recall how they felt—confident, excited, worthy, bold, proud, special—excelling as part of a championship team.

I attended eight consecutive President's Clubs in my first eight years at Xerox. But whenever I came home with my midwinter tan, I never missed the beach. I was revved up to get back to work. The celebratory trips were fantastic, and they were important to thank people for the year and to motivate them for the next. But the months spent inspiring my teams were far more nourishing. What mattered to me was the rhythm of it. Pumping people up. Walking the streets. Making the deals. High-fiving the team. Doing whatever it took to make my teams the best.

PART 3

INSPIRE

10

REAL

To thine own self be true.
—WILLIAM SHAKESPEARE, *HAMLET*

FIRST SEE JULIE at the end of the hallway outside my boss's office, seated on a couch next to the other job applicants. She has straight, shoulder-length blond hair and is wearing a black skirt and matching blazer with a white ruffled blouse and a flouncy bow tie. Standard eighties attire for professional women. Still, wow.

When she walks into my office an hour later, she is poised and friendly. I have no idea that Julie has already left her position as a financial analyst at the *New York Times* so that she can focus on changing careers and getting into sales, or that she quit with only two months' rent left in the bank. Nor do I realize that she is recovering from her earlier interview with my colleague, a tough sales manager who likes to break people down, with little interest in building them back up. When he challenged Julie to explain why her accounting background qualified her to be a sales rep in Manhattan, he was not interested in the answer. By the time Julie sits down for her interview with me, she doesn't appear flustered. But beneath the sheen of that smile, her self-confidence is almost as low as her checking account.

I look at her résumé long enough to see that she is a certified public accountant. But what I really want to know about Julie, and any potential new hire, is not what he or she wrote on a piece of paper. So I start asking my usual open-ended questions about where she comes from and where she wants to go. She seems surprised by my curiosity.

Julie grew up out west and majored in accounting at her state's university. *We graduated in the same year*, I note only to myself. After college, a major accounting firm recruited her to the nearest big city, where she stayed for two years before moving to Southern California. There, she worked as an internal auditor for a real estate developer before moving to New York City. *This woman has guts.* But she disliked her job at the *Times*. It was killing her, she says. Working in a cloistered cubicle as an analyst, Julie felt like a flower getting no sun, which was not what she'd imagined for herself when she left her home. *A dreamer!* Julie's father still lives out west, working for the state highway department. Her mother passed away from cancer when Julie was only fourteen years old. *I can't even fathom.* I am taken by this woman's courage and her ambition, and feel comfortable in her presence. Calm. Plus, she makes great eye contact—and Julie has beautiful blue eyes.

As I do with all interviewees, I hand her my business card before she leaves. *Keep it professional, Bill.* "You should hear something from our HR department in a few days, Julie. If you have questions or need anything, please don't hesitate to call me."

Later, when the sales managers come together to assess the day's candidates, even the guy who needled Julie's accounting background agrees with the rest of us. She is highly qualified. I am thinking that here is a woman who has come through the worst tragedy I can imagine, a parent's death, and has the strength to follow her heart. We decide to hire her into the training program.

Two weeks later, I smile because I have a phone message from Julie. I call her back immediately. *You gotta be kidding me*. She has not heard from anyone at Xerox and is being pressured by a life insurance company to accept its job offer. "Bill, I am wondering if you have any suggestions for how I might find out if I am still being considered for the sales position. I really want to work at Xerox." Her voice is professional—not a tinge of panic because she has only, I learn later, twenty-five bucks left in the bank.

"Julie, when we hang up, don't leave your phone. Someone will call you back in fifteen minutes."

Xerox's bureaucracy is no longer implausible to me, but it is infuriating. I call human resources. "We agreed to hire this woman two weeks ago. What's going on?" I get some pathetic explanation. "Save your stories. We're going to tell her today that she is being hired by the Xerox Corporation." An hour later, an HR manager calls Julie and offers her the job.

At twenty-five, Julie is one of the oldest sales trainees in her group of thirty, and she is very good. She wins the demo-rama and graduates at the top of her class. Three months after her start date, when it is time to assign newly trained reps to sales teams, Julie requests Team F. But I can't let her work for me. I urge my colleague Grace to take her. Grace is competitive, and thus suspicious of why McDermott isn't interested in the number one sales trainee. *I am interested; that's the problem.*

"Please, Grace, trust me on this one." She does. Later Grace will thank me when Julie becomes one of her top producers.

During the next few months, I see Julie at sales meetings, in passing, and on various company outings. One day she is waiting for an elevator when I walk up and pull from my wallet a torn piece of newspaper, half the size of a playing card. In the center is a fuzzy black-and-white photograph of a house. It's the second property I've purchased in Amityville, where I'm fancying myself a bit of a real estate magnate.

"Julie, what do you think of this house?"

"It seems very nice," is all she says. "Why?"

"I bought it," is all I say. I don't tell her why. I just smile at her and walk away.

From the moment I saw Julie sitting on that couch, I wanted to ask her out. I had dated other women, but my gut told me that Julie was special. And at twenty-five, I was ready for something special. For all the extracurricular socializing that comes with being a young businessperson, and for all the energy I put into charging up teams, I was most comfortable being alone with somebody in a quiet place. At my core, I was a family guy who preferred a quiet date night to a party. What I really wanted in my midtwenties was to be in a relationship with the right partner.

Eight months after we first meet, once Julie is settled into her job and proven her talents, I discreetly track down her home telephone number and ask her out on a date. Julie says yes, and over dinner my instinct is confirmed: the most beautiful part of this woman is on the inside. Rarely do I meet other people so curious about others. She asks me questions about my family, beyond what I usually discuss, and she likes to listen. The crush—*Thank you, God!*—is mutual. Julie tells me that every time we bumped into each other before I asked her out, she lost her breath just a little. She recalls a day when we walked together from Xerox's Midtown Manhattan office up to Fifty-Seventh Street. "I almost passed out trying to keep up with you," she says, laughing.

Two years later, we move to Amityville together, into the house from the newspaper clipping. "I bought it for you," I finally tell Julie. It sounds like a line, but it's true.

On April 20, 1991, we married in Myrtle Beach, South Carolina, near my parents' vacation home.

The wedding was magnificent. I was surrounded by my favorite things: Julie, my family, the ocean, my oldest friends, and even a few special people from Xerox. Team F's Everton and Hilvan drove twelve hours from New York in Ev's vintage Volvo, just to be there.

Julie looked beautiful. As we danced to the Righteous Brothers' "Unchained Melody," we joked that my taste in music was about a generation behind my own. I had loved this woman from the second I saw her, and I had no doubt I would love her forever.

Julie had always imagined a honeymoon in Hawaii, so we decided to overlap it with Xerox's annual trip for its top performers— which we both made that year. During the awards ceremony, someone pulled Julie and me onstage together and presented us with two custom-made T-shirts: Just Maui'ed. Too perfect.

The Xerox Corporation had brought me so much more than a dream job: real love, a soul mate, and a true partner.

EVOLVING

Nine years after joining Xerox, I still felt like the luckiest guy in the world, doing exactly what I wanted to be doing—now with the love of my life working down the hall.

My sales and management skills were maturing; the company, however, was aging. David Kearns had stepped down as CEO, and Xerox was being run by Paul Allaire. Paul's financial bent and serious manner were the yin to David's marketing orientation and charismatic yang. I liked Paul, and he was a good leader, but like a lot of people, I missed David's spirit. Most people agreed that he had saved the company by rallying us to embrace customer service and product quality while ushering in the 10-series copier models. And by the end of the 1980s, we had broken the dominance of overseas competitors to regain market share. In 1989, David's last full year as CEO, Xerox Corp. was one of only two US organizations awarded the Malcolm Baldrige National Quality Award. The Baldrige was the

Good Housekeeping Seal of Approval for business, and signaled an organization's operational excellence.

As CEO, Paul benefited from David's legacy, but he also inherited a crippled balance sheet. The lackluster growth in our stock price throughout the 1980s had not thrilled investors, in large part because the company also tried, unsuccessfully, to diversify its portfolio by getting into the insurance business. Not wise. Financial services was too far removed from Xerox's core, and losses from insurance liabilities deflated earnings from profitable operations.

Since joining Xerox, I had changed roles about every eighteen months. After managing Team F for two years, I headed an amazing group of account reps whose performance propelled us to the company's number one account team in 1989. My next account team was also talented, and earned the top spot in the eastern region, and number two nationwide.

In 1991 Xerox took me off the front lines to learn operations. Instead of managing salespeople, I began managing marketing programs, figuring out how to price and position new products. As a sales operation manager, I worked side by side with a regional vice president who was responsible for a $500 million business. Throughout New York and Connecticut, some four hundred sales associates were going out and selling new machines based on sales plans, collateral pieces, and pricing models I created. Brainstorming how to market Xerox's machines was a more sophisticated, strategic puzzle than selling them to individuals and improvising in the moment. Like sales, marketing was about reading people, but from a distance.

Xerox's first color copier, for example, was a tricky sell. We competed with Kodak and Canon, which were known for their technologies' high photographic quality. When it came to producing pretty pictures, Xerox couldn't compare. So we crafted a different story, one that highlighted the company's differentiating strength: our history of reproducing high-quality *business* documents. Our marketing message married that strength with our business customers' desire to communicate their ideas on paper. We targeted our sales pitch to industries that relied on written documents to sway opinions and sales. Financial and accounting firms were perfect for our pitch. You're an investment banker preparing a big presentation to distribute to a client's board, hoping to close a deal? Make your argument more enticing by emphasizing, on paper, important numbers in eye-catching red or green or blue. Those graphs and data will pop off the page—and for a lot less money than our competitors' extravagant color copiers.

The intellectual challenge of thinking beyond "the box" to how a new technology could improve a business outcome continued to intrigue me. But too often I felt trapped in meetings with people who took thirty minutes to articulate an idea I thought they could have communicated in thirty seconds. The pace could be glacial for my go-go mentality. I missed being on the street, in the field with reps, talking to customers. Still, I paid attention in those meetings, trying to learn more about finance and operations, and gather strategies I could use once I ran my own business unit, which I hoped would be soon.

AUTHENTIC

Without daily sales outings to absorb my energy, my enthusiasm stood out more than usual in Xerox's reserved environs. One colleague told me to stop using the word "passion." Another prodded me to quit telling my direct reports that managers were here to serve their employees. Some senior execs worried that I was too generous with my praise and allocation of power, or doubted that my perpetual optimism was authentic, or served a business purpose. Executives like Tom Dolan and Roy Haythorn, however, had come to know that behind my smile were hard skills, and results, so they let me do my thing. But those who came across me in a meeting or only passed me in hallways wondered if the guy who walked around so happy all the time was capable of making the tough calls and pushing underperformers up or out.

Channeling David Kearns, I tolerated skeptics because I knew my teams' performance could change their minds. But cynics, people who refused to believe in the power of a positive attitude, or who mocked it, I would not tolerate. Being a cynic took no courage, and cynics certainly weren't dreamers. Worse, they were toxic, diluting the optimism that made people believe they could make the impossible possible.

A cynic would never have believed that Xerox's worst-performing region was capable of becoming its best-performing one, which was probably why few people at the company were interested in managing Xerox's Puerto Rico–US Virgin Islands district. In the early nineties, the Caribbean-based business unit had such low sales that it ranked sixty-fourth out of all Xerox's sixty-four districts in the United States. The worst. To bring the sun-drenched region back from the almost dead, it needed an emotional overhaul, which was why, in the summer of 1992, my phone rang.

11

PAINT PICTURES OF SUCCESS

---

*The method of the enterprising is to plan with
audacity, and execute with vigor; to sketch out a map
of possibilities; and then to treat them as probabilities.*

—CHRISTIAN N. BOVEE

"BILL, GO DOWN to Puerto Rico and check it out," says Al Byrd,
the vice president of Xerox's southern region. "If you like it,
the job is yours." Out the window of Al's Washington, DC, office, I
can see the Washington Monument. It's a stunning view, but I can
only think, *Do I really want to lead Xerox's worst-performing district?*

Al has the same sharp style and warmth as Barry Rand, and we
hit it off. He wants to plug someone into Puerto Rico who doesn't
need to be micromanaged, he tells me. He wants a leader, not just a
manager. Puerto Rico is driving down his entire region. Anything is
better than sixty-four.

That night, back in New York, I don't sleep. A district manager
position is *the* job at Xerox, but is it a half compliment to be offered

such an undesirable gig? The district's performance is a horror story. And Puerto Rico? The land of flip-flops and piña coladas where gringos like me vacation? I am Mr. New York. If I am just a little patient, Xerox will likely give me a district manager position in Manhattan.

Two considerations prevent me from turning down the job. First, my optimism holds that the worse a situation is, the greater its potential upside. Maybe Puerto Rico can become a sensation. Second, unexpected opportunities have paved my path. When I saw that Help Wanted sign in a deli's window . . . when my boss decided to sell the deli . . . when I didn't get that early promotion . . . when an uptown sales manager position opened up, I always acted. Also, after nine years at Xerox, I know that people who seize opportunities get one reputation. Those who wait for the perfect job get another.

I lie awake, debating. Should I jam all our possessions into a shipping container and haul them to a US commonwealth where I barely speak the language? Especially now? A week earlier, our first son, Michael James, was born, serene and healthy. Our doctor swore that she had never seen a new dad jump so high in the delivery room. The pure joy I felt being a father was like no other feeling I had ever experienced. Plus, Julie and I are living in a lovely apartment a few blocks from Xerox's offices, in Murray Hill, which is close enough to Grand Central station that my mom can easily come into the city and help Julie with the baby when I'm at work. Not only is Puerto Rico far from everything we know and love, but San Juan, where Xerox's office is located, is not the safest place. Would a new mom and a newborn be okay there?

One of the secrets to my great relationship with Julie has been our ability to communicate our long-term goals and to trust each other in the short term. Before Michael was even born, we'd agreed that raising children would require a lot of attention from both of us. Family was so important to me that we decided, whatever my career brought, I wanted to do anything I could to be home by Friday nights and enjoy weekends with our family. If I was successful enough in my career, we agreed that Julie would stay home full-time and focus on our kids and the household. As much as she enjoyed her work, that's what my wife wanted, and I was grateful. I knew she would pour into our family and home life the same passion and skills that made her so successful at Xerox. Also, Julie already understood my pace, having witnessed the time I put into other people. We both knew I would not be as successful, or as happy, without that same level of intensity.

After a sleepless night, Julie and I agree. The Puerto Rico opportunity must be considered. I will fly down and assess the situation.

"Bill," she says, "I trust you completely to make the decision."

SPOT POTENTIAL

As I walk the sales department floor of Xerox's Puerto Rico office, my antennae go up. This place is in need of repair. From the matted rugs to the morale, everything about the thirty-year-old district feels worn. There's no bustle. Like its sales record, the place is flat.

The office is located on the seventeenth floor of a modern white, curved twenty-two-story structure situated on la Milla de Oro, or the Golden Mile, a manicured oasis where many global brands have parked their Caribbean headquarters. I am pleased to see that we have serious neighbors and that, in our office, employees aren't dressed for a day at the beach.

I pop into people's cubicles and introduce myself with my best high school Spanish, "*Hola, yo soy Bill McDermott.*" Photos of family and friends and group shots of smiling men and women are framed on desks and pinned to walls. *Okay, there is energy here.* Personal and professional lives seem to intersect. I take note. I'm met with occasional skepticism; above the expressive eyes of one sales manager named Giselle, I sense caution. *Who is this guy?* her inverted eyebrows ask. But most people greet me with smiles, and I sense something beneath the flatness, like a pot that wants to boil over if only someone would turn up the heat.

I meet with the district's two existing managers, Benjamin "Benny" Martell, who is in charge of customer service, and Severo Rodriguez, the district's business manager in charge of finance. If I take the job, the three of us have to function as a team.

For lunch, Severo and Benny take me to an elegant Argentinian steak house so we can get to know one another the proper way, over food and glasses of sangria. I probe to figure out if the three of us can work together. Collaboration among the sales, service, and administration divisions has been lousy, they explain. Their last sales manager was obsessed with cost cutting and wasn't all that collaborative.

I try to jar them out of their day's to-do list. Are these men with whom I can work, men with passion, men with vision? "What does Xerox's future look like to you, Benny?" "Severo, what drives you?" They appear relieved. Severo has an underdog's spirit. His family left Cuba in the 1960s, and he went to school and worked in New York for many years until transferring here. Benny was born and raised in Puerto Rico, and is just as extroverted and interested in shedding their sixty-fourth-place standing as I am. These are not men who deserve to be ranked dead last. Benny, Severo, and their coworkers don't lack a work ethic, they lack hope. *My goodness, they just want someone to tell them where to go, and to give them reasons to get moving.* By the end of lunch, I've made my decision.

Severo hands our waiter a camera, and the gentleman snaps photos of the three of us shaking hands, then with arms around one another, smiling like heads of state after signing a treaty. It feels surreal, but also right.

Before we return to Xerox's offices, Severo takes me on a quick tour of the city, and then a real estate agent whisks me to Condado, an upscale urban neighborhood where families from the States prefer to live. She shows me two buildings. I like the one on the beach, with a two-bedroom condo almost triple the space of our Manhattan apartment, and with direct views of the ocean. Exquisite. The neighborhood feels safe, the building has armed guards, and I see women walking babies in strollers. My attitude is shifting. *Who wouldn't want this job?*

Back at the office, a few hours before my American Airlines flight departs, I make two calls. "Al, I've got the condo's lease right here, and I am ready to sign. But I also need a car, and to be reimbursed for travel to and from New York to visit my family for holidays. And Al, you also need to get me out of my Manhattan lease. If Xerox is comfortable with all of that, my wife and I are ready to close this down." Al approves the package, so I dial Julie.

"Pack those bags. It's all good. We're moving."

SIMPLE QUESTION, SIMPLE ANSWER

"Yo quiero saber qué necessita." The sales managers seated in front of me are already stunned that I'd called them together at this lovely hotel, which obviously cost some money. Now I am asking them what they want, in Spanish. The words have been transcribed phonetically by my new administrative assistant, Leida.

Leida's patience with my Spanish, as well as her willingness to adapt to my chop-chop pace, is helping me parachute into the San Juan office and get my agenda moving. We'd already established a morning ritual: whoever arrives first makes the coffee. And, man, was that coffee strong.

At the hotel, the sales managers' surprise at my simple question evaporates into simple answers. Mainly, they want more support from senior management. David Ruiz, a dynamic sales rep who likes to play U2 on his BMW's CD player when we go on sales calls together, describes their former sales manager as a "no" machine, especially when asked for anything that cost time or money. In addition, the sales reps want better support from Benny's team in customer service. Internal strife between the sales and service departments was being taken out on customers. New machines aren't always delivered on time, and broken-down machines could take weeks to fix. Such inconsistent support is souring relationships with our clients. I do not need to be fluent in Spanish to realize how much our salespeople can get done with the necessary support.

The most heartfelt, universal request, however, surprises me. The district has not had a real Christmas party for years. If they did anything to mark the holiday, it was a gathering held in a lifeless Rotary Club facility. Worse, employees had to help pay for it. The people in Xerox's Puerto Rico office do not request higher pay or better benefits—they just want their Christmas party back.

It takes me about five minutes to grasp the significance of this request. I already know that Puerto Ricans love a good party. In New York City, the annual Puerto Rican Day Parade draws thousands from the tri-state area. The crowds close down Fifth Avenue. The celebration's flags and music and food spill into Central Park. Canceling a Christmas party in Puerto Rico, even to an outsider like me, seems shortsighted. It is, unfortunately, too late in the year to schedule a full-on bash for December 1992, so the party will wait for 1993. By then, I am confident we'll have a very good reason to celebrate.

I tell people that, by the end of 1993, the Puerto Rico–Virgin Islands district will have gone from number sixty-four to number one. That means our year-over-year sales growth will have to exceed the growth of every other US district, including Cleveland, Xerox's most consistently high-performing district. This goal is as bold an aim as I can muster. It reminds me of the coach of the 1980 USA hockey team telling his new recruits that they were going to steal the gold at the next winter Olympics from the undefeated Russians. That feat, when it happened, was considered a miracle. But Puerto Rico has to go for the gold. Who leaps out of bed to win the silver? Audacious goals motivate me, but they also get other people's attention. I describe our future as if it is not a possibility but a destiny. "Sí, we will be numero uno!" I repeat this mantra again and again and again, and my confidence in the far-fetched outcome is palpable. Besides, I've already planned the party.

At the end of the year, I promise everyone, we will throw the most fabulous Christmas party the office has ever experienced. Not some half-baked after-work event with store-bought pastries as we mill about the office playing Secret Santa. Instead, it will be a luscious Saturday-night affair, with music and food that will keep people and their spouses out of their chairs dancing, eating, laughing, and singing all night. Yes, everyone may bring a date. And no, employees do not have to help pay for the party.

As for the entertainment, I had asked around, "Who is the biggest act in Puerto Rico?" I'd never heard of Gilberto Santa Rosa, but he is the most popular salsa singer and orchestra leader with a crowd-pleasing reputation for improvising during live performances. When people find out that Bill has booked Gilberto—*Dios mío!*—they can't believe it. The morale meter spikes.

People not only appreciate that their Christmas party is back on, but also the prospect of being *los mejores*—the best!—awakens their spirit. For months, every time I remind people that soon we'll all be dancing with Gilberto Santa Rosa after leaping to number one, they wake up a little more.

It is amazing to watch the transformation. After years of poor performance, 275 people who had come to think of their office as a loser are now optimistic that they can win it all. A few even start to believe that *un milagro*, a miracle, is possible.

FUNDAMENTALS

There's a quote from Xerox founder Joe Wilson that was still as true in 1993 as it had been in the 1960s: "In the long run, our customers are going to determine whether we have a job or whether we do not. Their attitude toward us is going to be the factor determining our success." I included this quote in my districtwide business plan for Puerto Rico.

My first hundred days were spent repairing broken processes so that, come January, we had a solid foundation from which to begin selling, closing, and servicing customers, and striking bigger deals. On the back end, we first had to bridge the disconnect between sales, service, and administration so that they worked together on behalf of Xerox's customers. No more infighting. To help, I invited Benny and Severo to all of my sales meetings. But also, I attended their meetings, to listen as well as talk to their teams. When I sent out sales memos, I included the entire office and had Benny and Severo sign their names next to mine. I wanted to make the point that we were all in this together: a team. The three of us had agreed to act as partners, and we enjoyed the camaraderie. Seeing their bosses collaborate encouraged departments to come together, too, and day by day we cleaned up our sloppy customer service and delivery operations. Engineers were soon responding to complaints in the shortest time possible, and our finance department started processing new orders more quickly, so that a sales rep's promise—"I will have a machine delivered to you tomorrow at noon"—could be kept.

On the front end, I made our sales strategy clear: "In the past, you sold boxes. We're going to start selling solutions." More and more, companies were making purchasing decisions based on whether it added to their organization's sales or earnings. That became our district's mandate, to provide ideas about how Xerox's equipment improved customers' businesses. To bring in big money to make our big goal, we had to sell big machines—which required coming up with big ideas.

Xerox was selling a mammoth machine called the DocuTech Production Publisher. About the length of a car, the two-ton, $200,000 DocuTech scanned images and turned them into electronic documents, or received electronic images of documents from remote computers, and then stored the images so they could be manipulated and shared over a network, and quickly printed out in high resolution.

Together, our sales reps and I figured out how companies in our territory could be more productive with machines like those $200,000 DocuTechs. To reach potential customers, we held free symposiums, which were more sophisticated versions of my lobby demos back in midtown.

For individual companies, we came up with customized solutions. One of the best, and probably the most lucrative sale, was to La Lotería, Puerto Rico's lottery.

Playing the lottery was a huge pastime in Puerto Rico. When we got the call to see if Xerox could replace the lottery's outdated IBM printers, our sales manager for government accounts, Andres "Papo" Justicia, thought bigger. Papo and I spent a lot of time together. When I first arrived, he'd introduced me to one of the most delectable lunches I'd ever eaten, Cubano sandwiches packed with pork, ham, sweet cheese, and pickles. Julie and I would often join Papo and his wife, Sarita, for dinner. When Papo came to me and asked for my support to put together a technical solution for the lottery that would be complicated and risky, I was not a "no" machine. "Papo, of course!"

Papo explained to me that fraud was a huge problem for the lottery. On its flimsy printed tickets, numbers were easy for ticket holders to fake. Millions of dollars were being lost to false winnings. A technical solution to the problem could be worth several million dollars to the lottery's independent distributors, the government, and Xerox. We had to go for it. So in collaboration with the Department of Treasury and other vendors, Xerox digitized the lottery's antiquated printing process using several DocuTechs, going so far as to customize our machines and sourcing tamperproof paper.

The day we were scheduled to sign a five-year contract, I stood next to Papo and expressed to the government my own confidence in our solution. We signed. For Xerox, the contract's value, in hardware and services, was worth $5.5 million. Huge.

When deals like that closed, we celebrated back at the office. The *ding-ding-ding* of the bell I had brought with me from New York produced cheers and fist pumps in the office. Incremental incentives kept the momentum. We commemorated a record-breaking quarter with a night out eating and dancing. When a group delivered superior performance, every member of the team was rewarded with prizes that reflected the size of our ambitions. Rolex watches. Flat-screen televisions. Ten-thousand-dollar travel vouchers. Because people in our office loved to have fun—to laugh, to party, to dance, to put on silly shows—a little pageantry was injected regularly into long workweeks.

Still, trinkets and dinners were only short-term motivators. If I managed people like Pavlov's dogs, and only dangled expensive toys in front of them each month, I'd never have enough money in my budget to keep them motivated over time. Prizes were fun and intoxicating, but the high wore off. The more powerful, lasting motivator was *the idea* that we were all working together toward a crazy miracle.

SIMPATICO

The district accepted me, I think, for a few reasons.

They embraced my natural style. Here, when people met others for the first time, they assumed the best, not the worst. None of that thick Manhattan skin. Puerto Ricans also launched conversations with personal questions, like asking about one another's families. No one began a sales call talking about business. And hugs, not handshakes, punctuated meetings. Emotion and energy were intrinsic to the culture. When I walked through the office, people put their fists high in the air. "*Pasión!*" I'd shake my head and smile. *Yes, these are my people!* And when someone nicknamed me "220," the European equivalent of the US 110-volt outlet, it was a compliment. We were simpatico.

I tried to honor their traditions, dousing whatever I had to give in flavors my new colleagues would digest. The entire office spoke English, so I could have gotten away with little Spanish. But I realized just how important it was for me to speak their language. After starting my first speech to the entire organization in Spanish, I got a standing ovation not because of what I said but because I'd made a respectful effort. I ramped up my Spanish lessons, listening to Berlitz tapes in my car and meeting with a tutor at the office several days a week. At home, I read *Spanish for Gringos* while Julie and I passed Michael back and forth.

I incorporated Spanish into everything. Our district's mantra, *"Compromiso para excelencia"*—commitment to excellence—appeared on my business plans and interoffice memos. At my first meeting, I quoted a phrase from a political candidate running for mayor of San Juan: *"El pueblo hablo y yo obedezco,"* which meant, "the people speak, and I obey." I was finding my voice in Spanish.

Sometimes my attempts at integration flopped. Arsenio Hall's late-night talk show was popular then, and when I tried to translate into Spanish the cries of "Wuff! Wuff! Wuff!" that accompanied Arsenio's signature fist pumps, the result met with sweet laughter from my team. My chants of *"Puño! Puño! Puño!"* translated into "Fist! Fist! Fist!" I laughed at myself, but again, people appreciated the effort.

I also adapted many of my habits. Occasionally I swapped my tailored suits for short-sleeve shirts with island prints. I even bought a pair of white patent leather dress shoes. Instead of inhaling fast food at noon, I got used to multicourse sit-down meals. Lengthy lunches distracted from work in New York, but here they were part of the work culture, especially when customers were involved. Puerto Ricans were never too busy to eat. So I began incorporating meals and festivities into my meetings, bringing people together in nice restaurants and hotel conference rooms. To be heard, I created environments where people would be more willing to listen.

I also participated in work activities outside the office. I played on the company's basketball team. On Columbus Day, I gathered with people on the beach to celebrate the explorer's historic island arrival and cheered as several people dressed as Christopher Columbus paddled canoes into the surf to reenact his discovery. On one playful outing, someone from our office rowed a boat a quarter mile offshore and then pushed a small Canon copier into the water, which was later fished out. The little skit was in response to a statement I had made that we would "force our competition into the Atlantic Ocean." Such easy, uncomplicated fun was rampant in Puerto Rico. I got into it.

Not every aspect of island life was a pleasure. After one holiday, I was ravaged by sand fleas, little insects so tiny they were barely visible. In the middle of the night, hot with fever and unable to stop itching, I drove to the emergency room, furiously scratching my arms and legs. I struggled to explain the extent of my discomfort to the doctor. "Aha, you have *mimes*, the *mimes* got you!" He pronounced it *me-mays*. I was only a few months into the job, so my Spanish was not superb. "*Qué?*" I asked. "You're a rookie," he said in English, and then explained to me how to treat the insect bites, which mainly involved no scratching.

Aside from the occasional cultural blunder, my immersion was incredibly fulfilling. Twelve months after my original visit, the seventeenth floor felt like a different place. When a meeting was called for eight o'clock, no one came wandering in at eight fifteen. Afternoons were quiet only because so many reps were out at appointments. At the end of each day, we gathered to brainstorm how to help one another, and the orders kept coming in.

The people in our district did not fear change. What they feared was what most people feared, which was change without well-defined expectations, change without a plan, and change without a goal. Ambiguous change, that's what turned people off.

I had not anticipated the full-throttle effect of having 1,500 miles of ocean between my Xerox bosses and me. In Puerto Rico, with no one questioning my decision to throw a blow-out Christmas party or insinuating that it was a bad idea to tell my employees that I would "obey" them, even in Spanish, I thrived.

The entire experience, as well as the geographic distance from home, was also positive for Julie, Michael, and me. In between visits from our extended family, Julie and I became even closer as a couple, and the three of us bonded as a family.

COUNTDOWN

In March 1993 Puerto Rico broke a district record, exceeding our planned budget by 205 percent.

"That is an accomplishment the whole organization can take pride in!" I wrote in a congratulatory memo. I used regular communication like memos to keep everyone apprised of our performance, while reinforcing our plan and recharging people's emotional batteries. My language could get sentimental as I tried to escalate our mission: "In 1961 John F. Kennedy said, 'In this decade we will put a man on the moon, not because it is easy, but because it is hard,'" I paraphrased the former president after our record-breaking performance in March. "Without each of you committing total excellence, this could not have been achieved. *Gracias por su compromiso para excelencia.*"

In our quest to outperform the other Xerox districts, our most challenging national competitor was Cleveland. For years this large regional territory had dominated the stack rankings, Xerox's monthly progress report that compared each district's performance. Cleveland was led by one of the company's best sales managers, Frank Pacetta. Frank's ambition and commitment to his people reminded me of my own; his teams' loyalty to him was legendary. But his style reflected his name. Frank conducted himself with an uncensored edginess, a flavor of tough love that was anathema to me, from the four-letter words that sprinkled his pep talks, to his unapologetic disdain for senior management. Neither of our management styles was better than the other's. History showed that we both brought in high numbers. Frank just had more history at Xerox than I did.

In 1993 he knew that my district was gunning for the top spot. When we saw each other at district manager meetings throughout the year, we razzed each other. As fall approached, we each kept our eyes on the other's performance via the *Daily Flash*, another internal report that compared districts' sales every twenty-four hours. In Cleveland, Frank created a scoreboard, and every morning, when his reps entered the office, they immediately saw Puerto Rico's status from the previous day, versus their own. In San Juan, I kept the *Daily Flash* rankings to myself, believing that our people needed to focus on our customers, not on Cleveland.

Seeing each Xerox district's performance rise and fall on a daily spreadsheet was like watching a slow-motion horse race, with Cleveland the favored War Admiral to Puerto Rico's smaller, come-from-behind Seabiscuit. Going into the fourth quarter of 1993, I recall, we ranked about fifth place in the country. The leap from sixty-four to any spot in the top ten was success by almost any standard, but the difference between fifth place and first was gold.

"We're making great progress, but we're not nearly where we want to be," I told our team as I walked through the office. "This is your moment, Juan!" "Rafael, you are awesome!" "Giselle, we need your intellectual firepower." Fists popped up from cubicles. "*Pasión!*"

By the end of October, we were fourth. By the end of November, number two. In December I was reviewing the *Daily Flash* with fervor. At night, Julie joked that she would be surprised if Puerto Rico didn't sink into the ocean because of the weight of all the Xerox machines we were selling and shipping to the island.

On Thursday, December 9, 1993, a small weekly newspaper, *Caribbean Business*, in an article titled "Xerox Has the Right Formula for Success," wrote that sales for our Puerto Rico district were up more than 50 percent from the previous year. "Bill McDermott," the associate editor wrote, "credits the company's motivated workforce for the firm's sales success."

As Christmas neared, our margin in the *Daily Flash* was wide enough to hold off Cleveland, and anyone else. We had done it: *un milagro*.

Nothing beats the first time that underdogs prove themselves, in any language. Watching those first waves of achievement wash over Papo, Severo, Benny, David, Leida, Juan, Giselle, and the entire district was beautiful. In the history of Xerox, no group deserved a party more than these men and women. Thankfully, we had one planned.

CELEBRATING SUCCESS

A splash of glamor hit us when we walked into the grand ballroom of the El San Juan hotel, where everybody from the district was assembled, most with a spouse or a date. Everybody looked gorgeous. Sparkles popped from long black dresses, and the floor was a sea of gold high heels. Julie looked stunning.

The food was abundant, a sit-down dinner, and when the first chords of music from the horns in Gilberto Santa Rosa's band hit the air, everyone rose and ran onto the dance floor to salsa. Hundreds of people, moving their bodies in ways unlike anything I'd seen at the Silver Shadow. Gilberto kept the entire crowd on its feet. It was the most festive atmosphere I could have imagined. People came up to Julie and me, and we hugged and laughed. Can you believe it? We did it! *Pasión!* Severo said he had never worked so hard, had so much fun—and made so much money—in his life. We had set our minds on a target that many people did not think we could hit. But we did, and the pride that evening fueled the festivities. No one wanted to go home. At three in the morning I asked Gilberto if he would keep playing. "I'll write you a personal check, anything you want."

"No más, no más" was all the exhausted musician could say. We had worn out the famous salsa singer. Reluctantly, people emptied the ballroom, their joy overflowing into the parking lot, where they danced before heading home.

For me, my time in Puerto Rico was amounting to much more than ushering a fantastic group of people from last place to first. More than ever, the experience proved that I could seize an unexpected opportunity and turn it into something more powerful than even I had imagined.

I was also growing. Here family time together was intensified because we were so removed from our old routines. For all my hard work, the entire experience felt like an extended vacation. Our entire family benefited. When I flew my parents out once a month, our times together were extra special. Our beachside condo was a cocoon of familial joy.

I also realized that I was more than Mr. New York and could be happy outside the one place I had convinced myself was my mecca. I still loved the city every time I flew back—at Christmas I arrived at Xerox's offices all suntanned, while everyone else was pale and on life support—but now I saw a world beyond New York City's boroughs. Letting go of what I had known was leading to remarkable growth. In the new year, Julie and I settled into a new routine of work and socializing with local friends, who had come to feel like family. It was a beautiful life.

In the summer of 1994, my office phone rang, again. Someone at Xerox's headquarters in Rochester, New York, had a request. I listened. Another district, the biggest one in the United States, needed a turnaround. Everyone in Rochester knew how happy I was in San Juan, so I asked, "Is this important to the company?" Yes. I understood that Xerox was calling in another favor, and I saw another opportunity to get closer to my dream. After work, I drove back to the condo. As I helped bathe Michael, I turned to Julie. "Babe, how do you feel about snow?"

12

QUESTIONS OF REINVENTION

Change is the price of survival.

—WINSTON CHURCHILL

'VE BEEN THE new district manager in Chicago barely one month, and I am about to piss off the one guy I was told not to piss off. Bernard "Bud" O'Brien is twice my age and oversees our lucrative government clients in Chicago. His legend pre-Xerox is something about which people like to speculate, and I'd already heard just enough to know that, despite rumors of some youthful entanglements with the law, Bud is beloved and highly respected.

Chicago and its surrounding cities are a major market for Xerox, but business here has been lumbering along with average revenues and lukewarm customers. Turning around the district, which I was sent here to do, will require a more deft touch than I exerted in San Juan. Compared with Puerto Rico, this city by the lake is another planet. The terrain. The weather. The people. Not better or worse, just different. The Chicago office's culture is steeped in its own traditions and relationships that go back decades. To begin to earn others' respect, I first must earn Bud's respect.

A few weeks after I'd arrived in town with my Caribbean tan, Bud had shown up in my new office, a groomed elder statesman, unannounced. Even standing in my doorway, the man was a force.

"Your grandfather was the greatest pro basketball player that ever lived," he said. "Wanna go to lunch?" This was more statement than question. Technically, I was Bud's boss, but I sensed Bud wasn't into titles.

"Of course, Bud. I'm honored you think that about my grandfather, and yes, I'd love to have lunch."

"Where do you want to go?"

"Bud, it's your town. Please, you decide."

"Let's go to the Drake. Friday at this time, I'll pick you up, and we'll walk."

The legendary hotel was at least twenty blocks away. Bud left my doorway as unceremoniously as he had arrived, and after this brief interaction, coupled with what I'd been told about the man, it hits me: Bud O'Brien is the de facto boss of the Chicago office. I have just been introduced to the power base; or rather, it has introduced itself to me. Like the cat that launched itself onto my torso a decade earlier, Bud is in charge. As the new young manager, I best make nice.

On Friday, June 17, 1994, I arrive at my office ten minutes after our scheduled meeting time. Being late is unlike me, but Bud doesn't know that. I had just been on a sales call but couldn't find a cab, so I ran the three blocks back to the office, and it's humid as Hades today. By the time I get there, I am wiping sweat from my face.

"You're ten minutes late," my new assistant, Barb Taylor, says. "Bud already left."

"Where'd he go?" I ask.

"I don't know, he just kept looking at his watch."

"Can I catch him?"

"That's up to you."

I must catch him. Missing lunch with Bud is not an option. *The general*, I think, *has just put me on notice.* I hustle to the elevator and get down to the street, where I look around as if I'm searching for a lost pet. *Got him.* I spot Bud's dapper figure and run after him.

"Buddy, what are you doing?" He keeps walking.

"You're late. You missed lunch."

"I'm late, but I didn't miss lunch."

"Do you still want to go?" he asks.

"Do *you* still want to go?"

"Only if you want to go."

"Buddy, of course I want to go. It's an honor to have lunch with you."

He nods. We bound north up Michigan Avenue. Man, I love this street, especially its nickname: the Magnificent Mile. Perfect! Block by block, like a proud papa, Bud introduces me to Chicago's famous office towers. The Wrigley Building. The Tribune Tower. John Hancock Center. On our right, we pass a limestone building; a miniature castle tucked among the urban steel. Bud says it's the old Chicago Water Tower, one of a few structures left standing after the Great Chicago Fire in 1871. Amazing, how this city rebuilt itself around a little piece of history. We cross the street where the sleek, marble-clad high-rise, Water Tower Place, is named after its tenacious little neighbor. The juxtaposition of old and new is humbling, and inspiring. I tell Bud I love his city.

We arrive at the Drake, another ornate piece of history parked among fresh-faced façades. We walk up a wide carpeted stairway through the lobby's grand décor and are led to a table in one of its finer restaurants. Bud orders six beers, on ice. A half dozen bottles arrive in a champagne bucket. Even in Puerto Rico, I rarely drank, especially at lunch. But every city and every person has their rituals. "Sure, Bud, I'll have a beer." Besides, it's Friday. We order lunch, and two plates arrive with portions large enough to feed a small family. I open another bottle. Bud isn't eating fast. He seems in no hurry to get back to work.

We talk about basketball. As a kid, Bud and his dad saw my grandfather play pro ball at the Chicago Stadium, which is about to be demolished. "Bill, we'll go to a game before they tear down that beautiful stadium."

"Sounds great, Bud."

When we talk about leadership and my philosophy, Bud leans back just a little, sussing me out. *Is this guy a Rochester yes-man?* I imagine Bud's thinking. *Or is he like me; someone who likes to get stuff done?* I tell him why I'd replaced my executive assistant the day after I arrived. She was a nice woman, I explain, but when I asked her to copy some overheads for a presentation, she told me that her former boss, the prior district manager, copied his own overheads. She and I looked at each other like a bad fit on a first date, and to our mutual relief, I got her a job more in line with her ambitions, and I found someone more aligned with mine. "Bud, I'm not afraid of hard work, and I'll get anyone coffee, but you can tell a lot about leaders by their assistants."

When we talk Chicago politics, Bud says he'll introduce me to Mayor Richard M. Daley, and lets me know without lowering his voice that the mayor was not impressed when a top Xerox executive showed up at the mayor's office in a creased brown suit and without business cards.

We also talk a lot about Xerox's Chicago office. The district's performance was no horror show like Puerto Rico's, but unimpressive given the potential of its location. Chicago and its sprawling suburbs are headquarters for corporate giants such as McDonald's Corp., Kraft General Foods, Quaker Oats Company, Motorola, Caterpillar, Sears, Roebuck & Co. I tell Bud I think I was sent here to jolt the district out of mediocrity. We clink bottles.

"Should we go to the Cape Cod Room?" he asks, again rhetorically, about a half dozen more bottles and three hours later. "We'll have a couple of martinis." *I've never even had a martini.*

We walk back through the hotel lobby to a smaller, dark seafood restaurant and bar. I look up to see old frying pans hanging from the ceiling's wood beams; square tables are dressed in pristine white cloths. We pull into the iconic bar, and I rub my hand over its wood surface, covered with decades of knife-scratched engravings. Somewhere amid the drunken initials, Bud tells me, are Marilyn Monroe's and Joe DiMaggio's. I'm impressed with how this city treasures its history yet feels crisp. Even this sixty-year-old restaurant doesn't feel tired. Once Bud starts ordering those martinis, I stop expecting to return to the office.

Bud lets me in on his past, and I hear a fascinating tale about a young man who got caught up in some bad stuff early in his career, paid his debt to society, and recast himself as an account rep at Xerox. Bud knows that it's possible to lose something and rebuild.

Like my relationship with Puerto Rico, Bud and I are different yet simpatico, and on Monday, back at the office, I know he will tell his crew, "Bill's good people." I'm grateful. But even more so, I like Bud O'Brien. He feels real to me, yet bigger than life, no BS—the best of his Windy City and my Big Apple.

We part at about ten thirty. "Buddy, what a day. Thank you." He hugs me good-bye and says we'll go golfing at his country club. "Sure, Bud." I do not mention that I'm a lousy golfer and have never been to a country club. The Drake's doorman hails me a cab, and I ask the driver to please take me to the ParkShore, where Julie, Michael, and I are living in a rental apartment until we find a house in the more family-friendly suburbs. Unlike in San Juan, we want to live with grass under our feet instead of sand. Michael is walking, and we hope he will have a sibling soon.

I open the door to our fifty-second-floor apartment. After more than ten hours of keeping up with Bud, I collapse on the couch and squint to see the TV screen in my inebriated state. A thicket of black-and-white police cars are trailing a white SUV on a sunlit highway. Julie explains to me what's been unfolding for the past hour or so. O. J. Simpson, the Hall of Fame football player turned actor, has been accused of double murder. Instead of surrendering to police, he is, reportedly, in the backseat of a Ford Bronco with a gun to his head while his friend drives, leading police on a low-speed chase. This news is sobering. *The Juice! What happened, my man?* Now, on TV, the camera shot from a hovering helicopter reveals a white vehicle rolling along at about thirty-five miles per hour, as if it doesn't know where it's going but just wants to keep moving.

Before I head to bed, exhausted from my hours under Bud's influence, I join Julie and the rest of the country as we watch the life and reputation of a once-revered man unravel one mile at a time.

BRANDING NEW IDEAS

In the mid-1990s, Xerox was trying to re-create the glory of its own history for the digital age. Desktop computers, networked offices, the internet—all would change how companies created, stored, and shared information. Mass emails were replacing hard-copy memos. Electronic files trumped filing cabinets. And printing documents from a PC to a digital printer was easier than walking to a copy machine to make duplicates. These trends had dangerous implications for a company built on selling bulky boxes.

I was young enough, and maybe naive enough, that I didn't fear upheaval and its side effects. Markets, like people, mature. I got that. I'd thought about it with my customers back at the deli. Those high school kids that hung out playing video games would grow older and infirm one day, and, like the elderly folks I also served, they'd want their products delivered. If I refused to do so, I'd lose their business. Twenty years later, a similar phenomenon was happening with business customers: companies were maturing, changing how they wanted information delivered. Vendors such as Xerox risked losing their business if they didn't accommodate their customers' new preferences.

Our chief executive, Paul Allaire, recognized the market shifts, and in the early 1990s, Xerox rebranded itself the Document Company. The tagline reflected our shifting perspective, at least theoretically. Xerox's value to its customers was not in the quality of our machines, but in the quality of the documents that ran through our machines.

This more solution-oriented approach to the market—Xerox can help you figure out how to make better documents—resembled how I'd always approached sales. In New York and Puerto Rico, I'd trained reps to empathize and problem solve. But now that I was in Chicago overseeing several hundred people, I couldn't meet, travel with, or train every single rep. I had to figure out how to scale my consultative style. To do so, I rolled out a districtwide technique I titled The Great Document Hunt.

The Great Document Hunt began with a rep asking a customer, or a prospect, a question: "Which of your company's documents most control your success? A contract? A new-business proposal? Product manuals? The employee directory?" The point of The Great Document Hunt was to work with office managers or, ideally, CEOs to find their organization's most meaningful materials, and then examine how those documents flowed through the company, from creation to revision to dissemination. A Xerox "consultant" would isolate points of that process that siphoned off too much time and money and figure out how Xerox's document management systems could provide productivity gains.

The activity itself wasn't all that intriguing. What got people's attention was how we framed it. As a hunt. A game. A mystery. And everyone loves a good mystery. It was a refreshing conversation starter for our reps, and the conversations differentiated Xerox, elevating a dull administrative process into something stimulating. "Which five documents define your company? Express your values? Help you win accounts, sell more stuff, connect to your customers, determine your success? Let's hunt them down!" The essence of The Great Document Hunt was energy and empathy. And it scaled.

The reps had fun with it. At daily wrap-up meetings, instead of announcing how many units reps had sold, our people tallied how many critical documents they'd unearthed. Even the media were piqued. In November 1994 *USA Today* ran a cheeky front-page headline next to my photo: "In Chicago, It's Always Document Hunting Season."

The hunt was the Chicago district's most creative tactic in a portfolio of more traditional marketing techniques—direct mail pieces, telemarketing, database management, business symposiums—which, combined, turned relationships into sales throughout the district. By the end of 1994, my district was among the country's leading revenue contributors.

Yet even as the district's performance began to improve, something was bothering me about the overall business environment, and Xerox's place in it. As focused as I could be in any given moment, I took time to stand on the balls of my feet to peer above what was happening in front of me. Something new was always on the way.

A NEW WORLD

From spending time with our customers, I was seeing how, more than ever, companies were resisting spending big money, especially on big hardware. They were happy with Xerox's technology—they just didn't want to buy it, operate it, and staff it. Massive cost cutting was something to brag about to Wall Street. Reengineering and out-

sourcing weren't mere buzzwords but billion-dollar business decisions, as companies laid off hundreds and thousands of employees
and shed anything not essential to their core business. I was meeting
savvy CFOs who wondered why they were paying maintenance fees
on a hodgepodge of copy machines, or operating their own printing
facilities. A pharmaceutical outfit such as Abbott Laboratories
should be pouring money into new drug development, not into the
care and feeding of printers.

By reallocating spending, the market was demoting our equipment into costly commodities. This trend was painful, even insulting, for longtime Xerox executives.

As I saw it, outsourcing and the digital wave gave Xerox a chance
to reinvent itself. Instead of talking about how our machines were
better, there was a more compelling story: yes, Xerox machines are
better, but so is our know-how when it comes to managing them.
Let Xerox take over all your document production, and you'll wipe
hundreds of thousands of dollars in labor and asset costs off your
balance sheet. In short, give us your document headaches.

To a degree, Xerox had been telling, and selling, that narrative
for a while. Our outsourcing division, called Xerox Business Services (XBS), already managed many companies' copying and mail-
room facilities, as well as operating stand-alone print shops that
serviced corporate customers. XBS was the latest incarnation of a
business unit that had existed for many years, and by 1994, its business model had evolved to be a full outsourcing alternative that bun-
dled document copying, printing, and distribution services—as well
as outright equipment sales—in combinations that were financially
attractive for companies.

Intentionally, XBS was a relatively small piece of the company.
But it was the fastest-growing segment. From 1994 to 1995, Xerox's
revenue from black-and-white copiers grew by barely 1 percent. The
next year, those sales declined. During the comparable two-year pe-

riod, meanwhile, Xerox's outsourcing business—which ran the print shops and mail rooms that CFOs disdained—*grew by 50 percent and 39 percent*, respectively. You didn't have to be Sherlock Holmes to figure out what was at stake. As the box business was sending up smoke signals, Xerox's outsourcing business was exploding.

Unfortunately, a lot of people inside Xerox weren't interested in facing this scenario. In the company's year-end financial filings that outlined our business model and performance, outsourcing was barely mentioned, while paragraphs were devoted to our newest black-and-white copiers' features. It was as if Xerox didn't want to admit that its gold mine was no longer just a box.

One reason to ignore outsourcing was its slimmer net profit margins compared with the business of just selling or leasing a box. For every box that XBS sold as part of an outsourcing arrangement, the margin was greater than a machine that was sold independent of an outsourcing arrangement. What's more, XBS's customers bought all of their copier-related supplies from Xerox; a customer that bought only a box often sourced its supplies from another company. So XBS could bring in more revenue per box. But the additional labor costs that XBS adopted by taking over, say, a company's print shop, weighed down our *overall* profit margins. That worried many executives inside Xerox. Despite XBS's growing revenue, they saw XBS, and outsourcing, only as a lower-margin business, so they did not support it. Maybe they worried that if Xerox began touting a future based on a services strategy, Wall Street would see only a less-profitable business model versus a higher-volume model, and that would upset the company's valuation and stock price—at least in the short term.

I didn't have much Xerox stock, and instead of worrying about the value of my retirement account, I was interested in growing the business. Rather than ignoring the changing market, we should have been pouncing on it.

As someone who started at Xerox selling door-to-door and had grown up on the marketing side of the company, I was not as well schooled in finance as many of the senior executives. But because I spent a lot of time with customers, I'd become convinced that avoiding the outsourcing revolution was a toxic strategy. So what if margins for services were smaller. Demand was huge! And in a few years, as XBS became more creative in bundling services and more effective in its operations, outsourcing's margins would widen.

Another vision for our future was even harder than outsourcing for Xerox's box-heads to digest. The rapid migration of technology, especially in business, from analog to digital formats was creating an increasingly networked world. Xerox had an opportunity to be a leader in the business of storing and disseminating digital information. Along with other digital document zealots, I envisioned a sprawling global network of Xerox-operated data centers where our people could pluck customers' online information from a remote network and, on demand, print out and prepare any combination of documents for a local user. If I were a businessperson traveling from New York to Mumbai to run a meeting, all the documents I needed—agendas, presentations, reports, training materials—could be accessed, prepared, and set up prior to my arrival, by Xerox.

By 1995, I believed in the potential of digital document management. That's why I was easily sold when XBS's president asked me to leave my district manager position in the mainline copier business and work as one of his five direct reports, running XBS's operations in the Midwest. I was ready to take a more strategic role, helping Xerox enter the future instead of continuing to sell its past.

As head of XBS, Norm Rickard was not trapped in that past, despite more than three decades at Xerox. Since 1966, he'd worked in finance, planning, and operations. As the company's former quality officer, Norm had instilled rigor and higher standards. His leadership was a chief reason why Xerox won the prestigious Malcolm Baldrige National Quality Award in 1989.

Like other leaders I admired and wanted to learn from, Norm traded micromanaging people for trusting them. He'd set a few ground rules and then get out of the way. Most important, Norm and I shared a vision about where the office of the future was going, and thus where Xerox should go, too. XBS was a sleeper inside the company, we agreed, not because the market didn't love outsourced services but because many executives at Xerox didn't love them. The real fight for respect was internal, within Xerox's own ranks.

Big thinkers like Bud congratulated me on the move, but many people thought I was crazy to join the junior varsity team. With about $900 million in outsourcing revenues in 1995, XBS represented only 5 percent of Xerox's overall revenues. Others even tried to block my transfer to XBS, fearing the potential Pied Piper effect. People who had worked for me often asked to join my new teams when I moved on. I always felt blessed when I earned the trust of talented people. Norm was hoping that by getting me to jump the fence, I would bring to XBS some top talent from the "Big House." Some did join XBS, including my former team member and top marketing rep Greg McStravick, who became my sales and operations manager for Chicago's suburban clients.

It was also our hope that XBS's stature inside Xerox would rise. Imagine what XBS could be, we proselytized, if more people believed as we did: that outsourcing was the future. This new world was intoxicating, and at age thirty-four, there was no place I would rather have been than working for the company's underdog.

13

HIGHER PURPOSE

*For when people get caught up with that which is
right and therefore willing to sacrifice for it, there is no
stopping point short of victory.*

—DR. MARTIN LUTHER KING JR.

PEOPLE ARE MOST likely to change their minds when the world
they once knew no longer exists. A leader's challenge, then, is to
explain why the old world went away, show people what the new
world looks like, and get them excited to be a part of it.

Norm brought me to XBS to sell services in the marketplace but
also to sell Xerox's employees on *the idea* of selling services to the
marketplace. Everyone from our salespeople to our hourly staffers
had to be jolted out of indifference and pumped up about selling
document management services—an intangible offering.

In my first year with XBS, I had complete profit and loss responsibility for the $350 million central region. Ten general managers re-
ported to me, fifty-five managers were under them, and some two

thousand staff and associates worked in our offices and on client sites. Not long after I started, Norm brought in Tom Dolan to head XBS's US operations, which was the bulk of the business: the feeder for XBS contracts in dozens of other countries. Reunited, Tom and I were like Batman and Robin: he brought the senior statesman gravitas; I brought a next-generation energy. We operated like crusaders for change, sans the capes.

The outsourcing business was thriving. By the end of 1995, XBS had posted a 50 percent increase in revenue year over year and added hundreds of jobs. In 1996 XBS's document outsourcing revenues reached $1.3 billion. All told that year, XBS was servicing four thousand customer locations, and our customer retention rate was approximately 95 percent, up from about 88 percent four years earlier. Anyone who thought XBS was destined to remain an outlier only had to look at the numbers. The $17.4 billion in total revenues that Xerox Corp. recorded in 1996 was driven, the company told investors in its year-end filing with the Securities and Exchange Commission, by a 10 percent growth in equipment sales and a *47 percent growth* in document outsourcing. One year later, in 1997, XBS had $2 billion in revenues and was serving five thousand customer locations. Again, rocket progress.

To create the internal support that XBS deserved, my actions during those years were driven by one philosophy: people get most inspired not by money but by purpose.

A REASON TO BUILD

I needed a cause. A compelling cause was like kerosene. It could light up a work ethic. On my past teams, well-articulated reasons to achieve—beyond a monetary goal—had sparked people's imaginations and extended their stamina: Be your personal best. Become number one. Make history. Go for the gold. These aspirations transcended the need to hit a number.

To figure out what would matter to people at XBS, I considered what mattered to me. I loved Xerox. The company had given me my first professional job and trusted me to excel. I had given Xerox everything I had since 1983, and it hurt me to see us on a path that threatened our sustainability. More and more, I believed our company's survival did not depend on another line of machines or on restructuring our operations, but on doing something bold.

Just as I was learning from my own history, I thought back to Xerox's history. Back to that independent physicist Chester Carlson, who sixty years earlier, after toiling away in a homemade lab, had produced the first xerographic image. I thought about Joe Wilson, who in the 1940s had his photographic supply company, Haloid Corporation, buy certain rights to Chester's technology. Why? Joe knew that Haloid's own products were becoming obsolete, and for the next decade, Joe bucked naysayers and poured Haloid's revenues into commercializing xerography. Then I thought about how, in 1959, Joe's gamble began to pay off when his renamed company, Xerox, introduced the 914 copier, catapulting Xerox's sales from $32 million to more than $1 billion in less than ten years.

Like any great organization, Xerox had made mistakes, but we had an inspiring heritage. To squander it seemed a tragedy. To live up to it, aspirational. Xerox's heritage, I concluded, was not about building boxes; it was about reinvention. And *that* was a purpose worth fighting to sustain. For my teams at XBS, I needed to position the New Economy as a compelling opportunity for growth, not something for Xerox to fear. Although fear could boost adrenaline in the short term, it could also spur people to make bad choices as they grasped for instant relief.

My internal marketing campaign was coming together. Xerox had a history of bold decisions altering our trajectory for the better. Now, in 1997, we were at another inflection point. We had an incredible chance to redefine and secure our great company's future—if we had the courage, and the will, to make the right choices. In my tradition of wrapping ideas in whimsical language, I labeled this inflection point "Ground Xero."

I knew from experience that simple language expressing a big idea could communicate a vision while elevating the mundane to something special. Names like Feel-Felt-Found or The Great Document Hunt may have seemed kitschy, but the right nomenclature was as descriptive as it was memorable, and could make complicated concepts accessible, as well as relevant, to everyone. The most effective packaging also delivered a dose of drama, and that's what I was after with Ground Xero.

The term "ground zero" had yet to become shorthand for the World Trade Center site following the horrendous 2001 terrorist attacks. For decades prior to that, ground zero was associated with points of absolute destruction, like the center of an earthquake or a bomb blast. I chose the term because my own optimistic lens viewed any point of destruction as a point from which to rebuild. "We've done it before and we'll do it again"—those memorable words from my mom as our house burned were instilled in my attitude. Anything, from a home, to a company, to a person's reputation, might have to be rebuilt due to circumstances beyond control—natural disasters, new technologies, the passing of time, economic shifts, freak accidents, politics, whims of human desire.

At XBS, I designed my Ground Xero campaign to bring necessary drama to this moment in Xerox's evolution. To help bring it to life, I produced a black-and-red foldout piece of marketing collateral for our employees. On its thick pages, my argument unfurled with my unedited drama, as if I were trying to sway the entire Xerox organization to change course. "Be warned . . . ," large black letters announced, "nothing is the same after Ground Xero." Inside the foldout, my case for change read like a battle call:

Every significant movement had a single point of origin, a history making moment. We find ourselves at just such a point in time—an intersection of people, process, and technology that has presented us with a new world to be won. Call it a defining moment if you want, I call it Ground Xero . . . This once in a lifetime opportunity is in our hands. Each of us must now decide whether to seize the power of its potential.

To bolster the argument, I created a timeline summarizing what I identified as sixty years of Ground Xero milestones at Xerox, beginning with Chester Carlson's and Joe Wilson's. The timeline went on: in 1977 Xerox launched the first laser printers despite concerns that they would cannibalize core products, yet those printers became a multibillion-dollar business. In 1983 David Kearns's quality movement began to sweep the company to reestablish Xerox's market dominance. In 1991 Xerox branded itself the Document Company.

To paraphrase Winston Churchill, the further back we looked, the further forward we would be able to see. "Like so many Ground Xeros that preceded it," I wrote, "we will once again seize the opportunity to make record-setting history." I was unapologetic about the drama.

In 1997 Tom replaced Norm as head of XBS Worldwide when Norm was promoted to lead another, related Xerox business. I was offered Tom's job, heading XBS for the entire country. But I needed to work out of Xerox's headquarters in Rochester, New York. Julie and I were not eager to uproot from our cul-de-sac in Lake Forest, Illinois, where Julie had made dear friends. Plus, we had been blessed with a second child, a spirited, healthy son we named John Patrick. Once again the hospital staff told me they had never seen a new father leap with such joy. Like Michael, my second son enthralled me. Beginning a new life in a new city, however, while balancing a baby and a toddler, was not ideal. But we decided to do it.

On the corporate power ladder, the new job was a step up. But more than the title, it was exciting to have a bigger stage, and more resources, to broadcast what I believed was a time-sensitive higher purpose. As president of XBS in the United States, I also was a newly christened senior vice president of the corporation. I had no intention of keeping my voice down.

14

PAGEANTRY

Where there is no vision, the people perish.
—PROVERBS 29:18

"BILL, I HOPE you know what you're doing."

I had just told Tom that I was inviting all 1,800 employees that worked in XBS's US sales and marketing operations to our 1998 kickoff meeting in San Antonio, Texas. It would be a lush affair. Xerox was known for hosting lavish trips to honor its top sales performers, but those events were reserved for people with revenue-producing responsibilities. The support staffers I was inviting to San Antonio—administrative assistants; people who ran our clients' mail rooms or worked in human resources and accounting; and many more—rarely left their offices for work. Tom knew senior management would get huffy when they knew that eight hundred hourly workers were headed to a party. Especially now.

The company was in a cost-shedding frenzy. Amid that, I wanted to commit $2.5 million to fly hundreds of people from around the country to a city where we would house and feed them for three days. By the time I told Tom, there was no rewinding. I'd already reserved the San Antonio Convention Center, two Marriott hotels along the city's famed River Walk, and hired a company to help plan various events. Plus, XBS's own people were creating dozens of training and educational sessions.

"It's going to get a lot of visibility, Bill," Tom told me. "And as head of the US, you're accountable for it." I told Tom I was accountable for everything I did. "It's my P&L," I said. "Tom, trust me, I got this." I was not being reckless. I knew even before I talked to Tom that the kickoff would be controversial, but I believed in it.

My time in Puerto Rico had reinforced the power of pageantry to inspire people. By incorporating nice meals into meetings, attending silly skits on the beach, promising a magnificent Christmas party, I'd witnessed how an event could spice up bland topics, turning ordinary assignments into bigger deals and ratcheting up people's commitment. A nod of ceremonial splendor instead of a second-rate affair showed respect for all invited, and that respect was reciprocated. The kickoff event for XBS's 1998 fiscal year was the ideal chance to translate outsourcing into a compelling, 3-D affair, which could translate into growth.

A show of pageantry from a small business unit was a calculated move on my part against Xerox's culture of austerity, as well as its dominating "box" mind-set. XBS's investment in our people's education would be more appreciated because much of Xerox was cutting back on training, perks—even pay. Plus, the grand gesture of an all-hands conference would get people to believe as I did: that a future in outsourcing was as grand as the gesture itself. Abundance begets abundance. So in order to move people at XBS to expect more of themselves, I had to give them more.

I secured Tom's blessing, but the price tag was high enough that I had to defend it in front of a group of top executives. Gatherings a fraction of the size of the one I had in mind were being replaced by virtual meetings or conference calls. I clarified my accounting to show that my operating plan funded the budget. I urged people to see the big picture. XBS was going to ask its people to follow a vision so grand, to hit a sales goal so high, that we couldn't afford to let them hear about it only through filters—emails, memos, managers—that diluted original messages. XBS needed to unveil its purpose and vision in person, loud and clear, so everyone understood it.

"What's the goal?" the executives asked me. I told them: XBS, driven by the United States, would reach $4 billion in revenues by the end of 2000. That meant doubling our size in about three years. "It's an impossible dream," they insisted. While I believed that $4 billion was indeed doable, I was, again, not being reckless. My operating plan's real target—the number Xerox's corporate finance department could calculate into the company's overall targets—was less than the $4 billion I would ask XBS's employees to aim for. Three billion dollars in revenue by 2000 was a more realistic goal yet still a dream target. *So why not tell everyone $3 billion, Bill?* Because my hurdle—getting my people ecstatic about selling outsourcing—was so high that I needed to get everyone's mind to a place where the dream seemed so impossible that it was exciting to pursue. I deliberately overshot.

For more than a decade now, I'd watched teams rise to the expectations set for them. The more daring the target, the higher people rose. Big numbers got people's attention and heightened their belief in their ability to achieve something deemed impossible. A jet doesn't leave the runway to fly around the world without full tanks of fuel, and asking them to double our sales by 2000 wasn't a puddle jump. I was asking them to circle the globe twice. They needed to come away from the San Antonio kickoff bubbling with enthusiasm and confidence in the plan, and in themselves.

That's why we needed hundreds of support staffers to be in San Antonio, I explained. Administrative assistants, for one, ran our offices day to day. If the person that answered my phone and opened my mail and kept my schedule didn't know XBS's vision and embrace its strategy, how could he or she prioritize my day or decide who gets through to talk to me, or who could wait? XBS needed buy-in at every level.

I described the gist of the conference. We would unveil the revenue goal as well as XBS's corresponding theme for the year, "Go-4Growth in America." To bring it to life, the opening ceremony, and each morning's gathering, would be modeled after a political convention. The country was a little more than a year past Bill Clinton's reelection as president over Republican senator Bob Dole, and their respective campaigns weren't far from people's minds. We'd recreate a political rally to rally XBS's constituents.

More than spectacle, the three-day event would also give people the tools to perform. Two full days would be packed with education, training, and certification courses, so people would know what they needed to do once they returned to their offices. Plus, they would be held accountable for what they learned. Then, on Sunday, we'd cap the event with an awards ceremony honoring our top performers. By the time our people left San Antonio and returned to their corners of the country, I believed, they would feel like valued members of a national team. And they'd produce. The alternative, circulating a memo or throwing a halfhearted kickoff, may have saved a chunky line item that quarter, but it would never unleash the level of engagement we needed to sell an additional $2 billion of document management services.

Not everyone bought into my premise, but San Antonio was a go.

RIGOR REWARDED

On the morning of December 19, 1997, about a month before the San Antonio kickoff meeting, I was with Norm Rickard and Tom

Dolan in Washington, DC, where, in the Cotillion Ballroom of the Sheraton Washington Hotel, Tom accepted, on behalf of XBS, the prestigious Malcolm Baldrige National Quality Award from President Bill Clinton.

For me, being in the same room as the president of the United States was unbelievable. I was thirty-six, but I still felt like a teenager behind a deli counter, slicing meat and waxing floors. I was in a constant state of awe as my life unfolded, whether I was sharing beers with a guy like Bud O'Brien or standing in the same room as the US president. I appreciated every experience.

Of course, for XBS, winning the Baldrige was a momentous occasion. Applying for it had required a tremendous amount of due diligence. Every part of a business was inspected and judged. Norm, who had led Xerox Corp. to win its first and only other Baldrige, said that the reason to go for it was not necessarily to win but to learn and improve from the experience of meeting its high standards. Of course, like me, he also wanted the win, but in going for it, XBS honed its operations. By the time a half dozen examiners descended on our regional offices and client sites, we were ready, and in 1997, Xerox Business Services was one of four winning organizations. It was an incredible vote of confidence, one that we hoped would also elevate XBS's standing within the company.

Plus, watching Tom meet President Clinton gave me a killer idea for San Antonio.

POMP AND CIRCUMSTANCE

On a Thursday in the middle of winter, XBS employees from across the country are flying into the warmth of Texas and settling into their well-appointed rooms with a view. More than half have never been to a President's Club or a similarly amped-up affair. Hundreds, from office managers to information technology guys, are just happy to be away from their routines and on an all-expenses-paid business trip with beautiful accommodations in a beautiful city. By the time they arrive at the opening ceremony at the San Antonio Convention Center's auditorium, they're buzzing. No one knows what's on the menu, but the plan is to start the meeting with dessert. Let's have some fun, some laughs, stop taking ourselves so seriously.

From backstage, I peer into the red-white-and-blue-soaked theater. It feels like an opening night. The entire auditorium, from the aisles into the lobby, has been designed to look and feel like a national presidential convention. I'd hired an event production company out of Chicago, One Smooth Stone, that specialized in what it called business theater. Its founder, Kevin Olsen, believed in the power of pageantry to galvanize people and drive business results. The execution is already exceeding my imagination. The theater looks amazing. From the main floor up into the balconies, each business region is seated together, like state delegates. There are signs for everyone to pump up and down, plus flags and noisemakers on every seat. Red, white, and blue balloons would soon fall from the ceiling, and people are already blowing little New Year's Eve horns.

Roving the floor, actors role-playing TV reporters are interviewing people on camera. One of them approaches my wonderful assistant. "This is Tom Lockjaw," he says into a camera (for laughs, we'd given the stand-in anchors gag names), "reporting from the floor of the San Antonio Convention Center. Barb, what are your thoughts on the next four years?" The actors play it straight and get people smiling, but more importantly they get people talking about issues that matter to XBS. Every on-camera interview will be quickly edited and replayed on big screens during the next few days. Giving our people a voice was imperative. The kickoff was not about me or other leaders doing all the talking. We wanted people in the trenches to be heard and to hear one another.

The seats fill up, and the energy is akin to a live convention, bolstered by the shock element as people wonder what to make of it all. No one expected these sights and sounds. *What's next? What's all this about?* We've transported people out of corporate America.

A mock news anchorman takes his place at an anchor desk in the back of the auditorium, so that, on camera, the convention floor is visible behind him. After each presentation, he will summarize and ad-lib commentary, keeping the event's narrative thread, with a wink. When the lights on the stage go up, and I walk on, the audience is so revved they don't quiet down. I look out into a sea of red, white, and blue pom-poms and pumping signs: Central Region. Western Region. Chicago. Atlanta. They're all here. "Welcome to Texas, everyone!"

My role is to set the tone for what I'm about to ask each of them to do over the next two years: double our business by the year 2000. But before I launch into all that, I want to turn up the volume a little more. Time to get Tom onstage.

"Ladies and gentleman, your president of XBS Worldwide. Mr. Tom Dolan." Tom and I shake hands and hug, and I hand him the microphone. His expression is disbelief. Xerox hasn't seen anything this elaborate in years. Tom thinks it's as if movie director Cecil B. DeMille got his hands on a corporate conference. Only minutes earlier did I tell Tom I'd be calling him up onstage, so he has nothing prepared to say. He begins to address the crowd, but if he goes on too long, we'll lose the energy, so after about two minutes I rush the stage.

"Tom! Tom! Look!"

Secret Service agents walk out from the wings in dark suits and headsets. One walks to the podium and slaps a large US Presidential Seal over the hotel signage, while the other agents look up and around, their steely faces inspecting the theater. "Hail to the Chief" blasts from the speakers and out walks the forty-second president of the United States.

Onstage, at a Xerox sales conference, William Jefferson Clinton is smiling and giving everyone his signature thumbs-up. People are out of their chairs, a spontaneous wave of screams and applause. *This is unbelievable. The president? Here?* We had set the stage just right, and everyone is so hyped that they are primed to believe that, yes, President Clinton is indeed here. *Holy*—. The place goes mad. People are swinging their flags and blowing their horns. Bedlam. Even Republicans in the audience. Everyone is cheering and hollering as Clinton walks up to a wide-eyed Tom and shakes his hand.

"Tom, great seeing you again," says the president. "It was just terrific to see you in Washington, DC, for the Baldrige and have you and Bill stay in the Lincoln Bedroom." Laughter erupts. "And I just want to thank you and your whole ball team here for that significant contribution you made to my reelection." Clinton looks at the audience. Mouths hang open. "In fact, it's all of you I want to thank for that contribution because it came out of your 401(k) program." People start to clue in, and I jump in.

"Tom, we really should let President Clinton have a few moments with the team," I say. "I know he would like to say a few words today." At the podium, behind the presidential seal, Clinton goes straight for the jokes, and by the time he tells a slightly off-color one about a particular senator, the choreographed gig is up. Everyone's in on the joke.

President Clinton is being impersonated. As this revelation replaces the shock of seeing the nation's executive in chief, it sparks more joy. People love the gag, and they love that they're part of it. *Bill got us! He got Tom!* Overwhelmed with the spoof and the impersonator's string of jokes, people are laughing so hard they're wiping away tears. No way could this palpable reaction have been elicited over a conference call or a taped video.

Later, I unveil our goal: $4 billion by 2000. I explain why we must do it, and why we can do it. I tell them the new world we all work in doesn't care about copiers and printers and high-speed production;

the world has evolved into an economy full of knowledge workers and companies that care about maximizing information. But—and that *but* was why XBS mattered—those workers and companies didn't want to do it themselves. They want to hand their document management to an expert. The decisions each of us at XBS makes from this point forward, the creativity and the commitment we show, will determine if we are that expert, and if we can change with the world. This moment is our Ground Xero, I say. Xerox has done it before, and XBS will do it again.

Throughout the rest of the event, other XBS leaders join me onstage in support, as our mock news anchors keep the conversation light and the narrative tight. At the end, I leave everyone with a final thought:

"The success of this meeting will not be judged by this amazing show and how much fun we had but by what you learn in the next few days and what you will do with that over the next few years." I was clear that my role was to put each of them in a position to win. I could give them the vision and the strategy and the plan, but I wouldn't be watching over everyone's shoulders when they went back to their offices. They had to have the desire.

"Do you have the will to win? Can I count on you? If I can count on you, please, let me know." People jumped to their feet, and I know. Even Tom knows. We have their votes.

APPRECIATED

Was all this orchestrated ceremony silly? Was it soft? Did it even matter? I would never be able to capture the exact return on investment of a three-day conference. But the appeal of the pageantry elicited a higher level of trust and excitement within our organization. Tom said he could barely remember ten minutes from dozens of past kickoff meetings he'd attended, but he'd be able to recall this one a decade from now.

After San Antonio, people flew home feeling appreciated and educated. In the calls and emails I received from folks who had attended, they restated our goals and committed to them. And they thanked me. The message had not been diluted. People knew what to do, and why.

During the first hundred days after the kickoff, I visited XBS offices around the country to keep up the momentum, and to make sure that every office leader was out in front of clients, going after revenue and profits. The earlier in the year that we signed contracts, the longer XBS would benefit from each contract's annuity stream. Touring XBS's regional teams also allowed me to make an impression. Everyone had to hustle. I didn't want managers sitting behind desks punching out emails; I wanted them on the front lines, in front of decision makers, showing their teams how to sell well. I joined sales calls in every city, always hoping that my behavior would turn into other people's habits.

XBS took off. By the end of 1998, Xerox's outsourcing revenues hit $2.7 billion, up 35 percent. By the end of 1999, we were at $3.4 billion. By the end of 2000, Xerox's outsourcing services were bringing in a reported $3.8 billion. In the three years since the Go4Growth campaign kicked off, XBS had grown 90 percent. Was I upset that we fell shy of our $4 billion bull's-eye? Not one bit. The point of setting audacious goals was that we could almost hit them and still accomplish something amazing. Had we never strived so high, we never would have hit as high as we did.

Yet many people inside Xerox still weren't buying it. Despite the company's declaring itself the Document Company, there were those still in love with a boxy business model. Never mind that market dynamics were screaming that it was time for a divorce. As the nineties drew to a close, such misplaced loyalties were breaking my heart.

15

BETTER

No person was ever honored for what he received.
Honor has been the reward for what he gave.

—CALVIN COOLIDGE

"THERE IS NO more important task than giving Americans the chance to dream of a better life, and there is no better path to a better life than a job."

When I heard these words in the East Room of the White House on May 20, 1997, I got goose bumps. I was surrounded by US senators, governors, members of the presidential cabinet, global business leaders, and President Bill Clinton and Vice President Al Gore. (The real ones.) The man speaking was Eli Segal, a respected businessman whom Clinton referred to as the "father" of the national service organization AmeriCorps. Now he was in charge of a consortium of companies that would help implement the president's new welfare law. This morning, Eli and the president were announcing the Welfare to Work Partnership.

When I arrived in the gold-hued East Room, after standing in line on Pennsylvania Avenue and being patted down by the Secret Service, there were no seat assignments. Most of the executives clustered together in the middle rows. *But kids, this is the White House!* So I made my way to an empty chair up front, determined to get as close as I could to the podium.

As head of XBS's US operations, I was here to represent Xerox's participation in the Welfare to Work Partnership. As part of the program, more than a hundred companies—including United Airlines, Burger King, Marriott Corporation, and dozens of smaller, regional organizations—would each hire, train, and retain former welfare recipients to create programs that moved people off public assistance. XBS was qualified for this task. The American economy was in overdrive, with national unemployment so low that XBS was having difficulty finding applicants for hundreds of new job openings at our growing outsourcing sites. Many of the jobs we needed to fill didn't require a college education or even a high school degree. Hourly positions in mail rooms and copy centers, replacing toner and putting paper in machines, were ideal starter jobs for folks coming off welfare.

When Paul Allaire and Norm Rickard asked me to represent Xerox on the Partnership's board, my initial excitement was around how cool it would be to work with the president. At Partnership board meetings, I would watch how President Clinton operated, how he read the room, listening to everyone who spoke before him, jotting down a line or two on paper or the back of a manila folder. Then, when he spoke, he strung together everyone's ideas so beautifully yet made every speech his own. I also noted how he appointed talented people to run his initiatives for him, people such as Eli, who had the brains for a particular job as well as the heart. Bill Clinton, I observed from my front row seat on the Partnership's board, empowered us and let us run. And we got stuff done. Later, when I told my parents how I sat across the table from the president in the Cabinet Room of the White House, I was as giddy as when I'd dialed them from the pay phone at the Bun n' Burger to say I got the Xerox sales job.

Yet the more entrenched I became with the Welfare to Work program and with its participants, the more that cool factor was replaced by a more substantial one.

Growing up, I'd watched my dad work a hardscrabble job, putting in overtime most weeks to provide for our family. I knew the world was full of hardworking people like him, who toiled away for less financial reward than they deserved. Since leaving Long Island and joining Xerox, however, I'd been in a blessed bubble. Like any company, Xerox had its share of lackadaisical folks, but for the most part, I worked beside people in New York, Puerto Rico, Chicago, and Rochester who wanted to make a good living as well as a good name for themselves. They worked hard to make it happen, and they had the resources—the educational pedigree, the emotional support of family and friends, a little money either saved or borrowed—to buttress their aspirations.

Participating in the Welfare to Work initiative, however, exposed me to slices of America's working class that had the work ethic yet floundered when circumstances beyond their immediate control blocked their attempts to bring home a paycheck. I met people who couldn't find affordable and safe child care for their kids so that they could go to work, or who had no reliable transportation to get to and from work on time, or who were in abusive relationships that sucked their self-confidence on the job. One woman I met was chained by all three—no sitter, no car, bad boyfriend—until Xerox helped her find good child care, lose the boyfriend, and access regular transportation. The woman rose to become a manager at the Xerox facility where she worked. We also employed a single father of two children, who would leave his house at five o'clock each morning to arrive at work by seven; his kids would have to get themselves off to school. After about six months on the job, he was promoted to a supervisor.

Xerox's own welfare-to-work program set a precedent for how employers could help ensure on-the-job success. We created training and mentoring programs, made resources available to help people address personal circumstances, and formed tight relationships with community organizations. Our pilot program in seventeen locations employed some 100 people and hit retention rates of more than 90 percent. We expanded the program to fifty sites, and by 2000, 439 people had been hired through it, and we had a 65 percent retention rate; about one-third had earned raises or promotions. It was inspiring to see the power that Xerox's welfare-to-work program had to help change people's lives.

My experience expanded my perspective, enlightening me to the responsibility that companies and their leaders have to the wider community.

"You come here primarily as businesspeople," the president had said from the podium in the East Room the day the program was announced. "Some of you are Republicans; some of you are Democrats; some of you probably wish you had never met a politician." A chuckle rose from the middle of the audience. "But you all recognize that this is not a partisan issue; that it is a moral obligation for our country. It is America's business, and therefore, it must be the work of American business."

After the meeting, the president made his way down from the podium to shake hands, using a cane to support a healing knee, which he'd injured two months earlier after a well-publicized fall down some stairs. Clinton limped toward my side of the room. When his gaze met mine, I gave him a thumbs-up, which he returned. A photographer behind me must have snapped his camera, because the next day, on the front page of the *Chicago Tribune*, there appeared a photo of a smiling President Clinton with his right arm outstretched and his thumb up, and the back of Bill McDermott's head. It was as proud a moment as a kid from Amityville could have hoped for in his lifetime.

Press clippings aside, another memory stuck with me from the experience, and that was a sentiment President Clinton expressed at the end of one of the board's meetings. He said there were three things that we, as Americans, can choose to do with our lives: we can be better, we can be bored, or we can be broke. Welfare to Work, he stressed, was all about getting better.

Better. What an uncluttered, modest word. It gripped me.

More and more, I was seeing my work not as a series of accomplishments but as a parade of moments led by a desire for my teams, my districts, my divisions—as well as myself—to be better. As much as I loved celebrating success, the joy of a goal achieved was usually short-lived. I was never done.

ITHACA

Back in Chicago, before we moved to Rochester, New York, I had been accepted into the executive master's program at Northwestern University's J. L. Kellogg Graduate School of Management, one of seventy students. The timing had not been ideal. In addition to trying to lead change through XBS and assist with Xerox's welfare-to-work initiative, I wanted to be spending time with my family. Sitting in a classroom was not how I wanted to fill my hours away from the office, listening to professors talk over the tick tock of a wall clock. But both Julie and I recognized education's value.

I'd already completed the Wharton Executive Development Program at the University of Pennsylvania. Still, Norm had urged me to apply to Kellogg, believing that it would broaden my financial acumen and sharpen my marketing skills. Round out the businessman. Having a degree in my back pocket couldn't hurt, I figured, but not having it could put me at a disadvantage one day. Plus, Xerox would pay the annual tuition.

Sponsoring my MBA may also have been Xerox's way of sending me to finishing school, which was ironic. Despite the rawness of my personality, some execs, although not Norm or Tom, complained that I was too polished. A management coach assigned by Xerox to up-

and-coming executives told me to tone down my style. "Bill," he said, "you suck the oxygen out of a room when you dress sharper than your bosses. You look too pressed. Too perfect." He implied that some people were uncomfortable around me. It was suggested—at least for casual Fridays—that I swap the navy blue suits, cuff links, and black shoes for chinos, Ralph Lauren sweaters, and loafers with little tassels.

I went to the mall and bought some of their clothes. And for a short time, I wore them, but it was like being in someone else's skin. I could have kept up the charade, worn their clothes and cut my hair, parting it on the side like other execs. But I went back to my style, which reflected the styles of the Xerox executives I admired most, like Barry Rand, Al Byrd, and Emerson Fullwood. If it made me feel like myself, I stuck with it. There was a difference between aligning with people's needs and conforming to other's behaviors. If I accepted senior management's safe attire, would I also accept its safe business strategies?

Eventually, with Julie's support, I applied to Kellogg. I was honored to be accepted. Although I first saw graduate school's value as a stepping-stone to future opportunities, I was surprised how much I enjoyed and benefited from the learning at Kellogg. One of my fellow students, Amos, nicknamed me "Helicopter View" because, when we studied complex business cases, I tended to focus on high-level issues rather than get mired in unimportant details. We all learned from one another.

After two years, in December 1997, an MBA from a great school was in my back pocket. I had gone for the degree, but in retrospect I left with so much more.

Of course, I learned a lot, mainly about how to craft better business plans and be a smarter business operator. But graduate school's most indelible influence on me was not a skill but an idea. One of my courses introduced me to the Greek poet Constantine P. Cavafy. I'd never been interested in poetry, but his poem from the early twentieth century read like an epiphany:

Ithaca

As you set out on the way to Ithaca
hope that the road is a long one,
filled with adventures, filled with discoveries.
The Laestrygonians and the Cyclopes,
Poseidon in his anger: do not fear them,
you won't find such things on your way
so long as your thoughts remain lofty, and a choice
emotion touches your spirit and your body.
The Laestrygonians and the Cyclopes,
savage Poseidon; you won't encounter them
unless you stow them away within your soul,
unless your soul sets them up before you.

Hope that the road is a long one.
Many may the summer mornings be
when—with what pleasure, with what joy—
you first put in to harbors new to your eyes;
may you stop at Phoenician trading posts
and there acquire the finest wares:
mother-of-pearl and coral, amber and ebony,
and heady perfumes of every kind:
as many heady perfumes as you can.
Many Egyptian cities may you visit
that you may learn, and go on learning, from their sages.

Always in your mind keep Ithaca.
To arrive there is your destiny.
But do not hurry your trip in any way.
Better that it last for many years;
that you drop anchor at the island an old man,

rich with all you've gotten on the way,
not expecting Ithaca to make you rich.

Ithaca gave you the beautiful journey;
without her you wouldn't have set upon the road.
But now she has nothing left to give you.

And if you find her poor, Ithaca didn't deceive you.
As wise as you will have become, with so much experience,
you will understand, by then, these Ithacas; what they mean.

Wow. "Do not hurry your trip in any way"—I loved that sentiment. "Better that it last for many years."

Since I was a kid, I'd dreamed about winning, in various forms. As a basketball player, winning was about our team scoring more baskets. As a hardworking teen, winning was about saving my family from our cycle of endless labor and endless bills, and about securing my own financial freedom. As a young salesman and executive at Xerox, winning was about being "the best," which meant selling more than anyone else. All worthy goals, but in and of themselves, high scores and high sales did not encompass what it meant to win.

Experience, exposure, and maturity—as well as a Greek poem—were revealing a truth that I'd probably always known: winning was not about a specific end but about how an end was met, moment after moment. Winning was the process, not the destination. A journey of striving to be better—to be kinder, more compassionate, hungrier, more humble, more audacious, more inspiring, more rigorous—*that* was what turned me on, what inspired me. The quest was the best.

So what was I to do with my long-standing dream? Back in 1983, when I first came to Xerox, my goal was to be its CEO. I never gave that up. But in the late 1990s, I began to wonder whether that was still the win I wanted.

RECASTING THE DREAM

At thirty-six, I became the equivalent of a "made" man when Xerox named me to its executive board. The appointment also made me the youngest corporate officer in Xerox's history, and the post came with an unspoken contract for life and perks that would dissuade most people from ever defecting. It also was a quiet nod that I had a chance to be considered for the CEO post one day—which was ironic because I'd been debating whether my time at Xerox was up.

My entire career, all I'd known was Xerox. Like my dad, I'd committed myself to one company, yet I now worried if my lack of breadth would prove a liability. The world outside Xerox was changing. The New Economy, buoyed by the internet, was booming as investors threw millions at anything that smelled of innovation. Every day, twentysomethings were calling themselves CEOs at dinky start-ups valued at millions of dollars. Was Xerox a stodgy grandparent at a young person's party? Was I crazy for staying?

I also became the worldwide general manager of XBS, which had risen to about 25 percent of Xerox's overall business. Unfortunately, the corporation seemed no closer to embracing an outsourcing and services business model. Instead, Xerox was betting that digital machines, not digital services, would drive growth.

In the fall of 1999, as other issues also dragged down the company, Xerox's performance began a descent. I felt helpless. Instead of being out on the front lines whipping up revenue, or engaged in strategic conversations about the company's digital future, I was a corporate officer stuck in windowless conference rooms, chugging through spreadsheets and debating expense-cutting techniques. I felt as though I were strapped in the backseat of an old clunker as it made U-turn after U-turn on a dead-end road.

I thought back to the words I'd heard Bill Clinton speak in DC: We can be better, bored, or broke. I also thought about "Ithaca," and the value of the journey over the destination. Becoming the CEO of Xerox was fading as a goal as I took into account the larger picture of a working life. *How many lives did we make better? What organizations did we improve? What positive change did we effect?*

I wanted a career that bucked the status quo. That way of life would be a win. But to get it, I started to believe that I'd have to be in the driver's seat. In the past, that's when I'd been most successful, whether owning my own business, coaching my own team, or orchestrating a sales conference. That level of control at Xerox would not come for several years—if it came at all.

Intrigued by the evolving landscape of technology, and emboldened by my own conviction, I was feeling ready to exit. I even had a few choices. All I had to do was make the right one and land at a company that would not derail my career after seventeen magnificent years at the Xerox Corporation.

PART 4

THUNDERBOLTS

16

TIME TO FLY

Have the courage to follow your heart and intuition;
they somehow already know what you truly want to
become.

—STEVE JOBS

T'S NEW YEAR'S Eve, and instead of celebrating the millennium, I'm pacing. I have until midnight to sign an offer letter that will make me president of an internet company called Techies.com. The Minnesota-based start-up is on the verge of an initial public offering during the hottest stock market in American history—but I can't bring myself to sign the letter. What's wrong with me? Today, December 31, 1999, the Dow Jones and the NASDAQ closed at record highs. I now have a chance to take part in the gold rush—if I sign that paper and fax it back by midnight.

So what's up?

The home phone rings. I know it's Techies.com's VCs, the guys that faxed me the document hours earlier.

"Julie, tell them I'm stuck in a snow drift." She picks up the phone and looks out the window. It's not snowing.

Techies.com was not profitable, but that didn't seem to matter to investors. Like most online companies that started up during the internet craze, the excitement surrounding Techies.com was based on millions of dollars in funding and promises, not proof, of success. I'd met the management team and liked everyone well enough. The company's business model—to collect revenues from technology job postings and create a community of tech workers—was simple enough. Plus, the company was about to close $22 million in financing, and in January it was scheduled to file its S-1 with the SEC for its impending IPO. By spring, Techies.com could make me a billionaire, at least on paper. So why am I pacing? Am I not ready to leave Xerox?

I get on the phone and tell the investors I'm sorry, I can't accept their offer. Even as the words tumble out of my mouth, a part of me wants to shove them back in. The VCs ask why. I tell them what's in my heart: if I say yes, I'm fairly sure I'd be doing it for the wrong reason. "The only thing about your company that really interests me is the money," I admit. "And that's the wrong reason to work for anyone."

I hang up feeling relief and regret. *Did I blow it?* "Poof, there goes a billion dollars. Happy New Year." Julie looks at me, cool-headed.

"Bill," she says, "you didn't say no to the money, you said no to something that you didn't believe was right for you."

Julie is, as usual, correct. If and when I leave Xerox, it has to be for a company with a reputation I am proud to be associated with, a business I can get passionate about, and a name I want next to mine on a business card. Most dot-coms were babies, barely old enough to have a reputation.

My Techies.com debate did serve a purpose. It stirred my desire for something more. But as hungry as I was, the decision to leave a company and the decision about where to go were two distinct choices. I could not let my desire to fly exert too much influence over my choice about where to land next.

I returned to work after the holidays with a hunch that I would not be at Xerox much longer.

THE BODY REJECTS THE ORGAN

As if sensing my waning loyalty, Xerox promoted me. I became president of major US accounts in Xerox's $4 billion North American Solutions Group, in charge of our largest, most lucrative sales force. This post was big. A necessary step toward any future I hoped to have in the C-suite. I was on my way—*but to what end?* I took the new job with my usual gusto, but I couldn't banish reservations about my own future at the company.

My charge was to revitalize the sales force after a shaky reorganization that began a year earlier under Xerox's new CEO, Rick Thoman. Rick had come to Xerox after years at IBM to be our chief operating officer in 1997. Now, as chief executive, he wanted to push Xerox to take full advantage of the world's shift from analog to digital communications and expedite our transition from selling boxes to selling digital products—software and networks—as well as document management services. Doing so, he said, required significant change inside the company. Rick came to the CEO role with bold plans, but his execution, I believed, faltered because he did not embed his own brand of passion into the organization before he acted. Rick brought in some of his own leaders from outside Xerox, but his hopes of replacing all of Xerox's longtime executives did not materialize. As the new leader, he never won the full confidence of all the people he inherited. As a result, the body rejected the organ. It may not have helped that Paul Allaire had stayed on as an active chairman. Paul was not antiservices, but like a dad in your college dorm room, Paul's presence may have stifled Rick, as well as made it difficult for Rick to win over Paul's executive posse. Rick was not guilty of Xerox's original sin—he had inherited a company that needed to be transitioned—but as CEO, it was his responsibility to execute significant change.

From my position as a corporate officer, I observed the dysfunction at the top and watched how it cascaded confusion throughout the company. The situation reinforced an important lesson: if a vision is not supported by the workforce, even the most brilliant ideas risk being nothing more than lightbulbs in a basket.

If I stayed at Xerox, I figured that if I even got the top job, I could end up being chief of a company that had waited too long to reinvent itself. Or I would never be offered the top job, and, instead, I would have forfeited five to ten more years of my life waiting for it. Then what? I decided to reinvent myself before it was too late.

FILL THE GAP

The first time I sat down with Manuel "Manny" Fernandez was in the mid-1990s at the large oval table in his Stamford, Connecticut, office. His company, Gartner Group, had been wooing me. I knew, as Bud O'Brien would have put it, that Manny was good people. Prior to running Gartner, he'd founded a computer company and been a three-time CEO. He had grown Gartner from a $40 million private outfit to a nearly $1 billion public entity. Yet Manny's breezy smile belied his ambitious nature. Now he confided in me that Gartner needed a viable CEO succession plan. He was interested, he told me, in adding me to the bench.

Gartner Group was a highly respected Connecticut-based research and consulting organization that sold deep-dive reports and analysis of companies, products, and services in the IT industry. Wall Street and VCs tapped Gartner to assist with investment decisions. Companies bought Gartner's reports and hired its analysts when choosing technology vendors or to assess mergers and acquisitions opportunities. Journalists leaned on Gartner's independent analysis to report on the rapidly changing IT sector. Every IT company wanted to look good to Gartner's analysts.

A former Xerox executive, Follett Carter, had become Gartner's chief marketing and sales officer and instigated my recruitment. Follett was tenacious. Over hours of phone calls, he articulated his argument: "Bill, you owe it to yourself and your family to explore new career options. If you don't expand your bandwidth, you'll get lost in this economy." Follett had made these same points back in 1994, when he originally tried to recruit me. He and Manny made such a strong impression back then that I did resign from Xerox— for a whole two weeks. I had traveled with Follett throughout Europe, preparing to work for him as a regional VP of sales. As we hopscotched from the United Kingdom to Germany and Italy, Barry Rand, as well as Xerox's head of HR, Anne Mulcahy, let me know the door was ajar should I want to come back. Anne had started at Xerox as a sales rep in the mid-1970s, and for many years she reported to Roy Haythorn. During my own ascent, Anne was always nearby with a congratulatory smile if I was promoted or won an award. We talked frequently, and I considered her a friend as well as a mentor. Because I respected Anne so much, her heartfelt invitation to return made it that much more difficult for me to break away.

Follett's tactic in zipping me off to Europe was meant to erase Xerox from my mind, but overseas travel had the opposite effect. I missed Xerox. It was still home, and I was not ready to leave.

Still, once back at Xerox, I harbored a sense that Gartner and I had unfinished business. So when Follett approached me again, in 2000, and told me the company remained interested in me— although now it wanted to hire me as president—I was primed to consider walking out that door at last. Follett was leaving Gartner, but he knew that, as chairman, Manny and the newest CEO wanted an outsider to help the company with its growth by refining its sales force and professionalizing its operations.

I listed the pros of joining Gartner. The tech sector was undergoing a transformation that exceeded anything Xerox was capable of capitalizing on, given its internal gridlock. Connecting desktop computers to digital office printers was Stone Age compared with the IT systems many companies were investing in now. Most companies were deploying so-called enterprise technologies, software that automated business operations such as human resources, accounting, and logistics. The role of IT in business was becoming more strategic: technology was not just a way to save money and move faster but a way to make more money. Tech workers who had once toiled away in back rooms were being given bigger titles, offices, and multimillion-dollar budgets, and they needed advice about what to buy. Gartner was the *Consumer Reports* of IT, and it held their hands.

The opportunity at Gartner attracted me. Swapping the hardware business for the thought-leadership business would fill in gaps in my own experience so that I could grow in tandem with the knowledge economy. Plus, the brand was hot. I could feel good about casting it next to my own name. Unlike my feelings toward Techies.com, I was ready to sign on.

GOOD-BYE

I wanted my exit to be unceremonious. I would tell Tom Dolan I was leaving, not say where I was going, and then slip away, thanking the people who had made my Xerox career so amazing. No lunch. No party. No celebratory farewell. All I wanted was to get on with the rest of my life. I had checked out, and I didn't feel the need to sit through a parade of Bill stories. I'd already packed the ones I wanted to take with me.

The night before I told Tom about my departure, seventeen years seemed to flash before me—like a dream, but real. I saw my brother carrying me across the water in our flooded house so I wouldn't ruin my suit, and, just hours later, Emerson Fullwood promising to hire me as long as I hadn't committed any crimes. I saw Bob looking baffled as I clung to a flying cat and closed a deal on a hot August day. I recalled how my first bosses left me alone to bound around midtown, and all those doormen that lent me their lobbies. I saw Richard Reid's face, joyful at the birth of his daughter, and I heard David Kearns's voice telling me to forget his jackass of a neighbor. I felt grateful all over again that Roy Haythorn took me seriously after I'd barged into his Stamford office, and that Tom Dolan took the time to get to know the man beneath the suit. I heard the *ding-ding-ding* of the bullpen bell when one of the dozens of hardworking reps who worked for me over the years made a sale, and the smell of those damp meat patties as Everton drove us through the Bronx. How honored I felt at twenty-eight when Barry Rand walked over to my team's table at the President's Club to congratulate us. I smiled at the memory of Bud O'Brien's bluster, Norm's faith in me, XBS's caped crusaders, and Anne Mulcahy's friendship. I recalled sales reps hunting for documents in Chicago, secretaries waving pom-poms in San Antonio, and thousands of people around the country going for growth for XBS.

How many careers had I watched blossom? How many high fives had I shared? I had been blessed with teams of fantastic people from all backgrounds who had worked so hard to exceed expectations and achieve their own personal goals. In early May, I sent a letter to those who mattered most:

> *As I depart, I want to express my thanks for your contribution to my exhilarating experience and success here at Xerox. You have made the ride rewarding, challenging, and fun. Only the once-in-a-lifetime opportunity could make me give up what truly has been one of the best jobs in the world.*

Martin Luther King Jr. once said that you could tell more about people from observing them in one moment of difficult times than you can in years of good times. As we've confronted our recent challenges, I've appreciated the wisdom of this thought. In working side by side, I've gained an even more reverent respect for your character and indomitable will.

I leave on a high note, and it has been an honor and a pleasure to be associated with such a great group of winners. I wish you every success as you live your dreams.

I was not going to be the next David Kearns of Xerox after all, but I left feeling like a winner.

BOOKEND

On May 2, 2000, Techies.com rescinded its plans for an IPO. Had I taken that job, I would have lost the only thing about the company that interested me. The money. Bullet dodged.

Then on May 12 I opened the *Wall Street Journal*: "Xerox's Thoman Resigns Under Pressure." I'd heard the rumors through former colleagues. Now it was official. Paul Allaire would reassume the CEO role temporarily, and he was quoted in the *Journal* saying that Xerox "needed leadership in the company with more Xerox experience and background." The article went on to document the company's ongoing troubles. Xerox's stock had lost about 60 percent of its value in the last year, and the company had lost several "rising stars." The *Journal* called out my recent defection.

Rick, I knew, was not a bad leader. After all, he'd had amazing success at IBM. He and Xerox were simply not a good fit.

I still loved Xerox, yet the choice to leave was the right one. I only hoped that I had found my right fit.

17

LOST

The battles that count aren't the ones for gold medals. The struggles within yourself—the invisible, inevitable battles inside all of us—that's where it's at.
—*JESSE OWENS*

ONE MORNING, ONLY a few weeks after I left, it hit me: I had bet it all. Job security and financial security were guaranteed at Xerox, assuming that I did not screw up. Yet the kid who grew up stashing every dollar he earned in a hollow cross above his bed had traded security to pursue a new dream. And now I had two young children, a wife, and financial responsibilities. We had some savings, but all the benefits I'd earned through my tenure at Xerox disappeared when I walked out the door. So did the familiar culture.

Gartner, I realized, was another animal. Not worse, just different. The current CEO was its former chief financial officer and six-year employee, Michael Fleisher. Manny had retired to spend more time with his aging father in Florida. And while I was sorry I would not be working directly with Manny, I liked Michael. He was hungry. But at thirty-five, he was nowhere near retirement. The chance of my be-coming Gartner's CEO was slim, but I felt okay with that. Being pres-ident of such a strong brand as Gartner was still enticing, and I believed in the company and my ability to help it grow. I oversaw Gartner's existing operations, primarily its research and services units, as well as its sales force and marketing events. I reported to Michael, who focused on strategy, new business development, and Gartner's in-ternational division. About half of the executive team reported to me.

As Gartner was based in Stamford, Connecticut, Julie and I agreed that I would stay in a hotel and commute back to Rochester on week-ends until the school year ended and our family could reunite in early summer, and move into the house we'd purchased in a nearby suburb.

REALITY BITES

From my first few weeks at Gartner, I sensed the difference in our styles.

I saw it in the jeans and tieless shirts that even senior executives wore Mondays through Fridays. I felt it in Gartner's small-company, New Economy culture, which shocked my corporate sensibilities. As much as Xerox's bureaucracy drove me crazy, I found myself craving the predictability of protocol. Part of my job was to impart some of that big-company accountability and discipline, so when-ever a meeting went off track, I was quick to try and herd the mean-dering conversation toward a conclusion or try to wring decisions out of intelligent people paid to ponder.

My discomfort with the cultural differences was compounded by sadness. I was plagued, a bit to my own surprise, by the loss of Xerox in my life. David Kearns once described his own exit from IBM after seventeen years as painful as he imagined a divorce must feel. Julie and I were happily married, so only after I'd pried myself out of Xerox did I understand the emptiness that can set in after saying good-bye—even when good-bye was said for all the right reasons.

But there was no going back, and I refused to spend my time pining for the past. The only option for an optimist like me was to find a way to make my new work work.

TRADING PLACES

A monumental rainstorm flooding the East Coast has me stranded at the Miami International Airport on the Friday that Julie and the boys are arriving in Connecticut, after an emotional farewell with friends back in Rochester. They show up at a hotel room with wet luggage, empty stomachs, heavy hearts, and no husband or father to greet them.

Finally, at about four in the morning, weary from travel, I knock on the hotel room door and an equally exhausted Julie unlocks the bolt and lets me in. The boys have fallen asleep on the pullout bed, she says. I look at my seven- and three-year-old sons sprawled on the thin mattress. Julie and I are both spent. I hug Julie, and we try to get a few hours of sleep before the boys wake up. *Welcome to Connecticut*, I think before dozing off.

At seven o'clock that morning, no one in my family is excited, and everyone is starving, so I pull on yesterday's clothes that still smell like airport and head out in search of breakfast. The rain is torrential, and thunder claps as I tramp across the empty hotel grounds and down a slick slope toward the parking lot. With no umbrella or raincoat, the rain douses my suit. I am drenched when, on the wet grass, my lace-up shoes lose traction. I am airborne and then, *bam!* My entire body hits the ground facedown in a rock-filled, swampy pit. Muddy. Soaking. Filthy. My shirt is ripped at the chest and elbow. I see specks of blood.

Gotta get breakfast. So I stand up and forge toward the rental car. I get in. The front seat is as hard and cold as the ground. I start the motor, turn on the windshield wipers, make a random right turn out of the hotel lot, and pull into the first diner I see, where I walk though the door. I look like the down-and-out Dan Aykroyd after he lost it all in the movie *Trading Places*. At the counter, I pick up a menu, and some of the patrons watch as I order breakfast to go. They probably think I've been on a bender. It would be funny, if I weren't so miserable.

Back at the hotel, I walk through the pouring rain so I don't drop the disintegrating paper bag holding my family's meal. Inside the room, three wet-eyed puppies await eggs and their new life to start. Julie is so startled at the sight of her soaking, distressed husband, she bursts into hysterical laughter, which devolves into tears. Julie is not a frequent crier, but now the sobs do not stop. After months of preparing for the move, saying good-bye to friends, and holding the house together on her own, she is exhausted. And she is sad. I drop my muddy, bloody body next to her on the bed and hold my amazing wife. The boys look at us, stunned at the sight of their parents. I promise everyone, including myself, that our life will get better.

For now, however, we are stuck in this hotel until bits of our own furniture—including a baby grand Steinway & Sons piano (I had gotten my family one of those)—arrive. Our house in Rochester is still for sale, and we had to keep it furnished. Only the basics are being trucked, and, with the storm, they will likely be delayed a day or two.

After lukewarm eggs and soggy bagels, I rally. "C'mon, team. Who wants to see the house?" As we drive up a winding street, John and Michael peer out the backseat window and see the freshly built Nantucket Colonial. I know we are so lucky, so why doesn't it feel that way? Inside, empty of furnishings, the house echoes. Without neighbors a football-toss away like at our Rochester cul-de-sac, this place feels lonely. The boys had moved previous times when my work took me to new cities, but they were babies then. *Is this fair?* I don't know.

Despite the swirl of the unfamiliar, at home and at work, I continue to walk into Gartner's offices with a smile each morning, pushing aside doubt. I am determined to make this move successful. "The Laestrygonians and the Cyclopes, Poseidon in his anger: do not fear them, you won't find such things on your way so long as your thoughts remain lofty."

I was trying so hard to keep my thoughts lofty when the real thunderbolt hit.

18

FAITH

Now faith is the substance of things hoped for,
the evidence of things not seen.

—HEBREWS 11:1

BACK IN ROCHESTER, a week before we moved, Julie's medical tests had been inconclusive. Some doctors saw something suspicious in the X-rays. Others saw nothing. We'd been advised to repeat her tests as soon as we were settled in Connecticut.

When we did, Julie was diagnosed with breast cancer. The illness slammed into our already upended lives, a typhoon after a flood. Shocked, scared, confused, alone. We were a mess of emotions. Such a monumental family crisis had not hit me since I was a child. Unlike work problems, my family's health was not something I could control.

The only option was to tackle the cancer with questions. *Where are the best doctors? What's the best treatment? How soon can we start getting Julie healthy?* Two things I knew for sure: One, I would be by

Julie's side for every doctor's appointment, every procedure. Two, I had to stay focused at my new job. I owed it to Gartner. I also had two hefty mortgages and, soon, medical bills. More than ever, our family needed money and health insurance. For the first time, I viewed my job as more than a vehicle for fulfilling my own dreams but as a necessity to sustain my family.

Within days of Julie's diagnosis, we drive into New York City for appointments at the nation's top cancer hospital, Memorial Sloan-Kettering Cancer Center. There Julie and I sit down with doctors Hiram Cody and Peter Cordeiro. They are the best, and their prognosis gives us confidence. It's good that we caught the cancer early. But because Julie has a history of the disease in her family, we choose proactive surgery and six months of the most aggressive chemotherapy treatment. Mercifully, over the next few months, my parents will fly in from South Carolina and settle into our half-decorated house to help care for John and Michael. Throughout it all, Julie is strong, positive, amazing. I cannot bear the thought of losing her.

Julie is wheeled into her first major surgery on a Thursday afternoon in October. After slapping down my Visa card at the front desk to ensure her a private room, I'm left to wait with other nervous family members to think about what could go wrong. That's what I'm doing when a priest walks up to me and asks why I'm here. I tell him about my wife's cancer, and return his gesture by inquiring why he's at Sloan. He's visiting a fireman friend, he says. "I'm sure it means a lot to him that you're here, Father." We have a few minutes of genial discussion and shake hands. I go back to walking and worrying.

Dr. Cody emerges many hours later and assures me the surgery has been successful. Relieved, I walk alongside my anesthetized wife as she is wheeled to the post-op intensive care unit, where patients are separated by curtains and monitored by whispering nurses. I sit at Julie's bedside and hold her hand, not wanting to wake her. I love this woman so much. Her breathing and the beeping of machines are all I hear. After months and even years of hurtling one hundred miles per hour, this is a rare moment of pause. *What happened to our life? How did we get here, to a place full of so much uncertainty?*

"Mr. McDermott, a priest is here to see you." The nurse's voice breaks my thoughts. *A priest? Is there something the doctors aren't telling me?*

"Why?" I ask.

"I don't know, sir, but he says he knows you and wants to see you." I nod okay, paralyzed by fear that he is here to give Julie last rites. Into the ICU walks the white-haired, kind-faced man I'd met earlier. Without speaking, he bends down over Julie and puts his face an inch from hers, their noses almost touching, and begins softly saying prayers as he holds his cross. As if on cue, her eyelids open, and Julie looks into the priest's blazing blue eyes. As the priest speaks to her, I can see Julie absorbing his words as she fights the anesthesia. When he is done speaking, her eyelids close, and she retreats into herself. The priest rises and motions for me to follow him outside the ICU.

"Bill, I just want you to know that everything is going to be fine."

"That's great news, Father," I say, incredulous, "but with all due respect, how do you know?" Those blue eyes look up at the ceiling. "I have connections in very high places, Bill." He smiles.

"Well, Father, if God told you that she's going to be okay, that's good enough for me, I'll take you at your word." We chuckle about it. This time, instead of shaking my hand, he hugs me. That's it. He walks away. I don't even know his name.

A few nights later, Julie and I are alone in her hospital room. She is feeling much better, her prognosis excellent. The hallways are quiet with a Sunday-night hush when, at about nine thirty, there is a soft knock at the door, and the same priest walks in. He says hello to me, immediately walks up to Julie, and then, just like in the ICU, puts his face in front of hers and says his comforting prayers. Then, like an old friend, he pulls up a chair next to me and begins speaking with Julie, asking how she is feeling. This man is so affable, so easy to talk with, that soon we are telling him all about our boys and how we'd whipped the rug out from under our lives—new job, new neighborhood, new house—only weeks before Julie was diagnosed. He tells us about his life, too. He is the chaplain with New York City's fire department. His friend, the firefighter, is doing well.

Talking to this man feels like being with family. When he stands up to leave, I follow him out into the hallway.

"Father, please, you've been so gracious to us. If there is ever anything I can do for you, please do not hesitate to call on me."

"Bill, there is actually something you can do for me."

"Yes, Father, anything."

"Say a prayer for me. I see a beautiful young woman like your wife suffering through this horrible disease, and it makes me want to have a drink more than ever, and I have a problem with that. So say a prayer for me that I won't go get one."

"Consider it done." Once again he walks away, and I realize we do not know his last name. All he told us when we asked was that he was "Father Mike."

After my younger brother died, my mother had told me that I would always have a guardian angel on my shoulder. And whenever things got a little rough at home or at the deli or at school, she'd remind me, "Bill, don't worry, you have a guardian angel." I grew up believing that I did, and over the years, with all the good fortune I'd had, there was a part of me that continued to believe an angel had at least a little something to do with all of it.

At this moment, in the hospital and at work, when I need to stay strong for my family and my company, it feels good to believe in something greater than all of us. So I choose to have faith that Julie will be healthy again, and that there is a reason we are here. I trust in that angel, and in myself.

Faith, of course, gives us strength, but it is not enough. And neither is luck. I still have to rally every day to be the husband and father that Julie and the boys need me to be. Our children and our big, hollow house are all thirsty for attention, so I will make our breakfasts while Julie sleeps in, take the boys to school and to playdates and to the dentist and trick-or-treating so she can rest, and I will buy the Christmas presents, play Legos, meet the teachers, and call the plumbers. The responsibilities are so many and the hours in each day so few that to worry, or to complain to anyone at work about what is going on at home, is a waste of time and energy.

At thirty-nine, just when I thought I had my life figured out, I'd been punched in the gut. But I won't crumble. Like boxer Jake La-Motta in *Raging Bull*, nothing can beat me up enough to get me down. I am a dreamer, but I am also a fighter.

The weeks and months become a blur of doctors, hospitals, airports, sales calls, new faces, prayers, sales meetings, bedtime stories, and hard, hard work. Except for the days that Julie is in the hospital, or has a doctor's appointment or chemo treatment, I do not miss a day at Gartner—until I leave.

19

EPIPHANY

*I've learned that making a living is not the same thing
as making a life.*

—MAYA ANGELOU

THE HEADHUNTER'S WORDS were like a ray of West Coast sunlight piercing the haze that had become our lives.

"There's a job in California, Bill."

Since Julie's diagnosis and throughout her recovery, each day
had rolled into the next. Perhaps inevitably, the turmoil on the home
front had colored my experience at Gartner. It was impossible to
know how the job would have felt had I not been so preoccupied.
Despite Gartner's brilliant people and the company's progress—revenues were up, as were customer and employee retention—I could
not recall a period of my adult life so rife with uncertainty and pain.
I was not looking to leave Gartner, but the opportunity the recruiter
presented felt like an escape hatch.

The job, he said, was head of worldwide sales for Siebel Systems, a company that specialized in sales and marketing software and had about $2 billion in annual revenues. Except for the reports I read at Gartner, I did not know much about software or the burgeoning niche that Siebel served, but I was excited to learn.

Even after the dot-com bust, companies were investing millions of dollars in IT systems that could automate and help them better manage their operations. Some companies, such as SAP AG, made software for multiple business functions, the so-called software suite. A group of smaller companies, including Siebel, focused their IT solutions on a single business function, and thus were known as pure plays or "best of breed" technologies. Siebel dominated a category known as customer relationship management, or CRM. Siebel's software allowed companies to automate, coordinate, and track their sales and marketing efforts, including direct sales and customer service. The idea was to give sales reps, call-center operators, and senior management more information so that they had more insight and control over their sales pipeline and existing customers. CRM software capitalized on the notion that customer loyalty translated into higher profits. Several CRM products were on the market, but at the time, Siebel was the leader.

Tom Siebel founded the company in 1993. A computer scientist with an MBA, he was an anomaly in the flip-flop-wearing, Ping-Pong-playing office cultures that had cropped up throughout Silicon Valley. The man was buttoned up and disciplined, and he built his company by paying attention to details. In articles I checked out before we met, Tom talked about his "old-school" values and about the importance of proper "comportment." His professionalism resonated with me. He also shared my obsession with the customer, telling the *Harvard Business Review* that if a company focused on "understanding what customers need and delivering it," revenue growth and a high market valuation would follow. I was intrigued. Tom and I first met at his home. Not long after, we had a second meeting at his country club. At a table overlooking a golf course, we had a terrific conversation, after which he proposed terms of my employment on the back of a business card and slid it over to me.

In addition to the numbers Tom scribbled, several aspects of the job intrigued me. The chance to become an expert in enterprise software systems would broaden my knowledge in an area that I had always valued: serving the customer. Even tastier, though, was the opportunity to move my family. The idea of swapping Connecticut's cold, dark winters for a warm, sunny place that bustled with innovation was uplifting. Julie loved California. She also had completed her chemotherapy, her hair was growing back, and her prognosis was healthy. More than a career move for me, a new job on the West Coast would be a fresh start for my entire family.

KRYPTONITE

"Bill, that's him," Julie said in disbelief as the morning newscast played on our television.

"Who?"

"Father Mike, the priest who sat with us at the hospital." The news had just reported that a priest with the New York City Fire Department was the first confirmed casualty in the collapse of the World Trade Center. When his name was announced, Father Mychal Judge, we were shocked. When we saw the photograph of five ash-coated, grieving firemen carrying a sagging body over the World Trade Center's wreckage, the man's eyes were closed and his face lifeless, but Julie and I knew he was the priest who had given us a breath of faith through Julie's recovery. Only now did we learn to whom those blazing blue eyes belonged. Father Judge, the reports said, died in the lobby of one of the shattered buildings after running to the scene to be with his men. We barely knew this fine man but felt as if we had lost a dear friend.

In the early morning of September 11, 2001, I had been sleeping in our rental home in Hillsborough, California, when a friend in New York called our house phone and woke us up. "Bill, turn on your TV." I did. We stared at the screen in horror before I jolted myself out of shock and drove to Siebel's offices so I could check on our employees who worked in Manhattan. Thank goodness every one of our people was safe.

The tragedy, of course, reverberated everywhere, ripping apart people's hearts as well as the economy. In a New York minute, corporate and consumer spending, VC funding, investor confidence dried up. Gone. Running a technology company became more about survival than success.

As other technology companies went out of business amid the economic paralysis, Siebel continued to generate sales and earnings, although our sales were less than previous years. The money didn't come easy for any of us. Never, not at Xerox or Gartner or even at the deli, had I worked so hard and for such long hours as I did for Siebel in the months that followed 9/11. I was flying around the world to meet with customers and to rally the sales force, ensuring that every region delivered on its quarterly goals. Working until four in the morning in any time zone became normal for me. I was barely sleeping, and I was rarely home by Friday nights and free for family weekends. I missed Julie and the boys, and they missed me.

But something more than the pace nagged at me.

INNER MAGIC

As a manager, I always tried to capitalize on what I called the "inner magic" of each of my teammates and direct reports. To discover an individual's inner magic, I asked basic questions. "What do you want?" I'd inquire when we met. "What are your dreams?"

I did not, however, always pause to ask myself this question. *Am I getting what I want out of work and life, staying true to my original dreams while accounting for changes in myself and in the world around me?*

One of the few times I did ask myself these questions was when I first left Xerox and had that two-week stint at Gartner back in the early-1990s. I was thirty-one, and on a plane flying over Europe, I asked a flight attendant for some paper. On the back of her airline supply manifest I wrote, "The Most Important Things in the World: Bill's List." My personal goals included having quality time with my family; to love Julie with the enthusiasm and compassion of our wedding day; to help my son (and eventually his sibling) grow into a healthy, happy, well-adjusted adult; to love my parents and my brother and sister, always remembering my roots; and to live with passion every day.

Next, I listed my career aspirations:

1. To be a winner.
2. To lead others to the doorstep of their dreams.
3. To manage a career and not the other way around.
4. To never confuse that which is most important with that which is not.
5. To earn a living commensurate with my talent, but not be ruled by the shallow shadows of money.
6. To be the ruler of my own destiny, not to slave for what someone else wants my destiny to be—in control.

Not long after making that list, I had returned to Xerox.

Now, ten years later and one year into my job at Siebel, I looked at it. As I read through the list, I realized an unfortunate truth: my present work situation did not check enough boxes.

I considered how I got here. When Siebel's offer had been presented to me, I was vulnerable, primed to accept anything that felt sunnier than the dark uncertainty of Connecticut and Julie's illness. Cancer had been a snake in the grass that we couldn't see or hear. I lived in fear that it was sneaking up on my family to steal life from my wife. Living with cancer tainted everything, and the anguish was brutal.

What did I want now?

One late night when I was still at my office, I grabbed a blue pen and wrote the word "Goals" on a piece of paper. Once again I wrote down what I wanted:

1. Happiness and serenity for my family.
2. Balance between work and family.
3. Live in a place until the kids *go to college*.
4. That place has to be good for kids: schools, neighborhood, friends, wholesome.
5. The place has to be affordable enough for the adults to have a good standard of living without being strapped financially.
6. Career is *secondary* to the above.
7. Professionally, I want respect and a platform to be me and *influence others*.
8. "Lead" people to a greater good. "A Cause." "Goals." "Better life" . . .
9. Stability for the future.
10. Tell the story someday—

Looking over my new list, I realized that the themes were not that different from the goals I had written ten years ago. Yet I was not living up to all of those goals, especially number eight. I was hungry to lead, to be more in charge of my own destiny and the destiny of an organization. At this stage of my career, I wanted to do more than execute someone else's plays day to day. I also wanted to call them, if not for an entire company, then for a substantial slice of business. I wanted my freedom back. I was ready to be a CEO.

I knew I needed time and space to reassess my career path. I took my list of goals home and shared it with Julie. Days later, I left Siebel without another job. For the first time since my paper route, I was unemployed.

PART 5

FOUNDATIONS OF DISCIPLINE

20

SWEETNESS

The privilege of a lifetime is being who you are.

—JOSEPH CAMPBELL

HASSO PLATTNER IS on a phone call when I arrive a few minutes early to my job interview at his home in Portola Valley, California. It's a beautiful day, and I am led outside to a stunning backyard and asked to wait for him.

Immediately, a golden Labrador retriever bounces toward me. The dog's name, I will later learn, is Claude, and he motions me toward a spongy Nerf-like football. *All right, this dog wants to fetch. No problem.* I'm a righty, so I pick up the ball with my right hand and throw it across the yard. It's a decent throw, and Claude races to fetch it, and then bounds back across the grass, depositing the ball at my feet so I will throw it again. I look down. The soft ball glistens with Claude's saliva. I stare at the soaked football in the grass. I love dogs, always have, and normally I wouldn't care about a wet ball, but it would be disrespectful to meet and greet the co-CEO and cofounder of the world's third largest software company, SAP, with a slimy handshake. Even if it was from his own pet. And I shouldn't wipe my hand on my suit. *Sorry, Claude, can't do it.*

The dog, of course, doesn't care about any of that. He just wants to play. I cannot ignore this beautiful creature. *Okay, Claude, you got it.* Right now, Claude is the boss.

I pick up the ball with my *left* hand and start throwing left-handed pass after left-handed pass. The dog keeps fetching and running back to me, and I love it. By the time a gentleman with a flurry of white hair walks out into his backyard, Claude is leaping all over the place, and the two of us are playing fetch like best buddies.

"Oh, you really like dogs," says Hasso, with a smile, "and Claude likes you!" Hasso has an approachable majesty about him, one of those rare individuals who compel attention without trying.

"Hi, I'm Bill McDermott," I say and extend a dry right hand. Game on.

I am close to certain that I want this job.

HISTORY

In the week or so since leaving Siebel, I'd spoken to various head-hunters. But nothing grabbed me. I had faith something would, but I was antsy. Being home on weekdays, wearing jeans and sneakers instead of a suit, felt unnatural. More than once, I had shaken my head—*This is surreal, man*—as I walked our new puppy, Angel, in circles around our backyard. I had never *not* had a job. I had never *not* worked. And although we were not strapped for money, I did have a family to support. I also was itching to get back to work—but I knew it had to be the right work.

When a headhunter from Heidrick & Struggles said that SAP was looking for someone to head its North American business, my interest was piqued. SAP had great products, including CRM software that competed with Siebel's, but the SAP reps that Siebel came up against in the United States were like the Bad News Bears—the young baseball team in the eponymous movie, running the same losing plays every time but expecting a different outcome. I'd always thought SAP could be a formidable competitor in the States, if only its sales machine got its act together. First, though, it needed leadership. In six years, SAP's North American business had five different leaders. That business also had been consistent at missing its own expectations for twenty-three quarters in a row.

The recruiter wanted me to get on the phone with SAP's acting president of the North American business, Leo Apotheker. Officially, Leo was head of SAP's worldwide field operations, and he was temporarily running its business in the United States and Canada until a successor to the last president was in place. Honored to be considered, I scheduled a call.

Pow. Instant chemistry. I expected a hard sell, but Leo didn't push. He was as curious about me and what I needed as I was about SAP and what its North American business needed. More conversation than interview, the call felt like two guys who just knew how to talk to each other. Leo felt real to me.

Not long after, we met in person at a sales conference SAP was holding at a depressed Loews hotel in Philadelphia, near its North American headquarters. Leo arrived with his close advisor and the head of SAP's global marketing, Marty Homlish, a quick, affable man who whisked me into a hotel conference room off the lobby so I wouldn't see the sales meeting. From the little I did observe, it looked as impressive as an aluminum-siding convention. The conversation with Leo, however, was anything but tired. I liked this man even more in person. He was smart, with a global perspective, and he believed SAP's operating regions needed autonomy to be more successful. Together, Leo and Marty had coordinated the company's scattered marketing efforts and launched a new brand positioning and tagline, "The Best Run e-Businesses Run SAP." I liked that tag because it focused on the company's value to its customers.

I left the meeting accepting Leo's invitation to meet SAP's executive board—in Walldorf, Germany, where the company had been based since its inception.

On the flight across the Atlantic, I did more homework about the company's history. In 1972 a group of five German programmers were working for IBM in Mannheim, Germany, selling and installing computers. One of the engineers, Claus Wellenreuther, had developed a program to help an IBM client better manage its finances. Claus and two colleagues, Hasso Plattner and Dietmar Hopp, went to their bosses to ask if they could start selling the new product. IBM shot them down: "We have labs that develop software." They were told to go sell more computers.

Undeterred, the three men recruited two more coworkers, Klaus Tschira and Hans-Werner Hector, to quit Big Blue and start their own software company. They called it *Systemanalyse und Programmentwicklung*—German for System Analysis and Program Development. Their intent was to create standard business software to help companies automate and manage operations. By day, the five founders would be out in the field, selling and installing their first software products. They broke to play soccer now and again, but spent nights designing and testing new software at their customers' offices. Over the years, as the company grew, it continued to create new applications for new business processes, migrating its programs onto new technology platforms. SAP became known for its integrated "suite" of applications for manufacturing, finance, and human resources. This trio helped its client companies better control resources throughout their enterprise, which gave rise to the software's name: enterprise resource planning, or ERP. Over the years, SAP also created applications to manage supply chains, customer relationships, and other business functions.

It was not an exaggeration to say that SAP changed how companies around the world operated. And although I was not an engineer, I related to its founders' work ethic, and admired the courage it took to break away from IBM to create something they believed in.

The company was also huge. According to its latest annual report, almost eighteen thousand companies in 120 countries were using SAP's software. Coca-Cola, Colgate-Palmolive Co., DuPont, BMW, Burger King. Despite having more than €7 billion in revenues, SAP was not as familiar a brand in the United States as it was in other countries.

For someone looking to get back into the big leagues, I was definitely in the right ballpark.

Plus, SAP's North American business needed the kind of help I might be able to provide: top-line growth. In 2002 SAP's US revenues were down 5 percent from the previous year, pulling the company's overall results down with it. Its problems were exacerbated by the troubled economy, and one of the worst downturns the application software market had ever seen. Competition had also increased. Still, my sense was that SAP had the potential to go from a good business to a great one.

Visiting SAP's offices in Walldorf, I was not sure what to expect. The company's world headquarters was about a twenty-minute drive from the beautiful, historic city of Heidelberg, where the majestic Heidelberg Castle still stood, nestled into a hillside, itself a symbol of renewal after seven centuries of destruction and rebuilding. SAP's corporate campus was surrounded by farmland, yet its interior was sleek and comfortable, reminding me of the precision and elegance of German engineering.

What shocked me, however, was the sweetness. Big smiles. Warm handshakes. More than nice and polite, everyone was so kind, so gracious. From the receptionist to the senior executives, including SAP's co-CEO, Henning Kagermann, *sweetness* was the word that kept coming to my mind. It emanated from their curiosity and from the authenticity I picked up on in every meeting. For such a big company run by such big brains to have such a culture of kindness made an impression on me, especially after being exposed to the extra-large egos that dominated Silicon Valley. I also appreciated how transparent everyone at SAP tried to be about the company's problems, especially in the United States. Its senior leaders were serious about turning around the business.

The meetings went well enough that I was invited to meet with Hasso Plattner—one of the original five founders and now SAP's co-CEO—back in California, at his West Coast home. I understood Hasso to be the man who had the power to decide if I got the job.

PURPOSE

Hasso leads me into his dining room, where we sit across from each other at a table. Despite my mounting interest in working for SAP, I do not steamroll into the interview hyped to sell myself. I want to listen to what Hasso has to say about his company and the position. Maybe it was Julie's cancer scare, my own introspection, or the sum of all my experiences, but at forty-one, I am less concerned about proving I can get a job and more interested in whether I want the job for the right reasons.

Hasso talks, Claude at our feet and my left hand still sticky. Hasso tells me about himself and his company. He was born in Berlin. His father was a medical doctor; his grandfather, an engineer. Similar to my history, there were times in his life when his family had little. Hasso joined IBM at age twenty-four, which means he respects my Xerox background—a sentiment not shared by many in the internet age. I listen between the lines, and what I hear is an incredible intellect that prefers simplicity to complexity, and a man who enjoys asking questions rather than just supplying answers. His opinions are unfiltered, and I recognize the sweetness in him that I found in his German colleagues. Humility amid the intelligence. It is also clear to me that he doesn't want his company just to survive. At fifty-eight, Hasso is still a visionary who wants to change the world. But to do so, he acknowledges, SAP has to fix its business in the United States, which he admits is a mess.

Hearing Hasso describe the job's requirements, I think about how I might make this underdog a winner. Leading SAP America out of its doldrums is not just another job. This opportunity, I believe, is a mission. My mission. What I've been wanting and waiting to do.

Two years ago, I realize now, I never would have been considered for this role or given this incredible chance to interview for it. In addition to my Xerox experiences, I needed Gartner to broaden my understanding of how IT systems translated into business results, and I needed Siebel to submerge me in the application software business. The weight of uncertainty begins to lift as I realize that even imperfect periods have their purpose. I now feel certain that purpose is to lead SAP America.

I have only one outstanding question: Will I have autonomy?

At the risk of pressing too hard, I explain to Hasso, with respect, what I'd discussed with Leo: if SAP wants to empower someone to lead its US business out of its funk, if it wants someone to draft a new playbook, to execute, hold people accountable, and to be accountable, I am that guy. But if they want someone they can micromanage from across the Atlantic, I'm not. Even if my decisions or my style make a few people uncomfortable, I need to be given the freedom to lead.

Timing was on my side—and maybe that guardian angel, too. After its string of ineffective leaders in North America, SAP seems more willing to let an American take over that business.

I hope Hasso can sense my passion. With each passing minute, I want this job more, and I think maybe I have it when he says, "Now, Bill, you would have to move to Newtown." Hasso is referring to the location of SAP's five-hundred-acre US headquarters: Newtown Square, Pennsylvania, near Philadelphia. Julie and I are still worshiping the California sun, but I look Hasso in the eyes.

"Hasso, one of the things I've been blessed with is that I married right, and Julie and I always do things as a family and in partnership, and I'm sure my wife will be a hundred percent supportive of moving our family. So if you're making a commitment to let me lead and re-create the US business, then I'll make a commitment to you today to move near Newtown Square so I can be with the people." About two-thirds of SAP America's six thousand employees—20 percent of SAP's global workforce—were based in Newtown Square. "Hasso, do we have a deal?"

With Claude still sleeping under the table, we shake hands and agree that, yes, we have a deal.

I pet Claude good-bye and walk outside into the Northern California sunlight, where I take out my mobile phone.

"Julie, we're moving to Philly."

21

URGENCY

Fortune favors the bold.

—VIRGIL

"WHERE IS EVERYBODY?" I look around the empty marble lobby. One of the two folks in my range of sight answers.

"Sir, it's Friday," says a security guard, as if that explains it. *Come on, people!*

The end of SAP's fourth quarter is a few weeks away, and SAP America is on a course to miss its forecast *again*. Sorry, we all have families, but if we keep spiraling, we won't have customers, or our jobs. People should be on fire, on the phone, in conference rooms strategizing, writing, and rewriting contracts—doing *something*.

Instead, it's dead.

I look up toward the high ceiling. Three stories above me a man peers over a balcony and waves at me to come on up. Walking through the desolate hallways toward the elevator is like stepping over dollars. There is money to be made, and no one seems to know it.

My appointment to president and CEO of SAP America a few weeks earlier had ushered the company's challenges into the news. Richard Williams, an analyst at Summit Analytic Partners, told the *Philadelphia Inquirer* that SAP's problem was that the company "can't answer the return-on-investment challenge for customers yet." Wrote AMR Research, "It will not be easy to improve the morale of the SAP America sales team in this economy, but putting a sales professional in charge of the business certainly sends the right message."

My first day heading SAP America was October 7, 2002. Like taking the streets of New York City, I launched myself into the job with enthusiasm and optimism, but unlike almost two decades earlier, I had tremendous responsibility. This job was not about me, but about the well-being of thousands of employees. With so much more at stake, my energy was infused with a heightened seriousness as I prepared to combat the onslaught of problems—beginning with the despair that hit me every time I walked into SAP's headquarters in Newtown Square. Today, the Friday silence almost makes it worse.

I'm meeting Rob Enslin, the man peering over the balcony, who runs sales for the northeast region of the United States. I know that Rob has been at SAP since 1991, when he started in South Africa. He has lived all over the world and, like me, now lives in the quiet suburbs outside Philadelphia. For the past few weeks, I've been meeting with SAP America's leaders one-on-one, listening, assessing, making some decisions. I walk into the conference room, where Rob is waiting for me.

"Hi, I'm Bill McDermott. Where is everybody?" I ask again.

"Look, Bill . . ." Rob sighs and looks straight into my eyes. "The company is a mess. There's no other way to describe it. There's no direction, no leadership here. Most people have pretty much given up. Many of the best ones have left or are on their way out." I am grateful for the candor. Rob's assessment reflects what I've already heard and observed. I knew that SAP's US business was broken, and while I had some intimations why, it would have been foolish of me to assume I knew what needed fixing on day one. For the first several weeks, my goal has been to listen and learn before telling and selling.

STILL LISTENING, STILL LEARNING

During the three months that I waited for Julie and the boys to move from California, I lived on SAP's corporate campus in one of several Colonial-style cottages that served as temporary housing for visitors. The cottages had cozy living rooms, and shared kitchens and dining spaces—much more hospitable than the sterile hotels I'd camped out in back in Connecticut. In the morning, I walked from the cottage to my office, and back again every evening, occasionally spotting the deer that roamed the fields between SAP's buildings. The campus was so vast that local law enforcement trained its police dogs here. More than one morning, I encountered drooling, barking Rottweilers as I left the cottage.

Except for traveling for sales calls and customer visits, or dining with new colleagues, I rarely left SAP's headquarters. I would stop folks on my walk to work, or in hallways and in the cafeteria, introducing myself and asking who they were and what they did for SAP. (My memory for people's names would become a standing joke: Marty Homlish routinely asked me if I had a drop-down menu bar in my head that identified all employees' and their kids' names when they came into my line of sight.)

I read comments that employees had posted on our internal websites, held private meetings, and brought together small groups of programmers and support staff. When I convened the top thirteen leaders from across the United States in one room for the first time, I had a hunch that many of them would not be working with me a year from now. Still, I wanted to know them and hear everyone out. "Tell us, what was your greatest success? What was your biggest failure? What's your story, and please share something about your family." As we went around the table, what amazed me was how little many of the leaders seemed to know about one another. This was a group of people. Not a team.

With almost every interaction, I encouraged people to share their opinions about what SAP needed to do better. But I also asked what they would do about the problems if they were me. Not only was I curious, but that follow-up query changed the conversation from a one-way garbage dump to an exchange. People had to start feeling and acting as part of our solution, not just waiting for me to flick some magic wand.

As I took note of everything I heard and saw, I concluded what needed to change.

For one, the pace. The listlessness almost killed me. There. Was. No. Hustle. Plus, a sense of entitlement lingered, left over from SAP America's flush decade, in the nineties, when sales reps could just show up and win business. Some salespeople bragged about multimillion-dollar deals they'd cut years ago as if they'd closed yesterday. There was no urgency. The tendency to overengineer even the simplest tasks was maddening.

There also was a discipline shortage. Few if any measurements were in place to ensure that sales goals were on track. Money was being spent on things that had little or no return. Too much spending on too much travel for too many people, and throwing too many dowdy meetings instead of a few that mesmerized. Meanwhile, we were imposing silly costs on employees, for things like cans of soda or water, that chipped away at morale a few dollars at a time.

We also had to abolish the stultifying combination of negativity and insularity. People droned on about the ineffectiveness of this leader or that manager, and pointless processes. They gossiped about one another, with some making the mistake of doing so to me. The culture was so internally focused that no one talked about what should have been our obsession: the customer.

Few transgressions concerned me more than the absence of a performance-driven culture, which should have included a compelling year-end celebration for top sales producers. I discovered this discrepancy during my first few weeks on the job, when I asked how SAP America planned to reward the year's highest performers.

"Let's talk about the sales club," I asked a room. "What are the qualifications to make it to the year-end trip?" The answer landed with a thud.

"Bill, we don't have any." *You gotta be kidding me.* Apparently there were no metrics in place. The top fifty highest performers were simply sent on a trip. Because I knew the long-term value of expecting, measuring, and recognizing high performance, the lack of strategic planning was frustrating.

"Okay"—I took a deep breath—"when are you telling the sales force about the trip? To get them excited for it?"

"We've been planning on doing it, but it just hasn't gotten done."

"You're kidding me, right?"

"We're not kidding you."

"Okay, let's get the announcement out today. Where is the trip?"

"A cruise ship in the Caribbean."

"Personally, I am not big on cruises, but okay. Who's the entertainment?"

"Shirley and the Shirelles." I recognized the name, and although I had nothing against Shirley or the Shirelles, I had to wonder how many younger employees would know the group's early-1960s hits. A flashback band was fine, but had we flashed back too far? Would enough people jump out of their seats and rush to the dance floor when the Shirelles started singing "Soldier Boy"?

"Nobody cares, Bill," someone tried to reassure me. "The entertainment is just a sideshow."

Stay cool. I smiled on the outside, but inside, my body was rejecting the smile. We had to think bigger. No more shoestring-budget gatherings in tired hotels with amateur audiovisuals and entertainment that didn't excite. Everything mattered.

It was too late to revamp the top performers trip for 2002, so I accepted the situation. "Okay, we'll take people on a boat and listen to

Shirley and the Shirelles, but next year, we're planning the best trip anyone at SAP has taken. Ever."

To dream big, people had to feel big. There could be no more sideshows.

CHANGING MINDS

In November 2002, for my first all-hands speech in front of Newtown Square's employees, about eight hundred people crowded into an auditorium. I didn't have to hear the buzz to know it. *Who is this guy? What's he about? What's he going to change? Does he even know how to sell enterprise software? How old is he? He looks too young, too pressed. Is this guy for real?*

I understood the skepticism. These were good, smart people who did not deserve such instability. They had bills to pay and families to support and hopes and dreams. Five leaders had come and gone. Why would the new chief from Silicon Valley—America's golden land of innovation—linger in the freezing cold suburbs of Philly at a decades-old giant? No doubt people were betting on how many months would pass before another CEO abandoned them, too. They deserved better.

I addressed their fears, assuring everyone that I was not going anywhere. That I was committed to them, and that I harbored no love for companies that were consumed with raising their valuations instead of raising up their people. SAP was and would be different. We would serve our shareholders as a result of serving our customers and our people first.

The customer. No word came out of my mouth as much that one. The customer was our most important responsibility. If the customer had a problem, we had to fix it—no matter what. Everything revolved around the customer's needs. Drop anything internal for the external customer. If it's right for the customer, just do it. Everyone had to rethink how the job he or she did every day connected to our customers. Why? I channeled Xerox's Joe Wilson: the customer and the customer alone determines whether or not each of us has a job.

"If we each do everything we possibly can to make our customers successful, then everyone within SAP will benefit," I promised. Not just frontline revenue producers, but people in finance, in human resources, in facilities management.

Customer. Customer. Customer.

Repetition was essential. It bred belief.

MODEL BEHAVIOR

Many of my bumper-sticker philosophies became widely known: Make the news, don't report it. You're focused on the wrong stack of mail. None of us is as smart as all of us. If you have a problem, share it but help solve it. If you're busy, know what you're getting done. Excuses never built a single stair step to success. Phrases such as these came naturally to me, and they were easy to repeat and thus, I hoped, easy to digest and follow.

But my words had to be backed up by actions. All leaders' behaviors scale—for better or worse.

Every day, even Fridays, I dressed as if I were showing up to meet with the chairman of the board. I returned every email I received in a matter of minutes. If someone arrived late to my scheduled Monday-morning meetings, I let him know as he sauntered in. "Glad you could make it; the meeting started at eight." When someone came up with a good idea, and people around the table sat back in their chairs debating if it could be done, I leaned forward and asked *when* it could get done.

"Two months, Bill."

"How about next Monday." I didn't ask for perfection. "Just give me the best you can by then."

I kept my office door open, and when people asked to see me for a minute, I invited them in. "What's up? Let's talk." If they needed me to get involved in a deal or to call a customer, "Give me the number—I'm dialing." But if they came only to complain or talk bull, the conversation was over. My tolerance for gossip and pointless presentations and artificial conversations and bureaucracy and org charts and overcomplicated anything was slim, and I let people know it. "We're not here to play office," was another one-liner that began to snake through the building.

If I saw a problem, I didn't walk past it. Instead, I found the people responsible. "Why do we do this? Help me understand." More often than not, I was discovering that little strategic thought had gone into embedded policies. When I happened to pass by the company's gym and saw that it was empty and looked tired, I went to HR.

"What's up with no one using the gym?"

"People don't want to pay the high membership fee."

"Well, if no one is in the gym, did it occur to anyone that maybe we're charging too much? Give 'em the gym." So we brought down the fee, and brought in trainers as well as new equipment. Guess what? People started using the gym. Now whenever I passed, it was bustling. My intent with such actions was not to micromanage. I wanted everyone to start taking responsibility and questioning the status quo, and see opportunities where he or she saw dust or defeat.

I had given myself a hundred days to convince everyone we could do better. Change would be slow—I got that—but if I didn't win their agreement that change was possible by the end of January 2003, I never would.

INFLECTION POINT

Although I joined SAP in October, the first month of the last fiscal quarter, I still needed to take responsibility for SAP America's performance during that period. We were on track to miss our goals for the twenty-fourth quarter in a row. The easy path was to ignore those three months, telling everyone I was just getting situated into the new job and that real change would start in 2003. But to get people to believe a different future was possible, they needed to see immediate proof. I refused to accept a miss, and that required meeting or beating our own revenue expectations. It was too late to make significant operational changes, so we had to work with what we had in the sales pipeline.

I convened the top sales managers and explained that our mandate was to exceed our goal. To do that, I had to find out exactly how close we were. One by one, I met with each manager to find out if the sales numbers he or she had committed their territories to deliver were grounded in facts or a loose guesstimate based on assumptions. If someone anticipated $10 million in software revenue from, say, Acme Inc., I followed up with questions. My inquiry hit some managers like a fire hose.

"Who is the highest-level executive at Acme that told you that?"

"Bill, the chief information officer told me."

"Does the CIO have the authority to approve a ten-million-dollar deal? Or does that have to go to the board? And if so, does the CIO have direct access to the board, or do those requests have to go through the CEO? And if so, who at SAP has the relationship with the CIO, and have we even spoken to the CEO? And if so, do the CIO and the CEO both agree SAP is a central element to their business strategy? And please articulate the specific solution that we're selling for that ten million, and the business outcome Acme expects to get for its investment in us? Thank you. Have we given them a one-sheet document explaining that so they can take it to board members and get it done?"

Truth, I knew from experience, was often with the people closest to the action. So I also got on the phone with field reps in Cincinnati and Chicago and Seattle, salespeople who had the account relationships and could get me the details we needed. I was on conference calls with men and women who, in all their years with SAP, had never spoken to anyone above their direct boss.

The inquiries revealed which deals were likely to come through, which were on life support, and which were mirages. Eventually we compiled a list of some ten deals most likely to close if we nursed them. I got involved with almost every one of the accounts, guiding SAP's salespeople through tactics and strategies that harkened back to my earliest sales years, or calling CEOs if a peer-to-peer conversation could put us over the edge. I loved being in the trenches. It was fun and informative for me, helping me learn about SAP's products and markets; if one customer needed something, a dozen more would need it, too, and I wanted to be prepared.

A renewed sense of accountability started to take hold. The night before a complex government contract needed to be signed to count toward the quarter, a storm kept the FedEx plane carrying the signed contract for next-day delivery from getting off the ground. To make sure the contract had every chance of making it to its destination in time, the sales manager called up DHL Express and Airborne Express and had all three couriers ship the contract. And instead of going home that night—where his family and friends were waiting to celebrate his birthday—he chose to stay and monitor the delivery situation rather than leave it to chance. Incredible dedication. The contract arrived and was signed in time. A few weeks later, in front of the sales manager's coworkers, I shared the story, thanked him for his sacrifice, and presented him with a check so that he could treat himself and his family to the birthday dinner he missed, and that he deserved.

The heightened level of rigor paid off, and for the first quarter in five years, SAP America surpassed its own revenue expectations. Legally, we could not reveal the exact number for several weeks. But when we did, winds of momentum hit our sails, and many people felt something they had not experienced in a long while: hope.

22

ANATOMY OF CHANGE

A man's mind, stretched to a new idea, never goes back
to its original dimensions.

—OLIVER WENDELL HOLMES SR.

ENTERING THE NEW Orleans auditorium, I feel like a Ferrari barreling into a desert. It's opening night of SAP America's 2003 sales kickoff meeting, and as I walk onstage from my seat in the front row, there's only thin applause. Then nothing. Lifelessness slams into me as I turn to face about a thousand sales professionals slumped in their chairs. Silence fills the hall. I swear I can see tumbleweeds blowing down the aisles.

As I begin my remarks, the expression on my face does not reveal that, in my head, I am reassessing the room. The audience, which is the entire North American sales organization, reeks of doubt. So much so, I note, that these next few days cannot be about me trying to charm them out of their deep disengagement. Despite the progress last quarter, these people have been through too much during the past few years to be completely revived by a few speeches. More than inspiration, they need action bolstered by conviction.

So, what's my play?

The most powerful thing a leader can do is change minds. To begin to do this today, my tone must be positive yet as serious as the situation. I aim to plow through their doubt with my agenda and with certainty. I am confident that if we execute the right plan, we will not only turn around SAP America, but make it a winner. At no point in my career have I been so intent, or felt such urgency, to change people's minds, and their behaviors. *Here we go.*

THE GOOD NEWS

"Let's look at what's good," I say. Despite my heightened level of seriousness, I want to start the sales meeting on a high note. SAP is already a global market leader, not some start-up. What's more, our industry is converging, and only a few key providers are still standing, including SAP. Even in the internet economy, our size and our history are not liabilities, I point out, but competitive advantages.

"Gartner says SAP is the most viable business application vendor in the world," I proclaim. In the financial community, I explain, JMP Securities recently wrote that SAP's own competitors say we are doing a superb job of defending our own turf. I remind everyone: our market is growing, we are making money, we are regaining market share. SAP, I assure them, is a good business.

"But I didn't come here to be good. You didn't come here to be good. We came here to be *great*. And we are now starting to formulate the plan on how we go from good to great. We won't sit idly. We want to go big."

Then I unload it: the big.

ASPIRATIONAL

"Our goal is for SAP America to be a three-billion-dollar business by 2005."

If silence can get louder, it does. The numbers almost echo off the arena walls. Behind me, on the huge screen, tall yellow letters and numerals tower: $3 Billion by 2005. "In the next three years, we are going to increase our revenue one billion dollars." Since 1999, SAP America's revenues had barely grown by $100 million, in total. Now I am promising ten times as much growth in less than three years. Not only is this an audacious goal, but everyone also realizes that hitting $3 billion would catapult us to the number one provider in the North American market for software license sales, reversing years of being ranked third.

The only noise that breaks the quiet is muffled chuckling from the front few rows. Several SAP executives from around the world have flown to New Orleans to check out SAP America's new chief, and instead of nodding in support, some of them, I am fairly sure, are snickering. I shoot the front row a sharp look. *You can do almost anything you want at my meeting, but you cannot steal people's dreams.* I scream this thought so loudly to myself that I am sure I must have said it out loud. It's Sister Jean Agnes all over again! The smallest show of doubt can destroy people's belief in what's possible. Plus, there is nothing funny about reaching $3 billion. I didn't just pluck the number from the ether. I'd thought this goal through.

Given that SAP America brought in only $2 billion in revenues last year, its chief financial officer, Mark White, had cautioned me that a goal of $3 billion by 2005 would scare people. I appreciated honest opinions like Mark's. Disagree with me, but do it to my face.

"You're crazy," he told me.

"I'm aspirational," I told Mark.

I was also realistic. Mark's revenue models were based on SAP America's former ways of selling. We were about to launch a new approach. Plus, aiming high improved our odds. I would rather reach for the stars and hit the moon than reach for the moon and hit nothing.

Standing onstage, I absolutely believe SAP America can hit $3 billion by 2005.

"We can do it. And we will do it."

EXECUTION

The previous year, in the summer of 2002, the country had been captivated by a monumental effort to rescue nine Pennsylvania coal miners trapped more than two hundred feet below ground in cold, flooding tunnels for seventy-seven hours. Six months after their stunning rescue, I recalled their amazing story to our sales and marketing professionals in New Orleans.

"There was nothing these miners would not do for each other. That was their commitment." They shared the one sandwich they had. They made each other laugh. At one point, several men tied themselves together so should they die, they would be together. Meanwhile, above the ground, more than a hundred people—rescue workers, fire fighters, engineers, doctors, police, pastors, contractors, small-business owners, the mine's executives, the governor, caring citizens—worked for three days and four nights, making big and small decisions in the life-or-death race to pump air down the shaft, pump the dank water out, and drill an escape tunnel.

"The tools, the processes, the execution were amazing," I say. "And there were critical moments." When the rare, 1,500-pound drill bit that was boring the escape tunnel broke loose, a customized fishing hook had to be fashioned hundreds of miles from the mine and then shipped. Tasks that would have taken days took hours. Why? Because everyone believed in the cause: life.

"The miners came out alive. They went home to their families. These people achieved something that was remarkable. They never gave up. They stuck together as a team—both under and above the ground."

I retell this tale to remind everyone what can be achieved when belief in something grand is coupled with precise execution, creativity, and teamwork. Behind me, the large screen displays a photograph of one of the miners being raised from the ground through the rescue tunnel, with our own caption:

IT'S ALL ABOUT EXECUTION.

Belief alone is never enough. The audacity of any dream must be paired with the micromanagement of reality. Preparation, diligence, follow-through, hard work. A plan. If people are going to believe $3 billion is possible, I have to explain how.

"Get your pencils out." People rustle through computer bags. It's time to talk about the plan. It has four distinct parts.

Part 1: Grow Our License Revenue
Revenue from selling licenses to proprietary software is the biggest driver of any software company's growth. So it is imperative that SAP America drive its license revenue, now.

"Every account executive needs to get at least a half-million-dollar deal in Q1. That's five hundred thousand." The goal is aspirational, yet specific. "Do I have your commitment on that?" Nods and brief applause. *Okay, don't scare them off*, I say to myself. *Explain how they can keep that commitment.*

Part 2: Maintain a Rich, Rolling Pipeline
To ensure that sales reps perform quarter after quarter, they must keep their sales pipeline—their supply of potential deals—robust. How robust? I put a measurement to it: 3X. That means, at any given moment, each sales professional has to have three times his

quarterly revenue goal in his pipeline. Because I just asked them to commit to winning $500,000 worth of signed contracts by the end of Q1, each person must have $1.5 million worth of potential deals on any given day throughout January, February, and March. That way, if something falls through, backups are in place.

Not everyone will be up to maintaining 3X. Doing so requires each sales professional to be a mini-entrepreneur, and thus a wellspring of ideas. They must be able to juggle multiple projects at different stages of maturity, be willing to take risks, and be strategic enough to plot ten moves ahead. To many people, 3X is a daunting measurement.

So I do not just toss out the 3X requirement and wish people luck.

It is incumbent upon me, SAP's sales managers, and the entire field marketing organization to help each sales professional generate more opportunities through a combination of coaching, support, and targeted marketing campaigns. We are a team. Going forward, I tell everyone, SAP will invest more money and time in telesales, calling on companies we had not reached out to in a while. We will also broaden our pool of potential customers to small and midsized businesses, a population SAP has historically ignored, or that ignored SAP because they assumed we were too big.

And no more pitching tents at every tech trade show, hoping to snag a few new contacts. Instead, SAP America will start hosting our own topflight events, targeting industries and regions where our presence is weak. No paper-plate shindigs with doughnuts and fishbowls for business cards. We'll orchestrate sophisticated, content-rich affairs at four-star venues with marquee speakers. These events will attract senior executives to us, allowing us to form relationships with individuals who have the authority to approve multimillion-dollar deals.

Finally, we will fuel the 3X pipeline by reducing discounting. "I have a theory about sales," I tell everyone in New Orleans. "I believe that sales professionals that undersell their products are only underselling themselves. I think this is lazy. People discount when they can't tell a potential customer the specific business benefits of the product." Going forward, discounts above a certain amount must be reviewed *before* they are presented to customers.

By the end of my pipeline pitch, people are sitting up a little straighter in their chairs.

Part 3: Regain Partner Trust

To get to $3 billion, we also have to do a better job selling our software through SAP's business partners: the technology and consulting firms that help companies customize and install our systems. These organizations are in positions to recommend—or not—our software to their own corporate customers.

Unfortunately, most of our partners are not pleased with SAP America, and we must earn back their trust. During my first few weeks on the job, I'd started this process by inviting the leaders from our disgruntled partner companies to the Newtown Square campus. I sat them together in one room.

"We're not here to sing the 'Barney Song,'" I told them, referring to the signature "We're a happy family" theme of the purple dinosaur character, which anyone with children knew all too well. I told them that I knew SAP America had let them down, and promised that we were committed to reinvesting in our relationship.

In New Orleans, I give our salespeople this directive:

"Every account executive needs to meet with our partners by the second week in February so we can combine our companies' strengths and identify the two or three things we can do together to drive business. We are going to get this done."

Part 4: Refocus on Sales Excellence

The fourth pillar of our plan is to adopt a customer-centric mentality. Our new challenge is to give our customers what they want. What they want is *not* to buy more software but to make more money. We have to start showing how SAP's systems can improve our customers' financial performances. To deliver that level of value, we must get smarter about our customers' businesses. We will do so, in part, by reorganizing our sales force.

I announce that we will cluster our industry sales specialists in geographic locations so they can be closer to their customers and the industries they serve. The uncomfortable surprise: many salespeople are going to have to move. The level of commitment I am asking for has been ratcheted up.

Having presented the plan, I light the fuse:

"Vision absolutely requires execution," I say to the room. "And we're going to execute *now*. Not in the second quarter or the third. Now. I have walked in your shoes. I get it. I don't want to play office. I don't want to push around emails. And neither do you. We need to get this done. And there is nothing, professionally speaking, that I want to do more than come out of this meeting knowing that we are completely in alignment to deliver these results in the first quarter. I personally accept this challenge.

"Do *you* accept the challenge? Do you feel in your heart and your soul that this is something you truly want? Do you? You don't have to, but if you do, say it with me:

"I . . . accept . . . the . . . challenge."

The sound of hundreds of voices saying those four words reverberates throughout the arena. For the first time since the kickoff began, people clap like they mean it. There are even a few whistles, and no more tumbleweeds.

Perhaps minds are starting to change faster than I anticipated.

23

ART AND SCIENCE

Having a sense of mission that reaches beyond the present defines the final steps to individual and team significance. That means going beyond simply being the best, going so far that you leave footprints.

—PAT RILEY

WHEN I WAS getting my MBA in Chicago, I had the honor of meeting Gary Barnett, who was head coach of Northwestern University's Wildcats, a college football team that had a string of losing seasons until Gary arrived in the mid-1990s.

One day Gary spoke to my class and told us about his experience leading the Wildcats to the Rose Bowl championship game for the first time in fifty years.

"Every day that my players went to practice, I told them that if they gave their maximum effort, we would be ready to beat anybody. And we went through a ritual every single week, and our goal was absolutely clear: make it to the Rose Bowl. Well, we got to that Rose Bowl. And what do you think happened?"

I knew.

"We lost the game," said Gary. "We didn't lose because the team didn't have what it took to win that game. I believe we lost because, as coach, I had set the wrong goal: *to make it* to the Rose Bowl, not *to win* the Rose Bowl." I never forgot Gary's story.

By 2002, I had come to understand the difference between a goal and a dream—and my definition of *winning* also had evolved. A goal was a number. An outcome. A dream was something grander. More ongoing. Lasting. True winning was not about a specific end but about how that end was met. The journey was the dream.

VALUES MATTER

Achieving a goal doesn't matter, at least not to me, unless it's done in a way that lifts up people along the way.

During the early 2000s, when some of history's biggest corporate scandals were revealed, a lot of people got crushed. Employees, investors, and consumers were left with an aftertaste of distrust for big business. I was not perfect, but I always tried to lead and to win in ways that would make myself, my family, and everyone else I worked with proud. I would work you hard, but I would also work you right.

When I joined SAP America, the business had no formal set of values. No more. At the kickoff meeting in New Orleans, I introduced five values that would guide everyone's actions:

SUCCESS. ACCOUNTABILITY. PROFESSIONALISM.
TEAMWORK. PASSION.

I didn't come up with these values on my own. Nor had I outsourced the task to our HR or PR departments. Instead, I appointed an advisory council that worked with me, the management team, and employees to help define the kind of company SAP America wanted to become.

At the kickoff, a small "values" card was included in everyone's welcome package. I asked people to review the card and then keep it in their wallets—make it part of their DNA. Unlike other companies that framed their values on a wall in the lobby, we were going to live our values and reward those who did.

The five words could seem generic on paper, but they had meanings for me, and as I went through them one by one from the stage I didn't need to look down at the monitors. Like a coach determined to win the national championship, this stuff came from my heart:

Let's talk about success. We are successful when our customers are successful. That is it! We have to make our customers successful in the marketplaces as they compete. We must focus all of our energy and our passion on our customers.

Accountability. Don't pass the buck. I understand very well my own accountability to SAP America, and I accept that accountability. I want that accountability. And guess what? I expect nothing less from you. Each and every person in this room, regardless of the job type you have, you must be accountable for delivering results. And we, the executive management team, will recognize and reward performers who deliver consistent results.

Professionalism. Professionals are well prepared. They are always on their game. They would not think of going in front of a customer without understanding a scenario in great depth and doing the hard work to get ready for the meeting. To execute in a first-class manner. To exemplify excellence in all they do. Our transactions must be of the highest standards. We have integrity—

As if on cue, a cell phone rang from somewhere in the arena. I didn't ignore it but improvised to make a point. "We have integrity . . . but we also have cell phones. We should *not* have cell phones at business meetings." That was not the only time I had called out unprofessional behavior during the kickoff meeting. A number of seats were empty during our morning sessions, prompting me to assume that partying on New Orleans's infamous Bourbon Street had gotten the better of a lot of folks. I made my feelings about the absences clear:

"Those of you who *are* here, let everyone who *did not* make it here this morning know how much I respect *your* professional courtesy for soaring like eagles this morning after hanging with the owls last night. Tell your buddies that didn't make it to this meeting, it will be the last time they get away with it. I am keeping score on everything."

Back to the values:

Teamwork. Everything in life that really matters happens because a team of people decides it should. It is not just a sales thing. It is an SAP America success thing. Each and every function must pull together for the common good of the customer.

Passion. Passion is that differentiator between mediocrity, goodness, and greatness. Passion is when you will do whatever it takes to step up to the bar and deliver. We are fostering a winning culture here. The bar has been raised, and the expectations are higher. We have no interest in mediocrity. We really don't.

I reiterated these values in every talk I gave at SAP.

Cynics demean values as the soft stuff of leadership. For me, values are an essential part of the art, the lens through which we execute the hard stuff: the science.

REPEATABLE METHODOLOGIES

Playing basketball with my father as a kid taught me the importance of practice and preparation, of nailing the fundamentals of play before a game began. Even the most gifted players, my dad said, had to know the plays and follow the rules. Talent, and charm, only got people so far.

Dad had this philosophy in common with one of the best basketball coaches in history, the amazing John Wooden, whose accomplishments included ten NCAA championships for his collegiate teams at UCLA, seven of them consecutive. Coach Wooden also had played ball with my grandfather during the Depression.

One day, when I was older, I invited Coach Wooden to be the guest speaker at an SAP business meeting. Over dinner that evening, he and I chatted about his coaching philosophy and how he focused his team on the smallest details of the sport. By game time, his players' execution on the court was more about orchestration than invention.

Coach Wooden developed rituals that ensured his team had the basics down, from learning their competitors' weaknesses to how tight each player tied his shoelaces so a loose sneaker did not affect his concentration. Wooden wanted everything so locked down before his team hit the court that, in the heat of play, everyone could focus on the art.

Throughout my career, as I observed successful people, I recognized that they shared a respect for the fundamentals of play, each practicing behaviors that were the foundation for their recurring successes. The actual behaviors were different for everyone. But like any ritual, they provided consistency, especially during chaos. These "repeatable methodologies," as I called them, focused people. Improvisation was required, but instead of reacting emotionally, people acted wisely. Process trumped panic.

ENGINEERING VALUE

Late one Friday during my first few months at SAP, I received a panicked call. SAP was on the cusp of losing a major CRM contract to a competitor. Our sales executive had given up. But the contract was not signed, so from where I stood, there was time left to turn it around.

I scheduled a meeting with the prospective customer's CEO for Monday. Then I called Chakib Bouhdary, who was in charge of SAP America's business consulting unit and had arrived at SAP only six months before I did. The first time I had met with Chakib, a few weeks earlier, his resignation letter had been in his pocket.

"I've spent months dealing with internal politics and watching people walk around like zombies," he told me, unfiltered. "They think another reorg will fix our problems." A frank discussion followed. We agreed that the software market had changed. Corporations had become disillusioned with technology, and they had tighter budgets. Instead of talking about our software's functionality, SAP had to explain how our software helped a company make more money and become more competitive. But SAP America's sales force, we also agreed, was not able to articulate that level of value. Instead, we were making a classic tech-company fumble: assuming that product demonstrations and deep discounts were enough to sell more software. The way I saw it, SAP salespeople were telling a *technology* story when we needed to be telling a *business* story.

I asked Chakib for his solution. He proposed an experiment to prove that SAP would sell more software if we could better articulate our technology's business value. I was in.

"Chakib, what do you need from me?" All he asked for was my support as CEO, and the freedom to pick his team and pursue what he thought was the best approach.

"Done. Please come up with a proposal." Instead of handing me his resignation letter, he shook my hand.

A week later, a proposal was on my desk. A new "Value Engineering" team would send our top industry experts into select clients' companies to understand their business models, operations, and issues at a much more detailed level than SAP usually engaged. The team would compare aspects of each company's performance—

such as profit margins and inventory turns—to those of its competitors, and create industry benchmarks. The team would share what it had learned with specialists throughout SAP, and together assess which combination of products could help the client achieve its business objectives—not its technology objectives. The team would report its findings to the customer. All of this analysis would be free to the companies. The return for SAP would be honing a more value-based sales approach. For the time being, it would be an experiment.

Sooner than we expected, however, the experiment was in play.

"We have to fix this by Monday," I said when I called Chakib that Friday night to ask him to help prevent the CRM loss. He was packing up, about to leave his office to spend the weekend with his wife, Kathleen, and their three children. Instead, he unpacked his briefcase and called his wife to apologize because he would not be home for dinner. Then he called a half dozen colleagues from throughout the company into a conference room, and for the next forty-eight hours this dedicated team dropped their personal lives to dissect the company we were going after, collaborating to an extent that was rare for us. On Monday morning, the team delivered to my office a stunning proposal. I took it to my meeting with the CEO, and SAP won the CRM business.

More than winning a single deal, this moment proved pivotal. Value Engineering was a big idea if we could figure out how to repeat and scale the collaborative experience and build on the customer-centric sales approach. I unleashed the Value Engineering team. It brought in strategy experts from top firms McKinsey & Company and Booz Allen—professionals whose expertise was not in technology but in solving complex business problems. These people spoke the language that CEOs wanted to hear, not tech talk. The Value Engineering team supplemented our marketing efforts, and taught our tech-savvy account executives and salespeople how to be more business savvy.

To scale, the team trained people in a repeatable process of analysis: the questions to ask, which financials to examine, which operations among industry peers to compare.

Not every sales professional would have the ability, or the desire, to transition from a features-and-function pitchman to a value creator. Those who didn't would not be staying long.

By mid-2003, Value Engineering was changing how we sold. As the process took hold, the results were stunning. SAP America was winning 90 percent of the projects we went after using the Value Engineering approach. The key to its success was not just its intent but its institutionalization. It seeped into our culture.

MICROMANAGING REALITY

Coach Wooden's fundamentals-first philosophy gave his teams an edge at critical moments, when the clock started to run out and his team needed to score. He knew that as long as time was left on the clock, be it ten minutes or ten seconds, there was an opportunity to come up with a new play that could win the game—assuming no one wasted time tightening his shoelaces.

At SAP, we had to inject more discipline and transparency into how we tracked the sales process so that we, too, could improvise. The 3X pipeline requirement kept our sales reps' shoelaces tight, so they weren't scrambling with the basic task of finding new leads in the middle of a quarter. But only if my fellow leaders and I knew if our collective sales were short of our goal by, say, $3 million or $300,000—two months or two days away from the end of a quarter—could we bridge the gap.

The irony was that, despite knowing the value of our own CRM software, we weren't even using it. Seriously. People were tracking their sales status on paper via forms nicknamed Burger King Spreadsheets because everyone's was different, organized "your way." It would have been funny—if it weren't so unproductive. We *were* the shoemaker's kids. Barefoot. We had to start using our own CRM product so that we could track and update the stages of every sales cycle, and coordinate our accounts. Behaviors had to change.

We initiated a weekly process that became known as the Top 20 Call. The call was similar to how we dissected deals during the fourth quarter of 2002. Each week, our head of sales identified the largest twenty deals in progress, and everyone associated with them—from the regional manager to the sales reps—was on the "call," in a room with me or via phone. I asked people to bring to the meeting their most difficult account situations, so that the collective forum could help untangle the knots. Upward of one hundred people from the United States and Canada tuned in, including the heads of our other departments in case they were needed.

Once everyone was assembled, the curtain rose, and for about ninety minutes, a few senior VPs and I followed an interrogative script, assessing the status of key accounts and deals to sniff out speed bumps, dead ends, or likely home runs. At first, people approached the Top 20 Call as a punitive exercise, and I had to reset their expectations that these meetings could be tough, but the goal was to figure out how SAP could best help a company so that we might win it as a customer. One secret to the meetings' effectiveness was the optimistic way I framed it: the Top 20 Calls were not about figuring out how SAP could avoid a loss but how SAP could ensure a win.

That did not mean the calls were easy. The scrutiny shook people, as my friendly nature sometimes masked how process driven and disciplined I could be. "What's the business case? Have we presented it to the CEO? When is the next meeting? What, you just found out the company can't sign because its purchasing director went on vacation? What's your plan to backfill the loss?"

If someone didn't know his next move, he wasn't doing his job. If she couldn't articulate an ROI, she wasn't doing her job. We questioned people until we identified the next step, and who needed to step up. "The customer has credit issues? Let's get their CFO on the phone with our bank today and get them financing." "You're waiting on our head of consulting? You got it. Susan, get with Steve's team after the call and get it done." If a conversation with a customer had escalated to senior management, did we need to send in someone more experienced or sophisticated to close the deal? Sales is a team sport. The rep might be the quarterback, but he needed the rest of us to help him score.

When people knew their stuff, I let them know. "Fantastic work, Jason." "You're the best, Jennifer." "Beautifully said, David. Please circulate your proposal for everyone to learn from." When people couldn't provide a good answer, I didn't gussy up my disappointment: "The answer you just gave me failed the IQ test." Once, when a rep announced on the last day of the last quarter that he had met his quota and was "done," I made my position clear on the call. "No, you are not. We are never done." I could be blunt, but I didn't spit glass. For the caliber of talent on our teams, the desire to perform well and be rewarded for it was more motivating than the fear of screwing up, and I had no interest in nurturing fear or hurting feelings.

The Top 20 Call served another purpose. Unlike an annual training seminar, the live weekly reviews were productive teaching opportunities, especially early on. Unlike back in New York, my best sales managers and I could not be hopping in the car with every rep, visiting customers in every territory. Yes, I would hop on a plane and go wherever I might be needed to close a deal, but it was not possible to do that for hundreds of people. The Friday call helped us scale effective salesmanship.

Value Engineering and the Top 20 Call were two critical methodologies that helped our sales culture develop a cadence; a beautiful rhythm of preparation and rigor. Now we just needed leaders who could dance.

24

BIG ATHLETES

*If your actions inspire others to dream more, learn
more, do more, and become more, you are a leader.*
—JOHN QUINCY ADAMS

UILDING A NEW leadership team began by assessing the current
crop. I invited each of SAP America's current leaders to join me
for a one-on-one breakfast. As I learned, people inside SAP began
referring to these meetings as the Famous Breakfast.

Before each one, I had an idea of how it might go. Even if I felt
that someone was not the right fit for the organization, I kept my
mind open to the alternative. Plus, everyone deserved a dignified
conversation. Avoiding tough talks was a bad habit that some managers indulged because they lacked the temperament for honesty.
But whether someone was destined to stay or go, I always tried to
treat him or her to a civil, respectful dialogue.

The talk often began the same way: "What's your assessment of
the company and the market? What do you think we should do?" I

would ask, because I wanted to know. Then I would listen, learn, and eventually cast my favorite line: "What do you want?" This query was open-ended and unexpected, and got people reflecting. I hoped to discover not only what they were passionate about but also if they possessed a clarity about their own desires. I wanted to believe that they were interviewing me as much as I was interviewing them, and I was impressed when someone told me what he or she needed to be successful.

The best people for a role, I knew, would be those whose ambitions and passions fit the job. But I also had to assess skills. As much as I wanted people who worked for SAP to be happy, their success would be based not on what the mission brought to them but on what they brought to the mission.

Some of the managers I met with claimed my changes were too radical. My reply, "It would be radical to think we can get a different business outcome if we continued to do the same thing." Here the passion gap was obvious, at least to me. Other responses to my questions surfaced with unapologetic clarity: "Bill, I don't want what you want." Or "Bill, I got stuck in this job, and it was never right for me. I've been meaning to do something different." Such honesty was a gift! The sooner we got these people out and into a role they wanted, the better for them and for SAP America.

A few individuals were eager to play on the new team but weren't ready. Still, I was in no hurry to break their spirit. "Help me fill in the blanks," I might say. "Based on what I have seen and what you have told me, I cannot point to the thing you are best at." Or "You haven't yet made a case for what you want." Sometimes people had to be guided to the best outcome, not just ushered out. "Have you taken a solid assessment of yourself and concluded that this role and this company really are for you? Why don't you think about it overnight, talk it over with your family, and if you come to me in the morning and tell me this is not the right place for you, there will be no hard feelings. But if you want to stay, you cannot continue to do the same things that you have been doing and expect it to work out."

Giving people permission and time to ruminate often helped them reconcile conflicting feelings they already harbored about their careers. Our conversations often prompted needed self-reflection, preempting an inevitable fall. The end result, I hoped, was not degrading for people but empowering. Even if you left SAP, you did so contemplating what was possible. No blood was shed at those breakfasts. No one got up in a huff and marched out. On the contrary, many people thanked me. Some even hugged me.

About 85 percent of the leadership team I inherited moved on. I held on to our chief financial officer, Mark White, who hadn't hesitated to tell me what I did not want to hear, even about my own ambitions. Ed Lange was one of SAP's best big-deal closers. People liked and trusted Ed, and when we met, I understood why. We talked about his wife, Sharon, and his young children, and how he'd left SAP in 1999 to join an internet start-up. After his dot-com employer burst, he returned to SAP. As an SAP veteran, Ed had arrived at our Famous Breakfast assuming that he was already a dead man, so he didn't hold back his opinions. Ed stayed.

Aside from direct reports, I wanted SAP to retain Rob Enslin, whom I had first met that Friday night at the office, and whose product knowledge and commitment our sales and marketing organization needed. In Rob, I saw incredible leadership potential. SAP America's general counsel, Brad Brubaker, had been delightful throughout my contract negotiations, and exceptionally diligent once we began working together. Both Rob and Brad also had an integrity that would be hard to replace, so I didn't try.

To restock the empty seats, I first looked inside the company, but if the bench strength wasn't there, I looked outside. I needed leaders who embraced, and would spread, a renewed customer focus. I was not naive enough to think everyone at SAP would get on board with my new plan immediately. Some never would. But the best way to woo the doubters was to recruit faithful disciples. I also wanted people who not only had the passion and the acumen to perform but also the intellectual curiosity and humility to keep learning and growing. And because none of us was ever as smart as all of us, SAP America needed a team that complemented one another's strengths and weaknesses, especially my own.

I also looked for leaders who could create other leaders by distributing power as opposed to hoarding it, and who would speed up decision making by empowering their people to make decisions. Insecure managers chose to keep power for themselves. They also surrounded themselves with individuals who made them feel like the smartest ones in the room. On the contrary, I wanted people around me that were better versed in their areas of expertise than I would ever be. My dream team would be made up not just of executives that made me feel good but also those who had the courage and conviction to say, "Bill, the emperor has no clothes." I wanted people I could trust.

One of my most important hires was a new executive assistant. I had always believed that you could tell everything about an executive by the quality of his or her assistant. Supporting a CEO was an intensive, complicated task that required a mix of superior organizational, interpersonal, and business skills by someone who understood the company's strategic mission and prioritized. A big ego or someone who played power games would not work for me. My assistant also had to know shorthand to take dictation. This was becoming a lost skill, but I was a talker, and I needed someone who could get down my ideas and directives as they fired out of my mouth. I told the recruiter to find me the best executive assistant in America.

Barbara Rendina was working for the chairman and president of a major financial firm, and her résumé was stellar—and included shorthand. We met at an Italian restaurant in Newtown Square for lunch. Barb had the elegance, class, professionalism, and presence I liked, as well as an understated reserve. I immediately trusted this woman. Ten minutes into the conversation, I told Barb she was hired. I knew she was the one.

The sudden job offer took her by surprise. She barely knew me, and she had a family that her career helped support. Barb needed the security that she had in her present job. So in an unorthodox move, I promised her an employment contract. Even if we didn't work out—which I knew would not be the case—Barb and her family would be covered for a period of time. Bingo. Barb and I were in business.

Not everyone I hired checked every box, but all brought important assets to the team. When Terry Laudal and I met for coffee to discuss whether he would make a good head of human resources, he had a quieter personality than other people with whom I had met. But Mark had insisted that Terry was the best at what he did, and as much as SAP needed to up its energy level, we also needed discipline, especially in HR. I wanted someone who embraced HR's softer side and knew what motivated people, but did not shy from the hard conversations that came with the role. Like Barb, Terry was easy for me to talk to, and I sensed a valued confidant. In Terry I found our new head of HR.

Just as I tried not to push people out, I couldn't push them in. I did try to sway people in my own way, but to succeed in a job, a person had to want it—maybe even more than I wanted him. Snagging our next executive VP of sales took two months. No one thought we would hire John Nugent away from our largest competitor, but SAP needed an injection of Silicon Valley edge, and John's process orientation would free me from worrying about every detail of sales execution. He also had the chutzpah to stick with decisions when everyone else moaned. I understood, firsthand, John's hesitancy to leave his employer after an all-too-familiar seventeen-year run. Having been in John's situation, I recognized what he was feeling.

"John, I know this is very difficult for you," I said, calling him one weekend a few days after we first met. "How are you feeling?" We talked about how, for me, leaving Xerox had felt brutal at times, even though the decision was the right one. We talked about how this moment was an inflection point for him: if he did not make a job shift now, he was essentially signing up for a lifetime contract at his current employer. "Is that what you want, John?" I asked how his wife, Marilyn, felt about moving to the Philadelphia area. We must have had a half dozen conversations. Eventually John joined our cause.

I also plucked from my network. Former colleagues reached out to me, recalling our time at Xerox or Gartner or Siebel, and expressed a desire to recapture the experience at SAP. I was flattered, but careful not to hire only people with whom I had a good history.

Over time, more than a hundred people I had worked with in the past would find a place at SAP. Among them, I hired my former Xerox salesman Greg McStravick. In the past fifteen years, my once high-potential had reached his potential, so much so that he had joined me at Gartner. He never once lost my trust. Greg still carried with him fundamentals he learned from his earliest days. He also knew how to scale. Now I asked him to run SAP America's field marketing, which would pump deals into the pipeline and keep us steady at 3X.

I surrounded myself with people of substance, confidence, and aspirations. Most of them had been doing their jobs well for a long time. My job was to keep them happy, productive, and growing—or SAP would lose them.

TRUST AND ACCOUNTABILITY

The first time I had the honor of meeting four-star general and former secretary of state Colin Powell was at an event that SAP America was hosting. I asked him a question I often asked other leaders: "Please, if you would, share with me one of the biggest moments of your career."

General Powell told me about a day in 1988, during his time as national security advisor to President Ronald Reagan, when he was sitting in the Oval Office talking to the president, who was seated in a chair with a view of the Rose Garden. Powell was describing to the president a fight between various government departments, underscoring a problem that had to be solved that day. As he spoke, President Reagan kept looking out into the garden, distracted, so much so that the general became a bit uncomfortable. Finally, Reagan stood and interrupted.

"Colin, Colin, the squirrels just came and picked up the nuts I put out there for them this morning." The president then sat back down and looked at General Powell, who decided the meeting was over, excused himself, and returned to his office.

"Were you insulted or concerned?" I asked, thinking President Reagan was either ignoring one of his most important advisors, or not doing his own job by not engaging with him.

"No, Bill, he taught me a very valuable lesson." Powell explained: Reagan was the president, and as head of the National Security Agency, Powell was responsible for handling the minor details. In his remaining time working for him, Powell never upwardly delegated a problem like that to the president again. Instead, he and his team solved the problems they had been hired to solve. My take on the episode was that leaders must trust that the people to whom they delegate responsibility will do their jobs, and do them right.

As a manager, I trusted people to perform to high expectations without my hovering. That's not to say I did not inject myself when I felt the need, but I had no interest in micromanaging talent. If I prescribed too many solutions, I was merely insulting people's intelligence and stifling their potential. So I pulled back, allowing leaders to do their jobs if I felt what they were doing was right.

I also held people accountable for the ultimate outcome, as well as their behaviors. It was my spirit to want everybody to perform, but it was my responsibility to ensure there were no chronic under-performers.

"I assume by your behavior that you're telling me you've re-signed," I said more than once. Resigning was not just about writing a letter and leaving the building. If you showed up for work, but your mind and heart had checked out, you'd resigned from the pro-gram. That could not stand. I never judged someone based on a sin-gle quarter or even a single year. The most talented professionals have bad runs, so in assessing performance, I considered the larger picture as well as external circumstances. My bias was to be on some-one's side, not against him or her.

Still, allowing subpar performances to slip by, or tolerating bad behavior and attitudes, squeezed the juice out of those people work-ing so hard. As a leader, I had to hold everyone to the same stan-dards, even if I treated people differently based on their personalities, strengths, and weaknesses—and their personal circumstances.

BALANCE PRIORITIES

Supporting people on the home front was critical. As much as I ex-pected my colleagues to respond to emails or miss a birthday party when something big was on the line, I knew the importance of bal-ance. And of a strong home base. But balance was not just an issue of time. Everyone had a different set of priorities when it came to what was important to him and his family, and if I took the time to ask and listen, I could find each person's unique pressure point. I knew whose spouse disliked when her husband spent too much time in the air, fly-ing around the country. I knew whose children had special health needs, whose parents were ill, whose daughter was trying to get into college and could use a recommendation. Me? I always wanted to be home Saturdays and Sundays. Mindful of such issues, I did what I could to help people balance specific priorities. "No need to travel to the West Coast every week, Alan. A conference call will suffice."

Productivity was not my sole motivator. Just as my mom enjoyed getting to know our deli customers as she dished up her egg salad or poured cups of coffee, I was interested in the people I worked alongside. The lack of time in a given day often made long conversations difficult, but establishing a level of closeness with people—sometimes even a friendship—made the sacrifice and the work and the wins truly matter.

Some managers I'd observed had no interest in asking after employees' personal lives. They couldn't even feign interest for fear they'd get caught up in a conversation about a little league game or, worse, a family tragedy. But fueling and sharing the happiness of the people I worked alongside, even their traumas, mattered to me. If it didn't, the journey I was on would have been meaningless, and lonely.

Sometimes the nature of a relationship deserved more than just a conversation. When Terry Laudal's father passed away, I was traveling with John Nugent to a client on the West Coast. When we got word about Terry's dad, I rescheduled our itinerary and we hopped a plane to Grand Forks, North Dakota. John and I drove about a hundred miles to the funeral in Terry's hometown in northern Minnesota. Heavy rains delayed us, but we made it to the church before the service ended. After the funeral, I hugged Terry, looked over photos of his father, who had served in the US military, and spoke to his mother and brother before heading out. The look in Terry's eyes as we said good-bye confirmed for me that my trip's detour was well worth the time and effort, and would not be forgotten.

CELEBRATE MOMENTUM

By the end of 2003, the ambitious plan we'd presented in New Orleans, the bold declarations, the productivity improvements that kicked in after the kickoff meeting, had energized people. I could feel the pace quicken throughout Newtown Square and in our field offices. There. Was. Hustle.

The momentum showed up everywhere. We were selling the value of the "suite," and we won new business across the country and across industries: the food company H. J. Heinz became a client, as did medical device manufacturer Medtronic, a grocery store chain in Texas, and an elevator manufacturer in Iowa. Industry analysts who had once predicted the decline of SAP America conceded we were gaining market share. Our high-powered events were packed with guests, and global and local marketing campaigns were increasing awareness, reintroducing North America to SAP as a trusted alternative. We also held firm on limiting discounts. SAP America was expanding into new markets, penetrating the small and midsized business categories with a new software product designed especially for them, Business One, and generating more new-customer leads by strengthening our relationships with channel partners and other resellers. Meanwhile, as we blossomed, our distracted competitors were embroiled in contentious merger chaos.

Customer-centricity tied everything together. As I told *InfoWorld* magazine in spring 2003, "Everyone in this company, from executives down to the product line managers and their staff, are spending as much time with customers as they can. We are a totally customer-focused organization."

By May 2003, our progress was solid enough that Leo Apotheker stood in front of Wall Street analysts at a meeting in New York City and declared, "The US is fixed."

Well, not quite. But we were on our way.

The work was demanding but rewarding. A new compensation plan and bonus structure tied our performance to results and to customer satisfaction. It gave everyone, even non–revenue producers, a chance to earn more. Top performers could make a lot of money, and they would have a chance to really celebrate at the end of the year.

The 2003 end-of-year meeting for top performers, which I had named Winners' Circle, had to be special. People deserved a thank-you they would not forget. I had asked people to trust me, to stretch themselves, spend time away from their families, and to work harder than anyone had in a long while. Their faith and their efforts deserved to be honored, so I bumped up the event from coach to first class. I selected the venue. The Hawaiian resort was as stunning as it was expensive, but the message it sent was priceless: you are worthy of greatness, even though we are not great yet. Our numbers were improving, and the momentum was undeniable, but our dreams were big, and big dreams cannot sustain themselves in small environments. Just as Muhammad Ali called himself the Greatest before he ever was, the tone of the Winners' Circle set the expectation of how great we could become.

In addition to high-end, the celebration had to be fun. One night we threw a retro, disco-themed party. I invited one of my favorite groups from the 1970s, KC and the Sunshine Band, to perform. The group wasn't the Rolling Stones, but it also wasn't the Shirelles. I chose the band to take our people back to a decade they remembered, a period in their lives when they may have let loose. Their number one hits "Get Down Tonight" and "(Shake Shake Shake) Shake Your Booty" took the crowd back in time. Everyone was dancing. And when John Nugent and I showed up to the party dressed in white *Saturday Night Fever* suits, with open shirts and gold chains, forget it. People went crazy. The energy was so hot, so joyous, it was as if the slumping audience in New Orleans had undergone reverse lobotomies.

My favorite moment was standing in front of everyone, thanking them for their incredible efforts. As I did, a silence came over the entire team. The moment was meaningful not because it punctuated the end of something great but because it heralded the beginning of what I knew would be a winning journey.

The culture, the values, the discipline, the people, the methods we'd put in place in 2003 were giving us traction as we hurled toward 2005. We had established a foundation.

GROWTH

In 2005 SAP America delivered about $200 million more than our targeted $3 billion, with the United States exceeding $1 billion in software revenues alone for the first time in company history. I was thrilled, but more so I was humbled by what women and men who commit themselves to a mission can achieve.

The changes leading up to our goal had not gone unnoticed. "SAP AG's attempt to overhaul its flagging America operation appears to be paying off," wrote the *Wall Street Journal* in July 2004. In the *Financial Times*, a financial analyst from HVB Group summarized it well: "SAP is gaining market share, including in the US, where it is eating into the shares of the likes of Siebel and Oracle on their home base."

That year, I was appointed to lead a new business unit that combined SAP's North American and Latin American businesses. Soon India, China, and Japan were added to my plate.

Together, 2004 and 2005 had been a whirlwind of growth, for SAP and for me. The suburbs of Philadelphia had come to feel like my family's home. As much as I missed Manhattan's bustle and the West Coast's sun, I was fulfilling the goals I'd written down for myself during my last days at Siebel, which I kept folded in a drawer in my bedside table. My family was living in a community that was healthy for the kids, and affordable enough that we could enjoy a standard of living that felt indulgent compared with our working-class upbringings, but not over-the-top. I'd even bought my parents a condo nearby so that they could come for extended stays when they were not in Myrtle Beach. Between business trips, I was coaching John's and Michael's basketball teams while Julie continued her job as CEO of Team McDermott, taking steadfast care of our house, the boys, and me.

SAP was so much more than an employer. The company had become an intrinsic piece of our lives. I had found my post-Xerox family. Julie and I opened our home to my colleagues for formal dinners and parties. She and my parents attended every company Christmas party.

More than any other company, SAP was allowing me to be my full self. I still had room to grow, and I was learning from my own missteps as well as from the talent around me, but at my core, I was still the same person I'd always been.

Exactly twenty years after having graduated, I was invited to Dowling College, back on Long Island, to receive its Alumnus of the Year Award. I was also asked to become a member of Dowling's board of trustees. I mean, *wow*. I was honored. Julie, the boys, and I flew from Philly to New York to attend the Saturday-night reception, which was hosted by Dowling's president and its dean of students. Julie looked elegant in a black sleeveless dress, and Michael and John looked sharp in their suits and ties. My mother also joined us—as she should have. Her support of me never wavered. My mother's influence was a huge part of the reason why I was even here.

When a reporter from Long Island's *Newsday*, Mark Harrington, interviewed me about the award, I told him about growing up in Amityville, and about the deli, and how I'd built that business. When he asked me how I had managed to keep SAP America growing in a down market, I told him I did it by giving customers what they wanted. "A formula that hasn't changed," Mark wrote in his article's last sentence, "since the days he made sandwiches on the South Shore."

PART 6

BE BOLD

25

CRISIS OF OPPORTUNITY

It always seems impossible until it's done.
—NELSON MANDELA

THE GLOBAL ECONOMIC meltdown hit with the intensity of a house fire. On September 14, 2008, financial services firm Lehman Brothers collapsed, and the shock it triggered spread. SAP's corporate customer base panicked—and then froze. Many deals that were scheduled to close were canceled or delayed. In the third quarter of that year, $1 billion in potential revenue disappeared from our sales pipelines. Poof.

In the months that followed, cautious corporations began hoarding cash instead of reinvesting it in technology. More than ever, companies wanted a concrete business case to justify every purchase, and they wanted to see quick returns.

That fall, I was heading SAP's global customer operations and had just been appointed to SAP's executive board, the company's nine-member governing body. The executive board reported to the supervisory board, a larger group whose members included SAP chairman and cofounder Hasso Plattner, employee representatives, and external directors, all of whom were elected. Leo Apotheker, meanwhile, had been named co-CEO back in April 2008, serving with the existing chief, the well-regarded Henning Kagermann.

Before the recession slapped SAP hard, our performance in 2008 had been strong. The company was on its way to achieving its best annual performance in history. In August our share price on the New York Stock Exchange hit $58, just shy of a fifty-two-week high. The Great Recession, however, changed it all.

"This is the most challenging environment that SAP has ever faced," Leo told Wall Street during 2008's year-end earnings call. "I don't think it is prudent to expect that the macroeconomic environment will improve in 2009."

In response, SAP spent 2009 trying to drive sales volume for our existing products. But each quarter, year-over-year revenue from software licenses continued to slip. To preserve our profit margins, SAP cut costs. Some expenses needed to be shed, and when SAP made the painful decision to cut jobs for the first time in its almost forty-year history, already sagging morale deflated further. In May 2009 Henning stepped down, and Leo became sole CEO. That September, an employee survey revealed that SAP's workforce was losing trust in its senior management, of which I was one. Because I was never one to walk by a problem, I felt compelled to step up.

WHATEVER IT TAKES: RALLY IN THE FOURTH QUARTER

The last three months of every year, October through December, were historically SAP's most lucrative, when we closed the most contracts, and some of the largest. But given cautionary spending in the marketplace, many people inside SAP felt it would take a miracle to bring home 2009's fourth quarter with our usual gusto. As an optimist and an underdog, however, I saw opportunity. I was not alone in believing that, as long as there was time on the clock, a crisis could be overpowered by the right strategy and disciplined execution.

Jim Hagemann Snabe was head of SAP's product development, and another recent appointee to the executive board. Jim's intelligence and generosity were widely respected. Until now, Jim and I had been more social than collaborative colleagues. When we did get together, we always had easy conversations, and we genuinely enjoyed each other's company. Jim was born in Denmark and spent his youth in Greenland. His father was a fighter- and rescue-helicopter pilot. Jim was a schooled mathematician and spoke several languages. Despite our different histories, Jim and I soon realized that we were similar where it counted most. One night in the restaurant of the Villa Kennedy hotel in Frankfurt, Jim told me a story from his youth.

"Jim," a coach had once said to him, "the game is not about you, it's about the kind of team that you create around you. That's what makes a strong leader." Jim went on to explain the significance to me.

"Bill," he said, "I once thought that my math background could make me the smartest guy in the room, but I figured out a long time ago that my coach was right." I told Jim that my dad had taught me the same thing about teamwork when we coached together. "You can't make this stuff up," I kept saying as we compared more life stories over dinner. We were laughing so loud and for so long that someone in the restaurant approached our table to ask us to please keep our voices down.

Among the other traits that Jim and I shared was a customer-centric focus when it came to our respective areas of expertise, as well as the belief that SAP had to seize the crisis in the fourth quarter of 2009, as the company barreled toward the end of a very tough year.

Each of us had meetings scheduled with our respective leadership teams in October. We decided to combine the two and meet in

Newtown Square. Rick Knowles, my chief of staff—a meticulous executor and strategist who had been loyal to me since my earliest days at SAP America—quickly orchestrated a two-day gathering of the company's top sales and product development decision makers. Our goal: prepare SAP to close €1 billion in revenue before December 31, 2009. It was another chance to create *un milagro*.

The two-day emergency session began in a crowded conference room. The size of the gathering, about seventy-five people, seemed small for our ambition, but because execution, versus inspiration, was our agenda, I believed that a tighter group would get more done than a sprawling mass.

Sales took the floor and talked about the state of the markets, explaining the challenges it was hearing from customers, which included lingering uncertainty about the economy as well as companies' industry-specific software needs. When Jim's top product developers took the floor, they described various SAP software solutions that were either in development or ready to be deployed—including existing products that many of our salespeople knew little or nothing about. Amazingly, SAP had technology that we were not actively selling, and customers had requested products that we were not actively building.

This disconnect was unacceptable yet understandable. SAP had more than a thousand industry-specific software solutions. It was all too easy for newer, smaller solutions to get lost on their way to market. Vice versa, our customers' needs were not being consistently communicated back to our development teams. Throughout that day, Jim and I would look at each other and shake our heads as we realized how our value chain had broken down. But that's why we were here: to build it back up, and not just for the fourth quarter.

Next, everyone divided into miniteams to come up with go-to-market plans. The collaboration elevated the mood. Sales leaders learned about products that their reps could start pitching tomorrow. Developers got their innovations out and started tackling new ones.

Another directive I issued was to the sales force: every rep, I said, had to get in front of his manager and pitch his own plan to achieve his individual goals. I called these sessions "pit stops." Like changing a race car's tires on a track, the intent of the pit stop was to engage managers, and to ensure that every sales professional was equipped to race and win. Selling, I reminded everyone, was a team sport.

The cooperation did not end in Newtown Square. In the following weeks, as December 31 loomed, product developers joined our reps in the field, visiting customers, talking about their solutions. Pit stops were taking place around the world. Everyone hustled, including Jim and me, both of us going on sales calls, too. Day by day, SAP sold more to its existing customers and brought on new ones, cutting deals large and small, realizing incremental revenue from software sales that, had seventy-five people not rallied and done whatever it took, would have gone untapped.

Ultimately, we exceeded our own expectations and brought in more than €1 billion in software sales during that fateful last quarter. It was the first time SAP had broken through €1 billion in a single quarter since 2001. This achievement was incredible considering that the global economy was still recovering. And although SAP's total revenues were still less than the previous year, we never could have performed as we did had our sales and development leaders not rallied together.

What a galvanizing moment. We had proved that SAP could exceed expectations and work together toward a shared goal. The experience also cemented the mutual respect between Jim and me. At no point at the meeting or during the weeks that followed did either of us upstage the other. Acting together, we brought home a small but significant miracle, and we entered 2010 hoping that momentum would continue.

26

THE CORNER OFFICE

Everything comes to him who hustles while he waits.
—THOMAS EDISON

I N A TINY Phoenix hotel room, Julie and I are racing to pack for the airport so that we do not miss our flight to Hawaii, where I am hosting Winners' Circle. John and Michael, now teenagers, are traveling with us. My parents are en route.

SAP had, at my urging, opened Winners' Circle attendance to children and extended family members. I believed that members of our employees' own families deserved to celebrate their roles in supporting SAP year-round. Our people had to pay for any guests beyond themselves and a significant other, but they did so willingly. And each year in Hawaii, it seemed that more and more young people were filling the pools and the beaches. It was amazing.

I am about to close my suitcase when my mobile phone rings. We are too rushed for me to answer it. Yesterday our flight from Philadelphia to Phoenix was so delayed that we missed our connecting flight to Maui. We *must* be on this morning's flight. I take a quick look at the phone. It's Hasso. I answer.

"Hi, this is Bill."

"Bill, hello. Hasso here."

He has news. I sit on the side of the bed and listen. SAP's supervisory board, Hasso tells me, has come to an agreement not to extend Leo's contract as CEO. The contract, I know, ends in December. Today is February 6, 2010. Leo, I understand, is no longer going to be SAP's CEO, starting today. Hasso confirms that Leo has resigned. My reaction is mixed. Leo brought me to SAP and through the years supported my ascent at the company, which I have come to love like family. But now that family is hurting.

Hasso says he knows the company has gone astray. He believes we must refocus on real innovation, not just making incremental improvements to existing products. Hasso knows the world has changed. He also knows SAP has become too hierarchical and needs to regain the trust its top leaders have lost—with customers as well as with our own people. No one person is to blame, Hasso believes. But to return SAP to growth, he says we need to be a happy company again. The tone of my brief responses to each statement causes Julie to look at me inquisitively. She knows something is up.

What Hasso says next feels like destiny unfolding.

"Bill, the supervisory board has unanimously voted to make you SAP's co-CEO." A whirlwind of thoughts and emotions engulfs me as my mind slingshots back in time.

"Bill, what's your dream?" Emerson Fullwood had asked me when I interviewed at Xerox.

"Sir, one day I would hope to become the CEO," I had replied.

Hasso asks if I will accept. There is no hesitation. No trepidation.

"Hasso, yes." I thank him for trusting me with his company. I have only one question. "Who is the other co-CEO?"

"Jim Hagemann Snabe," he says. *Perfect.*

At the Phoenix airport, after my family gets through security, I call Jim, who I am assuming has also said yes to Hasso. Jim is home with his wife, Birgitte, and their two children.

"Bill!" I hear his smile over the phone and know we are in this together.

Our conversation feels like part reunion, part blind date. We've been set up together but know there is chemistry. Jim's joy is mutual, and we agree that each of us would not have been as confident had the "co-" been anyone other than each other. We don't talk logistics today, only dreams of what we want to accomplish for the company.

During the long flight to Hawaii, I am overwhelmed with gratitude and thoughts of possibilities for SAP. But the plane is packed with SAP families also headed to Hawaii, and the news will not be public until tomorrow. So in a hushed voice, I talk to Julie about how lucky I am to be working with Jim.

A two-headed chief would be an anomaly at some companies, but for SAP it is heritage. The company's history of shared, complementary leadership started with its founders. The culture is accustomed to balancing power and leveraging skills of joint chiefs as well as the executive board. And given what Jim and I had witnessed in the fourth quarter—the gulf between sales and product development, and our potential to bridge it—we seemed like a natural duo. We had harmonizing skill sets. We had proven to ourselves that we could collaborate under pressure and get people to work toward common goals. And neither of us was the type to hole up in a corner office, playing office. We preferred to be out among our people and our customers.

Plus, we genuinely liked each other. I admired Jim's patience and his calm demeanor; how he diagramed complex issues and potential solutions. Our differences would ensure a balance of expertise.

After six hours in what seems like suspended time above the Pacific Ocean, the plane lands, and the rest of my life begins in a flurry. We arrive at our hotel in Maui, where I immediately gather with my family and share the news with a few close confidants. *Break out the Korbel!* Joy fills the room. Having family here makes it complete.

Hasso wants to announce our appointment on Sunday in Germany, with Jim and me on a live, all-company global broadcast out of Walldorf. The only way for me to be present is via satellite, but with no adequate transcontinental satellite hookup nearby, I've got to hop a Saturday-night flight to Honolulu so I can be in front of a camera.

I leave my family and head to Honolulu, where in the middle of the night I drive to a windowless concrete building. A skeletal camera crew decides to film me outside, in the dark, at the rear of the building. *Okay, let's do this!* They set up the one camera near two industrial-sized Dumpsters. The moment their enormous spotlights flick on, I watch as a horde of large bees is drawn to the bright lights. Everything is silent as we go live. Standing there, I keep an eye on those bees as Hasso tells SAP's employees that Jim and I are their new CEOs. From two different continents, we express our gratitude and optimism.

The next morning, back in Maui, I call an impromptu meeting of my closest colleagues to discuss the news.

"Bill, what exactly did you say to Hasso when he called you?" someone asks.

"I told him that I had worked for this moment all of my life."

THE LAESTRYGONIANS AND THE CYCLOPES

Mixed reactions greeted SAP's announcement.

The head of an independent organization representing thousands of SAP customers and partners said he was pleased to see that SAP's new leaders had been appointed from within. Not everyone agreed. An analyst from Forrester Research, which like Gartner tracked technology companies, told one news outlet that he didn't think "SAP insiders" could turn around the company. "An outsider might wonder if congratulations, or condolences, were more in order for McDermott," opined a reporter on a Philadelphia-based website, reflecting on the company's challenging past year. Other speculators were even more critical. "The company's efforts to recoup lost ground may be too little too late," one financial analyst told Bloomberg News. Another industry analyst told *PCWorld* magazine that SAP "still needs to fill in many blanks about future product direction and strategy."

The various predictions made their way to me, but if I paid too much attention to naysayers or let encouragers bloat my ego, I'd lose focus on what mattered: the company.

Jim and I made our first appearance as co-CEOs at CeBIT, the big technology trade conference, which was being held in Hannover, Germany. "The co-CEO's appearance doesn't make an arrogant impression," read an article in the German publication *Wirtschafts-Woche*, titled "SAP's New Co-CEOs: Speaking Instead of Barking."

Our goal that evening had been to instill confidence and optimism in our leadership. If leaders do not themselves believe in their potential to succeed, how could anyone else? During the press dinner that SAP had hosted at Pier 51, a restaurant on the east bank of Maschsee Lake, we had mingled with reporters as they sipped wine and balanced appetizers. When we stood in front of the group, we committed to bringing new products to the market and returning SAP to double-digit sales growth. We hoped to make it a happy company again. But we offered no specifics. Not yet.

27

AIR COVER FOR THE TROOPS

It is time for a new generation of leadership to cope with new challenges and new opportunities, for there is a new world to be won.

—JOHN F. KENNEDY

A LOOK OF DISTRESS came across the faces of some of SAP's top leaders when they heard that, the next morning at eight o'clock, they would each have to explain the company's new strategy to a group of employees they had never met. It was mid-April 2010, and the company's top global leaders, about 250 people, had convened in Walldorf's cafeteria-turned-meeting-space—known as the canteen—so that Jim and I could introduce them to the company's new strategy. And now we were asking them to explain that strategy to others—tomorrow.

In the morning, the leaders would disperse in pairs throughout the building, where dozens of small groups of our Walldorf-based employees, from all departments, would gather for what we were calling "coffee corners." At each coffee corner, two senior leaders

261

would stand in front of the group and talk about SAP's new strategy, in their own words.

This assignment was risky. Rarely did people at SAP give extemporaneous presentations, especially about a topic they themselves had just heard about. But, as we also explained, our need to change course had urgency.

"SAP is in a weaker market position today than it was before the economic downturn," we had said. "While competitors shifted the playing field, SAP stagnated."

The global economic crisis had taken out many technology companies, but some competitors had recovered and were coming after us. With SAP's long-lucrative business model showing signs of fatigue, our defenses were weak. This truth hurt, but it had to be addressed.

CURIOSITY AND COURAGE

A leader's job is to provide air cover for the troops, and the first form of air cover is a bulletproof strategy.

The process of developing SAP's new strategy had been exciting. After years of executing other leaders' plans, I was finally in a position to influence directly which markets our organization entered, and how. I'd learned a lot observing from the wings.

A good strategy had to be easy to understand. Some people, I believed, confused complexity with a great strategy and equated volume with intelligence. The strategy for the delicatessen, for example, had been clear: provide exceptional customer service. A strategy also had to be true to an organization's core strength, which, too, was true at the deli.

Now SAP had a chance to rethink its own strategy, even reinvent its business model. But to do things differently, people have to see things differently. So SAP's executive team had asked ourselves some simple but telling questions.

First, *Do we matter?* Did SAP's core—our enterprise resource planning (ERP) systems, our business applications suite, and our analytics—still mean something in the marketplace?

Since 1972, SAP's core had been business software, and now, in April 2010, our software remained the central nervous system for thousands of organizations. Our solutions were used by thirty-five million people in twenty-four industries around the world. General Motors ran its entire supply chain on SAP. Bank of America relied on SAP to simplify its customer interactions. And Pepsi used SAP to manage its supply chain as well as its product promotions. We estimated that 65 percent of the world's transactions touched an SAP system in one form or another. What's more, hundreds of thousands of jobs made up SAP's ecosystem, from our own forty-seven thousand employees to the people who supported SAP systems at clients, partners, and vendors. Overall, business software installed at a client company's own location, or "on premise," was a $110 billion global market.

So to answer our first question, yes, SAP's core still mattered.

Next question: *Will the core matter tomorrow?* This answer was less rosy.

The $110 billion on-premise software market was slowing—growing only by single digits—which meant that SAP could not attain year-over-year double-digit growth by selling only our core product, or at least not in its current form. Even though I loved SAP's core, I did not want to be like some of Xerox's leaders back in the 1990s, who had trouble accepting that when markets change, so, too, must companies. Now I accepted that SAP products' present incarnation would not grow the company. We would continue to extend our core business, but we had to broaden our solutions.

If we wanted SAP to matter tomorrow, we had to add to our core, but without straying too far from it. We did not, for example, want to enter the consumer software market, competing with Microsoft. Nor was it wise for SAP to start selling hardware, competing with IBM or Hewlett-Packard.

The main thing, business software, had to stay the main thing. Therefore, we would continue to extend our leadership in the on-premise market by finding more opportunities, especially in industries and geographic markets with high growth rates, among smaller businesses, and by focusing on our most successful offerings.

To figure out which markets made sense for SAP, the next question we asked was the same one I had asked myself many years ago at the deli: *Who, exactly, are our customers? Who is our base?*

Back in April 2010, when our executive board listed its "10 firm beliefs," the very first item stated that SAP's current customer base of ninety-five thousand was one of its strongest assets. As always, everything had to revolve around the customer. And the customers were changing. Over the years, we had gone from selling software to back-office IT departments to selling to CIOs and chief technology officers, and then to CEOs. More and more, we were selling to the heads of lines of businesses, such as the vice president of human resources.

The number and type of employees that used our software had also expanded, from exclusively IT professionals to employees across disciplines; from executives in suits, to shop-floor workers in smocks, to interns in jeans. This larger user base had high standards for any technology it touched. Because more people used technology as part of their everyday lives, they expected every screen and device they interacted with, on the job or at home, to be as easy, attractive, and fun to use as, say, Facebook or Google.

For no segment of the population was usability more coveted than millennials, the approximately 1.6 billion individuals worldwide born between 1982 and 1993 and brought up in the digital age. By 2025, millennials would make up about 75 percent of the global workforce. The future success of any organization hinged on catering to the desires of this pool of employees and consumers—not at the expense of others, but millennials could not be ignored. Just like the teenagers that I wanted to frequent my deli, millennials deserved my respect.

Historically, SAP's software was not known for being user friendly but instead for its somewhat clunky interfaces. Going forward, we had to make our software easier for the consumer to use. I loved that this was how technology was evolving. Everything in my soul, and my inspiration as a leader, was based on having empathy for people.

Once we identified our base customers as everyone from executives to all possible end users of technology, we moved on to the next question in our quest for SAP's new strategy: *What do these customers want?*

In addition to enjoying their digital experiences, people wanted to engage with their work and with the world on any device they chose, from anywhere. Smartphones were like the Swiss Army knives of the global economy. And once I saw Apple's new iPad, before it was officially released in the spring of 2010, I could envision tablets becoming the new desktops. Mobility was disrupting the way business got done. Smartphone use alone would likely grow to include one-third of the world's population by 2017. For SAP, mobility expanded our current market of users, which meant that our software had to be compatible with multiple mobile devices. Mobility became a big idea for SAP.

What else do customers want?

Another change we observed within our base regarded software consumption, and the ways in which companies wanted to access the software that ran their companies. CEOs were still tightening their budgets, so few if any saw investing in more pieces of computer hardware as a strategic business decision. Buying ten new servers tomorrow to house more software would not improve the way a company operated. Software, however, was where business innovation happened. So instead of storing and maintaining software on their own computers, companies craved cheaper ways to access it.

Cloud computing allowed companies to use software stored on a vendor's own server—or in the cloud—and pay an ongoing subscription fee to use the software as a service. For SAP's client companies, purchasing software as a service from the cloud, or on demand, versus buying it and paying for it up front, was a compelling model.

Unfortunately, the attempts SAP had made to play in the on-demand marketplace had not gotten enough traction. The cloud business model was different from SAP's traditional one. Cloud's rent-versus-buy payment schedule meant that our revenue came in slower than we were used to, at least in the short term. This proposition was scary for some. But the more I observed the shifting marketplace, the more I believed that SAP had no choice but to lean into the cloud. If we ignored it, SAP would not matter tomorrow.

The executive board agreed that our company had to muscle its way into the cloud market fast. But it would not be enough for SAP to get into the cloud business; our cloud also had to be better than the competitors'.

The bottom line: companies large and small wanted choice—on premise or on demand, as well as on any device. If SAP did not give customers what they wanted in the form they wanted it, someone else would.

Asking such big, open-ended, if seemingly simple, questions can lead to big opportunities. Combined, these three markets—on-premise solutions, the cloud, mobile—gave SAP a much larger customer base to go after by doubling our addressable market from $110 billion to $220 billion.

Our strategy for SAP had become clear. By April 2010, we were ready to roll it out.

ANYTHING WORTH COMMUNICATING IS ALMOST ALWAYS UNDERCOMMUNICATED

Back in Walldorf, we had just immersed our top 250 leaders in our plan. First, we went through it in detail. Next, everyone divided into smaller groups to discuss what the new plan meant for them, as well as how their own business units and teams might execute. During dinner, we encouraged people to question Jim, me, and SAP's board members.

Jim and I got up onstage and role-modeled how to talk about the strategy. Neither of us had notes. We just tried to speak plainly. And although we each put the message in our own words, the main point we articulated was this:

SAP would focus on three areas: OnPremise (our core), OnDemand (cloud), and OnDevice (mobile). This doubled our addressable market and gave us an opportunity to ensure double-digit growth. By orchestrating and capitalizing on the nexus of these forces, SAP could become a €20 billion company by 2015, with 35 percent margins and one billion people touching our software in one way or another.

"We want to rewrite the headlines for 2015 together," I said. "We want SAP to begin right now on a journey to becoming the amazing growth company we know we are meant to be." Noted Jim, "We are lucky to be in an industry where the rules of the game change quickly. That gives us a great opportunity. But to take that opportunity, it is not enough to be big, we also need to move fast."

As the leaders geared up to put the strategy into their own words, their discomfort was palpable. SAP was a technology organization where many managers communicated through technology. Emails, texts, PowerPoint presentations. I had sat in board meetings and witnessed senior leaders read paragraphs, line by line, instead of talking to their peers around the table. That act could suck confidence out of a room. If leaders cannot trust themselves to hit the high notes *without* notes, how can others trust them?

As much as I loved technology, especially the mobile movement, an inescapable truth was that too many people were out of practice communicating with one another in person. There's no replacement for human interaction.

Before releasing leaders to their assigned coffee corners, we gave them permission to fail.

"It's okay not to have all the answers," we assured them. "The goal is for you to be prepared to go back to your offices and take your own teams through the strategy in a form that is easy for you to say and easy for them to digest and translate to their own constituents, so everybody knows what to do." The day's coffee corners would be a chance to self-correct before it really mattered.

Jim and I walked around SAP's offices separately, going floor to floor, observing coffee corners throughout the building. About half the gatherings we witnessed went incredibly well. We could hear excitement in people's voices as they explained how the market was changing and how SAP would change. We sensed the curiosity among employees as they sat up a little straighter in their chairs, or leaned forward to listen and ask questions.

As we expected, however, a few coffee corners were disasters. Some of our leaders, intelligent individuals, stumbled through explanations or did not sell it well. A handful did not even show up. Perhaps they did not buy into our plan, or maybe they were too nervous. But the few no-shows aside, the coffee corners made me very proud. It was important to break with history and let leaders loose without a script.

Later that morning, as we all gathered back in the canteen, leaders told us that by speaking with employees from different disciplines, they heard new perspectives. Listening to the feedback, we got wiser about how people throughout the organization might interpret the new strategy. The transparency of the exercise also reestablished some lost trust. Not because our leaders had all the answers about SAP's future but because we were sharing the thinking behind our journey, and thus involving people in the solution.

The biggest key, however, had been the opportunity for everyone to practice articulating the strategy. When a volcano in Iceland erupted during the summit, covering large swathes of European skies with ash, it shut down airspace and resulted in canceled flights for our people gathered in Walldorf. The result was two more days spent discussing and practicing. If ever there was a good time for our leaders to be stranded, that was the week. Ultimately, about 250 leaders returned to their home offices able to articulate SAP's new strategy more accurately and convincingly than they might have otherwise.

After the summit, it was time to summon the courage and execute.

SECOND FAMILY

The day SAP threw a picnic for its Walldorf employees and their children, the property surrounding our headquarters was transformed into a fairground with rides and animals and hay and color and, unfortunately, rain.

The beauty, however, was that no one seemed to care—twenty-two thousand people still showed up, including seven thousand kids—and many would stay until the early-morning hours. From a trailer, Jim and I served lemonade and beer. (Only after the event did someone inform me that, to each person who ordered a beer, I mistakenly served *Radler*: a local drink that mixed beer with Sprite. Out of kindness, no employee said a word to me; they all just enjoyed their beverages.) Later, when I walked around with Julie and the boys—careful not to slip on the mud—I shook hands and talked to people and met their families. All day, I experienced the same sweetness I had tasted back in 2002, and sensed a nervous excitement as people met the new co-chief.

The day of that picnic, and on most days, I felt supported by my colleagues—even when it rained, and when I watered down their beer.

28

TRUST IS STILL THE ULTIMATE CURRENCY

The secret to change is to focus all of your energy, not on fighting the old, but on building the new.

—DAN MILLMAN

BLOWN AWAY. THAT'S how I feel after checking out a new mobile application on my brand-new iPad as I sit in the backseat of a car, on my way to a trade show. Apple had not launched its tablet yet, but SAP already was jointly developing a new mobile customer relationship management (CRM) product with Sybase, a database and mobile technology company. A number of our customers, I'd been told, were already so impressed that they were placing orders. Now I know why. The look and feel of the interface on the screen is so beautiful, like nothing SAP has produced. Back in my door-to-door sales days, I would have loved this tool. Now it's what SAP needs, for itself and for customers.

I get on my phone to call Sybase's CEO, John Chen. We've known each other for years.

"John, it's Bill. Have you seen the prototype? Have you seen how good this thing is?" I am almost wiggling in my seat. John agrees that it's very special.

"John, we need to talk," I say. "SAP needs to have a closer relationship with Sybase."

"Sure, Bill. What do you have in mind?" he asks. "A joint marketing or sales agreement?"

"No, no, no. Closer than that."

"Okay, you want to resell it?"

"No. Closer." I hear John laugh lightly.

"Do you want SAP to invest in Sybase?" he asks.

"Nope. Closer than that." He becomes quiet. We both know there is only one step closer.

In executing our strategy, I had thought about where SAP could grow organically and where we could not. Breaking into the markets we had identified meant that we would have to look outside our own organization for certain expertise and infrastructure, as well as scale. A company such as Sybase had assets we did not, including a fantastic "unwired" technology platform that would allow SAP to more quickly move its existing software to mobile devices. We could continue to partner with Sybase, but that would not be enough. Too much was at stake, especially in mobile, where I believed SAP had to own the entire value chain, from innovation, to execution, to the consumer experience.

But for any merger or acquisition deal that SAP did, we had to trust the other company's leaders, not just love their technology. I needed to feel about them as my suppliers at the deli felt about me when they anted up free product to stock my empty shelves, trusting that I would pay them.

"There are times when dating is a great idea but times when getting married is even better," I tell John, about to present an idea that

I had discussed with Jim and SAP's board. "We should think about getting married. How would you feel if SAP bought Sybase?" I count silently to myself, *One one-thousand, two one-thousand . . .*

Finally, "John, are you there?"

"I am intrigued," he says, "but I am not there right now."

Sybase was not a company in play. It was doing well, generating cash, and a number of John's own initiatives were just taking off. I knew how much he enjoyed running his own organization, having turned Sybase from a loser into a winner since taking over in 1997. John also was a straight shooter and a pragmatist. I knew his personal history. Like mine, his family had faced its own struggles, and as a result, John faced life with a perpetual optimism as well as a strong work ethic.

"John, in all friendship and humility, this is a big, big play."

In addition to Sybase's unwired platform, it had a less obvious but equally valuable asset: 1,600 database engineers plus a database-savvy sales force. This population would help SAP ramp up in another market critical to our strategy: the database space. Sooner and faster than many people realized, SAP would have to scale its database expertise.

"Let me think about it, my friend," John says. "Let's talk after the quarter closes."

In April, after Sybase announced its strong quarter, I called John again. Eventually SAP presented Sybase with a purchase price, and John took the offer to his board of directors.

The deal needed to be done quickly and quietly. The only reason we could even fathom getting away with it was that John and I trusted each other. I trusted that no significant problems would crop up once the deal was done. In turn, John trusted that I would ensure SAP saw the deal through. The risk for Sybase was that if word got out it was being courted by SAP, it would go into play and have to entertain other offers, which could result in a drawn-out, uncertain period that could shake its customers' confidence and its employees' morale. And that in turn could affect Sybase's performance and its stock price. Entering into negotiations with us was not something John took lightly.

Nor was this a deal that SAP entered lightly. We had done only one multibillion-euro acquisition since the founding of the company. But I believed it was the right move, and we stood by it.

True to my word, SAP kept the pending deal as quiet as possible to prevent leaks. In early May, when global stock markets dropped, as did the euro, amid fears of Greece's contagious economic instability, people close to John speculated that SAP would lower its purchase price or walk away. We did neither, staying true to our original offer. And when John assured me that he would stay at SAP for at least two years to help us integrate Sybase and extract its full value, I trusted him to fulfill that commitment, even though he did not want to sign a standard employment contract.

On May 12, 2010, less than sixty days from the moment I first called John from the backseat of that car, SAP announced that it would buy Sybase for $5.8 billion.

The move got people's attention.

"There's some skepticism on the street," CNBC anchor Melissa Lee told me during a live TV interview after the news broke. "Is this a desperate move, as some Wall Street analysts have mentioned?" she asked.

"This is an exciting move!" I responded, smiling, and then explained why Sybase was a have-to-have asset for us.

"Hey, Mr. McDermott," another CNBC guest chimed in, "do you guys plan on other acquisitions? Is this the strategy going forward, to look for growth?"

"We are primarily an organic growth company," I said, "but the world is changing quite quickly." It was not the time to reveal what else we had in mind.

There would always be doubters claiming that this strategy or that tactic was unwise. But because I believed so strongly in where SAP was headed, and how we planned to get there, such noise did not cause me to question our plan. I was not deaf to the risks, but we were taking calculated risks—acquiring companies we trusted.

Bold moves unleashed naysayers, but bold moves were also necessary to capture imaginations. Bold moves pushed people to push themselves. Should SAP fail or make a mistake, I believed the world would be more forgiving—and I would be more forgiving of myself—than had we never attempted to be bold in the first place.

THE BEST PART OF ME

It's a Saturday night in October 2010, and Julie and I have just arrived at a neighbor's party when I feel compelled to leave and go see my mother. She and Dad are in Pennsylvania, staying at their condo nearby. When we arrive at my parents' place, Dad lets us in. He wants to know if everything is all right, and I say, "Yes, but I want to see Mom." He nods. He knows. I follow him into the bedroom.

"Hi, Mom," I whisper as she comes out of her sleep. She sees me and reaches for my hand, and for the next hour, we sit in the dark bedroom and talk. I tell her how well John and Michael are doing in school, and that next week I am going to New York City to give a speech at Radio City Music Hall for a business conference. We chat about Christmas. When we talk about how much fun we'll have seeing Tony Bennett perform in a few months, the thought of the show brings out her hopeful smile.

In the middle of the night, Mom has the clarity and the humor and the warmth of her greatest day. It's magic, because I know this day is far from her greatest. Three years earlier, my mother had been diagnosed with cancer. Amazingly, after undergoing major surgery as well as radiation and chemotherapy, my mother had been doing well, until these past few months. Now, as she returns to sleep, I place her hand on the bed.

The next day, Sunday, the clarity and ease from the previous night have faded. On Monday, Mom is having trouble breathing and is rushed to a downtown Philadelphia hospital. I am in my office when I get the call and tell Barb to cancel my afternoon appointments. Mom is in the emergency room when I arrive, and I am told she must wait here until a bed becomes available in the intensive care unit. I push aside the flimsy white curtain that separates her bed from others in the ER, and there she lies, a tube snaking out of her arm. Mom looks frail when she smiles. For the next eight hours, nurses sweep in and out, poking her with needles, taking blood, updating her chart until, finally that night, they wheel her into the ICU, where I sit by her bedside with my dad, my brother, Kevin, and my sister, Gennifer, as Mom dozes, in and out of sleep. I cannot fathom saying good-bye.

I look at my watch. In seven hours, I am scheduled to take the stage at Radio City Music Hall to speak to the theater full of businesspeople. My speech is sandwiched between a seven o'clock interview with a reporter from Bloomberg and a speech by former GE CEO Jack Welch. On a Philly street corner near the hospital, a car waits to whisk me the hundred miles to Manhattan.

"Mom, I'm not going." I mean it. I am not interested in leaving that hospital.

She insists I go.

Outside the ICU, I pace. On the first day of kindergarten, my mother dropped me off at the school, and I still remember how I climbed up onto the classroom's windowsill, inconsolable, clawing through the thick plastic blinds to look through the window and call her back. She returned for another hug. In elementary school, when I messed up on a test or felt down, coming home to my mom always lifted me up and out of my emotional muck. "Move on. You will get past it. You are still you." With her, the sky is forever blue and limit-less. For my entire life, my mother has turned piles of dirt into specks of dust; her presence has made everything that was already great—my wedding, the birth of my sons, promotions, holidays—even bet-ter. Just being next to her in the sterile ICU feels like home.

I think about the idling car on the street corner and about going on with the show because my mother taught me that the show goes on, even during the most difficult moments.

At one thirty in the morning, I slump into the waiting limo, and the driver heads to New York. We drive in silence. I shouldn't be here. I want to be sleeping on a chair outside the ICU. I want to be holding her hand even though she may not know. Instead, I arrive at a Manhattan hotel at three o'clock.

At three thirty, my phone rings. Dad says Mom has been intubated.

"I'm coming home," I say. I know she tried to resist the breathing tube. She never wanted any type of life support. Someone at the hos-pital must have talked her into the tube. "Dad, I'm coming back to the hospital."

"Bill, you know your mother wanted you to be on that stage and give that speech." *Yes, I know.* I wonder if she knows she is dying. I think she does know, and that's why she wants me anywhere but there, with her.

With no sleep I shower, dress, and a few hours later I show up at Radio City Music Hall to do my job so I can get back to my mother. I do not want special consideration from anybody, so I don't reveal my circumstances. At seven o'clock I answer a Bloomberg reporter's questions about SAP and technology and the economy. At seven thirty I make small talk backstage with Jack Welch and an editor from the *Wall Street Journal*. When I hear my name, I walk onstage and talk to a packed house about leadership and going after your dreams. By two in the afternoon, I am back where I want to be, by her bedside. She is no longer able to speak.

Three days later, on Saturday morning, the eighth of October, 2010, my mother passes on. This time, no matter how hard I claw at a window or call for her, she is not coming back. I have lost my mother much too early. She was only sixty-seven. I do believe, however, that the shadow of her smile will forever color my dreams and light my days. Still, the ensuing weeks drown me in a sadness I have never known.

TEAMWORK: PLAYER-COACHES

In the days following my mother's passing, Jim proved once again that he was the best business partner anyone could have asked for, as well as a true friend. In addition to his empathy and respect, he stepped up and covered for me at a global leadership-team meeting so that I could take a few days to be with my family. I did not stay away long, however, so as not to interrupt our momentum. Mom would have wanted me to get back to work.

The collaboration with Jim was working because nothing we had done since taking our jobs had been about us as individuals. We agreed to avoid jealousy and power plays and instead dedicate our energy to SAP's higher purpose. We even agreed to some explicit rules. We vowed to show each other respect in all of our interactions, even when the other was out of earshot. We promised not to let anyone come between us, or allow people to play one of us against the other. We agreed to honor each other's decisions, because there would be some we could not make together. We committed to speaking with candor to each other, and to discussing problems directly. And when we did debate—and there would be plenty of those debates—we would do it in private.

We found our groove. Although we collaborated on foundational issues such as strategy, Jim focused on improving product development and shortening our innovation cycles, and from his home base in Walldorf, he made sure that our operations were more disciplined and our people were happy. I focused on field operations, sales, marketing, customer service, our brand, the ecosystem. From my home base in Newtown Square, I made sure that our global customers were happy.

We bridged our geographic distance by maintaining one office of the CEO; my longtime chief of staff Rick Knowles now worked for both Jim and me, ensuring that our agendas and schedules were aligned. The two of us also erred toward overcommunicating. In the early days, we copied each other on emails and spoke daily, with Jim calling me when it was evening in Europe. We'd update each other and review the next day's agenda. Eventually we cut back to a call every Friday.

More productive than the scheduled calls, however, were our impromptu conversations, the FYI emails, the one-on-one dinners when we were in the same city. During these informal moments, we talked about business but also shared more personal issues. We were both parents—Jim's son and daughter were just a few years younger than John and Michael—trying to balance the demands of work with our desire to be home. In between business decisions, a deeper friendship blossomed.

SAP's culture was responding well to our shared authority, I believed, in large part because of the mutual respect we showed each other. Jim's more even-keel demeanor tempered my high-octane enthusiasm. All in all, the co-CEO model was ideal for this moment of SAP's evolution. The two of us were different in the ways that SAP needed us to be. But we were similar in the ways that mattered for two people to coexist, and colead: our shared commitment to communication, our respect for each other's differences, and our values.

A CAUSE

On a cool, sun-drenched day in Camden, New Jersey, dozens of children and adults were painting walls and putting up enormous green-

and-orange structures. They were building a playground, and among the volunteer crew were SAP employees and famed rock musician Jon Bon Jovi, clad in a leather jacket and red scarf. Jon's Soul Foundation assists communities in need around the United States.

"When we asked the kids to draw their ideal playground," Jon told the other volunteers, "they came up with a wide array of ideas, from a seesaw to a rocket ship. It was important for them to participate in the planning because that's the first step to envisioning dreams that can come true. I mean, if I didn't dream to one day strum a guitar on the world stage, who knows where I might have ended up."

It was only one playground, but one was enough for the kids at Rafael Cordero Molina School.

For a company the size and scale of SAP, the potential to make a positive difference on the world stage was greater than anything I had ever been in a position to effect. The executive team shared the belief that SAP had to become an even more responsible corporate citizen.

One of the first things we did was craft a broader vision: "Help the world run better and improve people's lives." The sentiment framed the benefits that our products already provided our corporate customers. Going forward, we would donate more of our software, talent, and resources to more schools, libraries, and charitable organizations. We would support other important causes. To help prevent and treat HIV and AIDS, tuberculosis, and malaria, SAP would provide technology as well as financial resources to (RED) and the Global Fund, working with (RED) founder and lead singer Bono of the band U2. After the disastrous 2010 earthquake in Haiti, SAP would partner with a local social business network to support the country's smallest and most-in-need entrepreneurs. And in America, we would donate money and technology to help preserve children's health and welfare.

But in light of the world's complex challenges, our assistance had to go beyond donating to full-on innovating. As SAP got into the mobile market, we had the potential to bring simplified versions of our business applications to remote corners of the world, places where mobile phones were the only technology people had. Mobile banking was already benefiting independent business owners in Third World countries. SAP could, and would, create a mobile app that, for one example, allowed a shop owner in rural South Africa to order products, like sacks of maize, from her cell phone, as opposed to closing her store for an entire day and paying for a taxi to drive her to the nearest town so she could visit her supplier, see how much maize was in stock, and then place her order. To further assist entrepreneurs in emerging markets, we would encourage our employees to take a "social sabbatical" and spend extended time away from their daily jobs to share their specific know-how with small-business owners.

Internally, we set targets to reduce the company's own direct and indirect carbon emissions and other heat-trapping gases by 51 percent by 2020; this would return SAP to its year-2000 levels. When we announced this goal, passionate employees throughout the company volunteered to help us deliver on it.

We also ramped up our community service efforts. In 2005 SAP had begun coordinating employee volunteer events in North America. Now, in 2010, an official Month of Service was a growing global event. Our hope was eventually to have employees spend more than a million volunteer hours each year in communities around the world, painting schools, tutoring children, helping entrepreneurs— doing whatever was needed. Like building a playground.

A cause is not a slogan or a motivational tool or a recruitment technique. It is a worthwhile reason to exist, and it comes with responsibilities that all corporations, regardless of location or industry, must respect. The entire executive board was committed to ensuring that SAP did not just benefit itself, its customers, and its shareholders, but also used its scale and its innovations to improve lives.

LOOKING BACK, LOOKING AHEAD

I viewed 2010 as a time of great joy and great sorrow. My mother's death was painful, yet I had a dream job. And SAP was performing.

In the fourth quarter of 2010, the company delivered more software sales than in any quarter of its thirty-eight-year history: about €1.5 billion. We weren't just closing big deals, we were also doing more volume. It helped, of course, that companies were emerging from their recessionary caves and investing in technology again. Plus, our product development cycles were speeding up. Our most exciting innovation was a secret project internally dubbed T-Rex. It had been delivered on time, in November 2010, to fifty trial customers, who loved it. In the years to come, T-Rex was going to be big for SAP. Like the company's previous innovations, T-Rex had the potential to change not only how organizations conducted business but also the business they conducted.

29

BIG IDEAS

The world of tomorrow belongs to the person who has the vision today.

—ROBERT H. SCHULLER

N 1963, WHEN I was two years old, my grandfather died. He was only forty-nine.

For all the blessings in my life, one of the great disappointments was that I never knew him. To honor his memory, my dad and I lobbied to ensure that he received his rightful place in the Naismith Memorial Basketball Hall of Fame. In 1988, when Bobby McDermott was inducted, my dad accepted on his behalf.

"My father's greatest asset was his competitive spirit," my dad, a carnation pinned to the lapel of his suit jacket, told a banquet room full of our family members and basketball luminaries. "Fans, players, coaches, teammates, and opponents—especially the opponents—remember him well. He never gave up. He gave it one hundred percent."

Behind my father's words was a powerful sentiment: the true

value of any sport was not winning, but the pleasure of watching great players in action. Living their dreams.

In 2013 the past collided with the present. I was participating on a panel at SAP's annual SAPPHIRE NOW conference, a huge event that brought together tens of thousands of our customers and partners in Orlando, Florida, each spring. Onstage I was flanked by three leaders I admired: Jed York, the strategic CEO and owner of the San Francisco 49ers football organization; Kevin Plank, the visionary founder and CEO of athletic apparel company Under Armour, on whose board I was proud to serve; and Adam Silver, the deputy commissioner and chief operating officer of the National Basketball Association, and soon to be the NBA's commissioner. Their organizations were also SAP clients, and they were at SAPPHIRE because each had a unique understanding of the intersection between athletics and technology.

Exercising my penchant for pageantry, I had a mock sports-anchor desk constructed onstage. I also had the host from CBS's *The NFL Today*, quick-witted anchor James Brown, moderating the panel. The setup, I hoped, would inject the tech-heavy conference with unexpected play, while showcasing SAP's newest products.

Before the panel got under way, though, Adam surprised me.

"Many of you may not know this, but Bill McDermott's grandfather was one of the greatest basketball players of all time." Then Adam stood up from his seat behind the mock anchor desk and handed me something small and flat. "Bill, I found in our archives one of the original trading cards of your grandfather." I couldn't believe it. There he was, Bobby McDermott, all five feet eleven inches of him. I was incredibly touched.

I had known Adam for a while now, and I appreciated that, like my father, he understood that the business of sport was not solely about creating winning teams but orchestrating amazing experiences for fans. When I first met with Adam and then–NBA com-

missioner David Stern, they had explained their problem. The NBA
had official stats going back to its earliest days of the league but a lot
of its data was inaccessible, even to the league's coaches and teams.
Many of the stats were inaccessible to fans. As basketball fans ourselves, David, Adam, and I knew this was a missed opportunity.

The NBA wanted its fans to engage with the statistics, whether
that fan was sitting in a stadium, on his living room couch, or logging
onto a digital device from the beach. SAP was not officially in the
sports industry, but we were about to be. Together the NBA and SAP
brainstormed, and our co-innovation yielded a big idea for the NBA.

Now, onstage, Adam explained that any fan could use any mobile device to access and crunch sixty-six years' worth of basketball
league data. Anytime. Anywhere. If my sons wanted to compare the
career statistics of Hall of Famers Chris Mullin and Dominique
Wilkins, all they had to do was to log onto NBA.com. Using technology to interact with its fans was a literal game changer for the
NBA, and indicative of another trend: where once technology had
been about supporting the business, now technology had *become* the
business.

"We want to empower the fans with software so they are bringing back to us new ways of using our own data," Adam said at
SAPPHIRE, another sentiment that echoed more truths from my
past.

EMPATHY AND ECOSYSTEMS

The next morning, on day two of SAPPHIRE, the rock band
Queen's lyrics to "We Will Rock You" blast through the main exhi-
bition floor of Orlando's Orange County Convention Center. The
enormous space is black except for spotlights that dance across the
seated business audience. The pumping music belies the nine o'clock
hour as people balance cups of coffee and laptops, and then clap as

SAP's cofounder and chairman, Hasso Plattner, walks out onstage in a gray suit and silver tie. Hasso, more professor than performer, begins his speech by getting straight to the punch line.

"After four years of preaching HANA, I think we have reached a relative climax. It is not about HANA anymore, it is about the applications on HANA."

Sitting in the front row, two years into our roles as co-CEOs and with eleven quarters of consecutive double-digit software revenue growth in our wake, Jim and I know that Hasso is about to discuss SAP's own game changer: that innovation once known internally as T-Rex.

Hasso had spearheaded the development of a revolutionary new data analytics platform in collaboration with a posse of PhD students attending the Hasso Plattner Institute, in Potsdam, Germany; SAP's highly respected chief technology officer, Dr. Vishal Sikka; and SAP's own brilliant engineers. The technology, called High-Performance Analytic Appliance, or HANA for short, stored and crunched tremendous amounts of data in a computer's main memory, or "in-memory," which could be accessed as much as ten thousand times faster than data residing on traditional disc-based systems.

HANA was another game changer. Every eighteen months, the amount of data in the world had been more than doubling thanks to the proliferation of devices that collected it. From supermarket cash registers, to radiofrequency tags on clothing, to traffic-light sensors, to internet sites, companies were amassing more information than ever about consumers, about their own customers, about their own operations. The glut was overwhelming many of SAP's own corporate customers, and mounds of "dark data" were going untapped. With HANA, SAP would become a more formidable force in the database business. And because HANA also ran in the cloud, it would help distinguish SAP's on-demand offering, which was critical to our new strategy.

HANA was more than software, however. It was a platform on which SAP's own software could run, as well as new applications built by third parties or even competitors. As an innovation that bred more innovation, HANA was capturing imaginations. More than 450 start-up companies, funded in part by SAP, as well as multibillion-dollar corporations, were building new applications exclusively for HANA. One app did human genome analysis in real time. Another alerted drivers about nearby services, store offers— even parking spaces—near their car's location at any given moment.

I had long understood the power of ecosystems to grow a business. From my deli's suppliers to those secretaries and doormen that eased my entrance into Midtown Manhattan's offices, supporting characters were as important as main customers. For comparison, HANA's ecosystem of developers was similar in power to those who provided the hundreds of thousands of products that populated Apple's App Store; SAP's developer ecosystem, from start-ups to big companies, could make HANA bigger than SAP could make it. Ecosystems were co-innovation on steroids.

Customer-centricity was a driving force behind HANA's creation. Its development teams followed a popular problem-solving framework called design thinking. Empathy was at the heart of design thinking's approach, which dictated that creators of any product, technological or otherwise, answer yes to three sets of questions to determine if an idea was worth pursuing:

Is the idea desirable? Do people want it?
Is it feasible? Could it be built to work?
Is the idea viable as a business? Will people pay for it?

If all three questions could be answered in the affirmative, as HANA was, then an invention could be more than an idea. It could be a product, and a company's big idea.

"Did you have fun?" Hasso asks the twelve PhD students that he invited onto SAPPHIRE's main stage to take a bow for their work. "Did you have fun building these applications?"

How could anyone not appreciate Hasso's enthusiasm? The man I first met after playing fetch with his dog was no different from the man I knew today: sincere, curious, passionate.

Most people, myself included, are not inventors. I respect those who are. I marvel at how their minds work. Although I do not write code or engineer software, I love to envision how the technology that others create can win customers and grow a business. I may never come up with the next amazing mousetrap, but I'm able to see where markets are moving, and I'm addicted to the challenge of building a winning culture and a growing company that can sell millions of mousetraps, and the traps after that, and the traps after that.

In every job I ever held, I stood on the shoulders of giants. Without others' innovations, I had no ideas to package, no teams to inspire. No way to win. Companies need inventors of products *and* builders of businesses—and we need each other.

30

THE WORK OF DREAMS

*If one advances confidently in the direction of his
dreams, and endeavors to live the life which he has
imagined, he will meet with success unexpected in
common hours.*

—HENRY DAVID THOREAU

EVERYTHING THAT I experienced in my life started with a winning dream.

A winning dream is an ideal state that people imagine for themselves. A goal so magnificent that the passion for that dream gets into their hearts, giving them the self-confidence to believe that not only can they achieve their goals, but also that they must achieve them, whatever the obstacles. Lack of money. An untraditional pedigree. Corporate hierarchies. A losing history. A bad economy. Disease, death, doubt. None of these hurdles had halted my own winning dream. If anything, obstacles fueled my desire.

A leader's role, however, is not just to dream but to architect dreams into reality.

After all the envisioning and motivational talk, leaders have to plant their feet on the ground and get to work, executing with precision. If dreaming requires optimism, audacity, and empathy, bringing dreams to life is a more concrete endeavor, demanding hard work, discipline, teamwork, communication, and courage.

HARD WORK: THE 24/7 PROFESSIONAL

Many of my work habits had not changed much over the years. I was as hungry and as hardworking as ever. I still stressed the importance of selling value versus products, I still liked to be in the field, and I monitored SAP's sales pipelines daily, although now I did so from my iPad. SAP was now running its business on HANA, so I could access any information I needed from my tablet as I traveled the world. I continued to demand the sales process be disciplined and measured, and I stuck to my own repeatable methodologies, scaling what worked well versus reinventing.

And I still believed that victories should be celebrated. SAP's annual Winners' Circle had become a sought-after event that inspired thousands of our sales professionals to achieve miracles on behalf of the entire organization.

Every week, I worked the equivalent of 24/7, but still tried to be home on weekends. But even on Saturdays and Sundays, I answered most emails within minutes, although now I was also texting, and I answered those pretty fast, too.

Most of my weekdays were wall-to-wall appointments. In one day at SAP's SAPPHIRE conference, for example, I hopped from the sports-desk panel to a room full of seventeen Asian journalists, whom I spoke to through an interpreter; and then skipped to a live press conference; and then jumped to a private room where, for two hours, appointments paraded in and out, each with its own agenda. When an Australian analyst asked me why Jim and I worked together so well, I told him it was because we nurtured a culture of trust. "No trust, no conversation. That's why cultures eat strategies for breakfast." He scribbled my answer in his notebook. When one of SAP's clients arrived to inform me that his implementation was going too slowly, I listened and then responded, "I'm not interested in who is wrong, only how we can get it right. What can I do?" He said SAP's project manager was being "too nice" and needed to hold the client more accountable for deadlines. I turned to Barb and asked her to send emails to the appropriate people. "Done," I assured the client, who left content. Next, a half dozen tech industry analysts filed in and unfolded their laptops, and for the next thirty minutes click-clacked away as I answered their questions. One wanted to know how SAP was keeping its talent from fleeing. "People don't quit companies, they quit managers," I replied. "And I have a low tolerance for managers that do not treat their people well." Another inquired how SAP planned to beat all the nimble start-ups flocking to the cloud. I leaned forward and almost whispered, "Co-innovation."

"What about the core?" another analyst demanded to know.

"We're still the only ones who do what we do, the way we do it," I responded. "And don't worry, we're making preemptive moves to protect the house," I added, alluding to the possibility of more acquisitions. Their time up, the analyst herd packed its laptops and left to write its reports, and I left to return to my hotel room to get ready for the evening's entertainment.

For all my consistencies, however, I had honed my ability to adjust my style so it fit different cultures and environments, which I had come to more fully appreciate. I had grown into the job. SAP's own operating model balanced power across internal and external boards—unlike the command-and-control approach common in the United States. This also had given me more appreciation for what I called my "abundance mentality," which was the notion that every individual at a table has something meaningful to contribute. Wise leaders absorbed insights from colleagues, ensuring that their organizations benefited from a team's cross-functional skill set.

Leadership, I also had come to believe, was not about providing all the answers but about looking for and presenting the next questions.

SELLING TO BUY

As I was led through SuccessFactors's glass-walled office space in Silicon Valley, I spotted the company's founder, Lars Dalgaard, and smiled. Lars smiled back. He was a smart entrepreneur with a hard-driving reputation, and probably had a hunch why one of his competitors was here, even though I had not told Lars that I had scheduled this meeting to decide if SAP wanted to buy his cloud-based HR software company.

Increasing SAP's top-line growth and expanding into new markets was always a question of whether to grow organically or through mergers and acquisitions. More and more, it was becoming clear that as the cloud became part of SAP's new DNA, much of that DNA had to be acquired. During the past two years, Jim and I had broken SAP out of its organic-only growth mentality, and added to its arsenal several companies whose technology, market position, and talent could push SAP forward in ways we could not do fast enough or well enough ourselves. As with Sybase, we did not acquire companies for their revenue or for their profits but for their DNA, because it either matched or needed to replace ours. Not everyone at SAP agreed with our approach, and with each acquisition I had to convince various people inside the company that it was the right move.

Lars and I sat down in a conference room, and an amiable conversation got under way. I found him charismatic, and as unapologetically honest as his glass office space. Within a few minutes, I became convinced that a marriage would be right for both companies. But Lars, I had a hunch, would not be interested in selling.

When I eventually broached the possibility, I heard Lars's concerns. SuccessFactors was his entrepreneurial labor of love. SAP, I promised, would not erase his company's identity and culture. Like Sybase, SuccessFactors could join SAP and run semiautonomously, and leave its brand intact. I also told Lars that we wanted him to hasten SAP's entrance into the cloud market.

"You can have the keys to the Ferrari," I told him. "You take it, you drive it, you park it."

"I'm confused," he said. "I already have the keys." As chief of his own company, Lars certainly did. We discussed how SAP could put him on a faster highway.

Once again SAP shocked the markets, this time by acquiring SuccessFactors for $3.4 billion. We were not buying the company to wipe out our competition or absorb its margins but to create a cloud powerhouse in a lucrative human-capital line of business. As I told *Fortune* magazine, "What we try to do is buy 'crown jewel assets' that have attributes that either in their own right or in combination with SAP allow us to lead in a category."

We did this again when we bought Ariba for $4.3 billion. Ariba was a cloud-based business network that connected 730,000 suppliers with millions of potential buyers; a sophisticated marketplace with the same potential as social networks to connect and foster relationships. Ariba added tremendous value, while expanding us into other markets. Plus, I had known Ariba's CEO, Bob Calderoni, for more than a decade. The trust box was checked.

All of my deals were first sealed with people, not paper. Trust was the glue. Most of the leaders whose companies SAP wanted to acquire were not ready to sell. As I spoke with them, I listened and moved with each company's rhythms. And like a courteous dancer, I was careful not step on any toes with SAP's own intentions. I could be persuasive and persistent, but I also wanted leaders of any company we bought to come to their own decisions. Entrepreneurs have deep emotional attachments to their organizations, and I respected that.

The second time I met Switzerland-based Hybris's CEO, Ariel Luedi, and Carsten Thoma, its president, chief operating officer, and cofounder, was after they arrived in Philadelphia following a grueling sixteen-hour, storm-delayed journey from Munich that included a train, a plane, a helicopter, and a car. When they arrived at the restaurant where we were scheduled to meet three hours earlier, I was still there, waiting, with SAP's head of mergers and acquisitions, Arlen Shenkman. When Ariel and Carsten finally walked through the door, they were the exhausted ones.

"Ariel! Carsten!" I greeted them. "Please, relax. I am sorry your journey was so difficult. Let's get you a drink and a wonderful meal."

The stress of their trip subsided, and we enjoyed the evening. Carsten was a sports fanatic, and we talked soccer and basketball. Teamwork and loyalty were important to him, an intrinsic part of his company's culture. Ariel discussed their interest in taking Hybris public in a few months, and his excitement about this possibility was palpable. Who was I to hold them back? But I, too, was honest about my intentions. I wanted to leave no doubt how valuable their company was to SAP. Hybris's multichannel software helped companies interact with consumers via all the shopping channels available today: online, in-store, on any device, on TV, and others. This "omnichannel" approach was the perfect fit to push SAP from a business-to-business company to a business-to-business-*to-consumer* mentality.

"Of course, you must do what your hearts tell you," I said. "But even if you become a successful public company, I will not give up!"

Then I shared with them some ideas for how to structure a transaction to preserve the integrity of the company they had built.

By the fall of 2013, when SAP acquired Hybris, Carsten, Ariel, and Hybris's employees became part of SAP's family.

I understood that the nature of entrepreneurs would mean that many of the CEOs whose companies SAP acquired would not stay at SAP forever. So while I hoped that leaders would stick around, I expected they would eventually be enticed by more entrepreneurial opportunities. During the years we worked together, I intended to tap as much of their talent as would benefit SAP in the short term and long term.

What's more, the markets needed to see SAP making these types of bold moves. History was rife with companies that did not get the memo to redefine themselves, organically or otherwise. As co-CEOs, Jim's and my role was to sell the right companies on selling to SAP.

NO ONE THING

Although mergers and acquisitions were essential to the new strategy's success, no single tactic or area of the company could be credited with transforming SAP. Sales and development were fueling each other. Our twenty-thousand-person development organization was innovating faster than ever, thanks in large part to Jim's efforts to reduce the time it took to bring new solutions to market and increase overall efficiency, and Vishal's innovating breakthroughs, especially with HANA.

Revenue was coming from multiple sources. We had repackaged some of our standard software into specific, simplified solutions that were easier to sell and easier to deploy and faster to return value. Especially in recessionary times, customers ate these up. In addition to our core on-premise ERP systems and HANA, we also were making and selling software that powered other companies' software. Our ecosystem, too, was proving its power; the partner companies that had soured on us years back were now the source of more than one-third of our revenue, almost double the rate they delivered in 2009. Most importantly for the new business model, SAP's huge software support organization, whose experts maintained our technology and customer relationships after the sale, was itself transitioning, providing customer service at levels higher than in the past, and driving revenue.

We were also expanding our reach. SAP plowed into emerging markets, making bets in China, Russia, and the Middle East. We engaged new industries where SAP had not had a significant presence, mainly banking, health care, sports, and entertainment. What's more, SAP was becoming a more recognized brand on the global stage.

Our shift from a business-to-business brand into a business-to-business-to-consumer brand was imperative. The popularity of cloud-based technologies and mobile devices meant that more non-IT professionals were in positions to purchase technology products. From heads of HR to heads of smaller sales departments, this new customer base needed to be familiar with, and trust, the SAP name.

I pushed to amplify our brand's recognition outside its home continent. I was especially thrilled that sports had become the twenty-fifth industry SAP entered. Now we had professional teams, leagues, and venues as customers. Even more importantly, we had fans! Our core ERP products helped sports organizations improve operations for ticketing, concession sales, and even athlete recruitment. More exciting, however, our mobile and analytic apps were being used and seen by millions of cheering fans. And by advertising during championship events such as the Super Bowl and at world-class venues such as Madison Square Garden, SAP was getting in front of more eyes than ever.

Becoming more familiar to end consumers and not just IT professionals also meant that SAP had to have a higher profile in the world's most popular urban areas, cities where decision makers as well as talented young people worked. We were a global brand. How we showed up around the world mattered.

In Manhattan, a city where brand names stood as tall as sky-scrapers, SAP had long maintained quiet, loft-like office space in Greenwich Village. The place was comfy, but its low profile diminished SAP's global status. It was time to move uptown.

In 2012 I toured the still-under-construction Hudson Yards, a massive twenty-eight-acre real estate development project reshaping midtown's West Side. Walking around, I envisioned what its prescient developer, Steve Ross, did: a dynamic city within an already amazing city where millions of people would flood to eat, shop, play, and work. Convinced that SAP needed to be part of this new New York, I shook Steve Ross's hand and committed SAP as a tenant. One of Hudson Yards's first. In April 2013 SAP signed a lease for the top floors of the development's stunning South Tower. Our new domicile would help us attract the talent and the attention the brand had come to deserve.

For many reasons, SAP had earned the right to change the perception of our brand because we were reframing our mission as a company, what we were capable of doing, and for whom. "SAP has got its mojo back," an analyst from Morgan Stanley had declared. "Under co-CEOs Jim Snabe and Bill McDermott, with the influence of Hasso Plattner, SAP has rediscovered innovation." Our products, our customers, our markets were evolving SAP into the kind of growth company that Jim and I started to envision when we first came together.

AN END AND A NEW BEGINNING

Almost four thousand miles from Manhattan, in the gravel court-yard of the Europäischer Hof restaurant on the banks of Heidelberg's Neckar River, Jim and I sat at a small round table under a white umbrella. It was a warm evening, closing in on midnight. We had spent the past several hours laughing and recapping moments from the past three and a half years.

Once our meal was cleared off the table, our waiter emerged from the kitchen with a congratulations dessert plate for Jim. Tonight the two of us were celebrating a fantastic run as co-CEOs, although it was coming to an end. Next year, in May 2014, Jim would step down to embark on the next phase of his career. Ridiculous rumors that he had been pushed out or that there was friction between us were not true. Jim had made the personal decision to leave the co-CEO role. After more than twenty years with SAP, he wanted to expand his impact beyond the IT industry and spend more time with his family while his children were still at home.

Jim's move was bittersweet for each of us. I was losing a day-to-day partner, and he was ceding day-to-day oversight of the company.

"Bill," he told me over our empty dessert plates, "the only reservation I have about my decision is leaving you." In no way did I feel as if Jim were abandoning me or SAP. Our years together had taught me so much and put SAP on a new path.

Indeed, he was leaving at a moment of strength. The industry transformation we had predicted and planned for was happening at full speed, and SAP was prepared for it. Our revenues and profits were growing, and perhaps most gratifying for each of us, we had earned the trust of SAP's people. In 2013 a report from Glassdoor, a career website that collected millions of company reviews, ranked the fifty highest-rated CEOs in the tech sector, from Amazon to Xerox, based on employee feedback. SAP was one of only two companies where the CEO (or in SAP's case, CEOs) received a 100 percent approval rating.

But new challenges lay ahead. I knew SAP's strategy would soon require another reboot. The market would demand it. But I felt ready, and had ideas percolating.

Thankfully, Jim was not retiring. Nor was he leaving SAP. He would exit the executive board but become an elected member of SAP's supervisory board. The company and I would still have access to his expertise and guidance. But it was important for me that he never second-guess his choice, even though his departure had been announced.

"Jim, there is no law that says you can't change your mind. So if it's in your heart not to go through with this, I'll be the first one to stand arm in arm with you to reverse this course." Jim felt confident that, come May of next year, the time would be right. Already he had accomplished what we'd set out to achieve.

Jim and I had come into the office of co-CEO when the company was in a state of chaos. Working together, we found clarity amid clutter, and we had changed minds and rallied an entire ecosystem around a winning strategy, inspiring people to go into markets that others assumed impossible for SAP to tackle. The company's spirit and market leadership were reviving because we all made bold choices and bold moves—and those had made all the difference in the world.

LEGACY

The true measure of a leader is not only what you accomplish while in office but also the feelings and memories that linger once you leave. To affect others' lives so profoundly—because people trusted you, respected you, were inspired by you, learned from you, felt emboldened by you to achieve magnificent outcomes—is to be a leader of consequence.

Back in February 2011, when I heard that Xerox's former chief and one of my professional heroes, David Kearns, had passed away, I had flown across the country to be in Rochester, New York, for his funeral. At the wake, I was among the first people in the door after his family. I was there because, from the moment I first read about David, I admired his integrity and commitment to excellence. I was there because when I called David from the New York City pay phone to apologize for having offended that angry executive who happened to be his neighbor, he told me to keep doing what I was doing. I was there because, in 2003, when a profile of me that appeared in *USA Today* mentioned that David Kearns was one of my role models, David, then blind from cancer, called me after his caretaker had read him the article, and thanked *me* for never forgetting *him*. Unbelievable.

I had gone to Rochester to pay my respects to a rare leader whose humility and courage resonated with me two decades after he left office. Every day, even under stress or when I was disappointed, I strived to make a difference in people's lives as David had made a difference in mine.

Numbers were one way to track whether leaders succeed. But sales growth, stock prices, and earnings per share never told the real story, or the most important one. More valuable for me were emails like the one I received on May 6, 2013, from Sean McGee, one of the hotshot Xerox trainees I had convinced to join my first sales team back in 1987, Team F. Sean went on to work for Xerox until 1995, when he left to join a financial services firm. We had not spoken in years.

> *Dear Bill,*
>
> *I am at a point in my Wall Street career where I realize that it's time for me to move on. I no longer have a passion for doing what I'm doing. Deciding that you've lost your passion for something is the easy part, figuring out what you want to do in place of that takes some introspection. What I have realized throughout this process is that I have an intense desire to be part of a winning team again. I am at my best and I am most valuable to my teammates when I'm work-*

ing with a team whose mission and most importantly whose leaders and players I believe in.

    Bill, you know me. I would be doing my training from Team F a disservice if I didn't ask you for the order. So, while it may seem a bit unusual because I can't be sure what specific role I can play, I know that given your leadership, I will add value. Bill, I'm asking for an opportunity to come to SAP and put my skills and experience to work for your organization.

    I respect the fact that you are extremely busy. I am available to discuss this further at any time.

All the best,
Sean

With Sean's words, I went back in time to 1987, when I asked a Xerox district manager to please give me a shot at being a sales manager. She did, and a few weeks later, as I recruited my team, I had asked Sean to give Team F a shot. He'd agreed, and his work ethic and talent helped propel Team F to number one. Now, even as SAP's co-CEO, it was not my place to hire Sean into a senior position at the company. But I could give him a shot. I put him in touch with SAP's HR department.

In August Sean emailed me to say that he had received an offer as an account manager in SAP's financial services business. He had accepted. "I have a great deal to learn," Sean wrote to me, "but I can't wait to have an impact. I thank you for the opportunity and your friendship."

If I still had a bell in my office, I would have walked over and rung it.

31

THE JOURNEY

The cause endures, the hope still lives, and the dream
shall never die.

—SENATOR EDWARD "TED" KENNEDY

THE DAY BEGAN in the dark.

At five thirty on a chilly February morning in 2014, four members of my staff and I left our quaint hotel in Heidelberg and were driving south to SAP's Walldorf headquarters. As early-morning commuters' headlights sped past us on Bundesautobahn 5, we huddled in the backseats of the SUV, reviewing the final draft of the company's earnings script, which documented SAP's performance throughout 2013.

As SAP's fourth consecutive year with double-digit revenue growth, 2013 had been a validating period. We were shifting to the cloud and growing the core. SAP now had 35 million cloud users, while HANA had amassed more than 3,000 customers, including companies such as Levi Strauss, Pepsi, and Bosch and Siemens.

HANA's ecosystem had grown to include 1,200 start-ups building their own solutions on the platform.

What's more, with a market capitalization of about $92 billion at the beginning of 2014, SAP's valuation had grown 75 percent in the four years since Jim and I were named co-chiefs. Also since that time, SAP's total revenue was up 57 percent, from €10.7 billion at the end of 2009 to €16.8 billion in 2013.

Feeling confident that SAP was on track to surpass our €20 billion revenue goal by 2015, we recast our growth target to €22 billion by 2017.

The only delicate news was that our margins were not growing at the rate we aspired to hit. As a result, SAP's executive board decided to extend our 35 percent margin target until 2017. The short-sighted markets might interpret this move as a miss, but the board and I knew our transition to the cloud required urgency as well as patience; it just needed to take its course, and once it did, *pow*. We stood by our strategy that day. If leaders flinched with every hiccup, so would everyone else.

By ten o'clock that morning, the live press conference got under way.

"We're proud of our track record," I said at one point, "but more importantly, I think we're significantly excited by the courage it takes to change when you're strong and to really go for something that you believe in. And that's where we're at now. We think it's time to take our strategy to the next level."

THE POWER OF SIMPLICITY

Even a great strategy can always be better. Like tectonic plates beneath the earth's surface, the business world shifts. Sometimes these shifts are incremental; other times a major move changes everything, seemingly overnight. This pace of change is humbling for any executive; no company can ever declare absolute victory. Every quarter, I was reminded, and I reminded others, that winning was a process, not a destination. Victory, a state of mind. SAP always had to be looking for new ideas, adapting, winning, and, the next day, looking again.

On days that SAP announced earnings, we looked back and forward at the same time. Today every hour of mine was scheduled, from meetings with analysts to interviews with journalists, and eventually for a gathering of SAP's employees. There was barely time to refuel. At three thirty, I did have time for a quick bite and ripped open a small container of Joghurt mit der Ecke, a popular German snack. I had a few spoonfuls before heading to the company's all-hands meeting in the canteen. In front of at least one thousand employees seated in rows of red and black chairs, and thousands more tuning in online, I took my seat next to Jim on a low platform, excited.

Leaders came in many forms, but I had long believed that they shared two undeniable traits. First, they brought others to places no one had ever been. Second, leaders had followers. Basic, but without a vision and without support, there was no leadership, only words. Not only did I desire that support, but SAP's newest strategy would demand it. As one financial analyst firm would observe accurately: "SAP's 2017 plan is well laid out—Now comes the hard part: Execution." They were right. The innovate-strategize-execute cycle never ended.

To start the all-hands meeting, my new chief of staff, Alex Atzberger, a longtime SAP employee whose interpersonal skills equaled his business acumen, spoke.

"I personally like the first all-hands of the year the most because we do two things," Alex told his colleagues. "First, we look at the scorecard of how we did in the past year, but we also think about the future and where we are going."

Jim, in his final all-hands as co-chief, talked first. "You will all remember that in 2010 we made some big bets. The dream became reality not because of the strategy itself but for the hard work that each of you did, the trust that this was the right strategy, and your willingness to team up." After Jim reviewed the past, I talked about the future.

"Jim was right giving you all the credit; you deserve it," I said. "And as much as it's in my DNA to want to keep celebrating, I have to bring it down to a more sober level now, because this is not just about celebration, it's about the reinvention of SAP. The world," I went on, "is littered with a lot of companies that, when they were strong, decided not to change. We're not going to be one of those companies."

From the deli to SAP, a business strategy had always evolved out of my own curiosity about what was next. Even as my teams executed one plan, I was in a constant state of observing the shifting markets, listening to customers, analyzing my own organization, talking with colleagues, and connecting the dots until the next strategic play came together in my mind.

For several months now, a single word had been in the forefront of my thoughts: *simplicity*. It was a deceptively big idea.

Whether I knew it or not, I had always embraced simplicity as a leader. Not because I feared or could not grasp complexity, but because it was so easy for other people to walk away from complexity. If leaders wanted their teams to follow their plans and to execute, their vision had to be so clear, so succinct, and so resonant that anyone could get it.

Too often, businesspeople took refuge in large words and dense language, believing that doing so made them appear smart, or smarter. I never bought into that. Simplicity was not about being small, simpleminded, or easy. On the contrary, simplicity was sophistication in disguise. Simplicity prioritized. Simplified ideas invited everyone in and freed people to see the world from a sharper but shared lens.

Complexity, on the other hand, could intimidate and confuse. Tangled language and multilayered strategies gave way to a briar patch of indecision. Arguing pros and cons was important, and could be enjoyable, as long as doing so did not overcomplicate the issues. In business, endless discussion could kill a company; healthy debate birthed action.

Through my conversations with Hasso, I knew that he, too, was a strong believer in the power of simplicity, particularly when it came to innovation. "If you cannot articulate in a simplistic form your real purpose and intention," he had said, "you will have difficulties developing something meaningful and efficient." This same philosophy, I believed, applied to building and growing any organization.

Going forward, SAP had to embrace simplicity on a few levels.

First, by how it operated internally. "Things at SAP are too complex, too hard," I announced in the canteen. This was not news to anyone. Inefficient internal processes were one of the top complaints on our latest employee survey. We were all responsible for fixing this. "You will be rewarded—in fact, you will be applauded and promoted—if you can help us simplify SAP. Don't feel like you need management to come up with a program; every little step matters." None of us should walk past a problem.

Second, SAP needed to sell simplicity to our customers, because that's what our customers wanted. "CEOs around the world want to get complexity out of their organizations so they can grow," I said. "They feel trapped. They've got fragmented hardware and applications everywhere. We've got to simplify how we give our customers our innovation and our technology. Leaders," I added, "remove complexity, and it's our time to lead."

This was why focusing on HANA and the cloud made so much sense for SAP now. The software behind HANA made accessing information easier. Delivering HANA via the cloud could eliminate the swamp of technological infrastructure that was overwhelming so many companies.

"Our future, ladies and gentlemen, could not be any clearer: we have to be *the* cloud company, powered by HANA."

Transitioning SAP into this new business model continued to be a daunting proposition. The vision and messaging around it could not be. Eventually, I realized that simplicity *was* the vision.

"We have to simplify everything, so our customers can do anything," became my new refrain. "Run simple" became the vision for SAP and our entire ecosystem:

Run simple
For employees to live by.
For customers to demand.
For developers to embrace.
For partners to adopt.
For influencers to amplify.
For investors to value.

Run simple had the power to change minds.

NEW NEIGHBORS

Finally, it was time for my favorite part of the all-hands meeting: questions. For the next half hour, we fielded queries from people in Walldorf as well as those listening and watching online. Nothing was screened. People asked about what the executive board was doing to ensure the quality of HANA; how we planned to accelerate diversity and inclusion when it came to recruiting talent; and the effect of our growing cloud business on our all-important software support organization. Jim and I spoke with candor.

Then, toward the front of the room, a gentleman wearing glasses and a green sweater over a blue and green checkered shirt stood up. Smiling, he introduced himself as Uwe Riegler and directed his question to me.

"I've been with SAP Germany for twenty-one years, and I'm from Heidelberg, so welcome to Heidelberg," he said, referring to my impending move; Julie and I were house hunting. "Here in Heidelberg, we love growth. Maybe you can share your views on growth in two areas particularly: growth regarding the age of SAP employees, and your views on growth regarding money that goes to employees, like double-digit growth."

I loved this question. It was direct, bold, and important. In addition to his words, however, what also resonated with me was his colleagues' reaction: applause and approving laughter. This was the first time people had laughed since the meeting began. It was as if everyone relaxed. The room was now full of people, not employees.

"First of all," I responded, "not just because you're my new neighbor but because you're my kind of guy, I formally invite you over to my house for breakfast or lunch or dinner when I come to town. Is that acceptable?" He nodded, and his colleagues clapped again, more than a little surprised. "I'll tell you a little story about my philosophy on the age thing. First of all, Hasso Plattner turns seventy today; does anybody know a younger man? I don't. He has as much energy as my seventeen-year-old son." Then I recalled something Frank Sinatra once said about age; that it was just a number. "And I don't care if you're seventeen or seventy. If you're a winner, if you stay intellectually curious and you execute and give everything you have to your work every day, we want you here at SAP."

Next, I told a story. Not long ago, the lead board member of Under Armour, on whose board I was a director, turned seventy-five, which was the maximum age a board member could be, according to that company's policy.

"As the chairman of Under Armour's governance and nominating committee," I said, "it was my duty to either change the policy or find a new board for him to go to. But he is fabulous. We wouldn't want to go on without him. So we changed the policy. That's how I feel about age when it comes to talent."

As for the question about employee bonuses, I explained that the executive board works hard to safeguard employee bonuses, so when the company does well, the employees also do well.

"I'm going to close on this thought about the wallets of the employees," I said. "With the innovation cycle we have now and with the commitment of sixty-seven thousand passionate people, is it possible to do better next year? Yes, it's in our control. But everybody's got to want it equally. Then you will see a double-digit gain in your wallet. I swear, nothing would make me happier: then *you* can buy *me* dinner," I said to the gentleman. "How's that for a deal?" Uwe nodded again, smiled, and sat down to more applause.

We moved on to the next question, but something felt different after our exchange. The huge room felt a little cozier because what transpired was a sweet, simple conversation between two people. Not between an employee and his CEO, or between a German and an American. We were two guys laughing and talking about getting older, getting paid, and getting together for a meal.

About ten minutes later, in the midst of answering a final question, I saw Uwe in his green sweater walking toward me with something in his hand. He popped onto the stage to give me his business card. I presumed he did not want me to forget who I had invited to dinner. Again, terrific. I looked at the card: Uwe Riegler, Sales Operations Manager. I smiled.

"Now that I'm getting to know you, maybe it better be dinner over a glass of wine. You are a good man! Thank you very much," I said.

Again, this exchange was small. So simple. Yet it felt profound. Not long after the all-hands meeting, I received an email from another SAP employee, Rita Marini:

Dear Bill,

Thank you for opening up during the recent all-hands and allowing us to get to know you more as a leader and as a person. I personally feel more honoured to be part of SAP after listening to the message you and Jim delivered.

Four years ago, when you were in Beijing, you took the time to shake our hands and said "thank you for your great work." It could be pure manners but to me, you showed sincerity and thoughtfulness that's left an impression on me. Personally, that simple gesture really encouraged me to push forward.

Thank you, Bill.

Best,

Rita

Letters such as Rita's meant so much to me. More than SAP's stock price on any given day, more than any media headline, analyst report, or a board review of my performance, her words reinforced that the journey SAP was on as a team—and the journey that I continued to be on as an individual—was the right one.

NEVER FORGET WHERE YOU CAME FROM

Storytelling is one of my favorite ways to simplify the world. That's why I always relish the opportunity to recall my days at the corner store or selling on the streets of New York City. The clarity of the goals back then, and the customer-centric approach and tactics I used at the deli and going door-to-door, transcend industries and cultures. These stories seem to resonate with so many different types of people at different stages in their lives, from CEOs to students.

The day I arrive to speak at Howard University in Washington, DC, I am greeted by the dean of the School of Business, Dr. Barron H. Harvey. Visiting with faculty and students at universities, and younger people in general, is a priority for me. I recently spoke at University College London and Capital University of Economics and Business in Beijing. In a few months, I would go to Harvard University to meet with MBA students who were conducting a case study on SAP's new strategy.

As a company, SAP maintains educational and recruiting relationships with universities around the world. We give them our technology so that students can learn it in classrooms and be more qualified to land jobs that require SAP knowledge. Another reason I love going to universities is that SAP is after the best young talent; having a campus presence ensures that we are top of the mind with bright, ambitious graduates. What's more, one of my goals is to put millennials in key jobs at SAP, reporting to a board member. Currently, my own office-of-the-CEO team—Deepak Krishnamurthy, Nick Tzitzon, Anke Otto-Jungkind, Corina Lam, and Hannah Datz—are each under thirty-five years old.

Third, *speaking* to students is always followed by *listening* to students, and in my quest to understand younger generations, I want to know what matters to them. Today's young people want a future that indulges their intense curiosity but also has a purpose beyond just making money. Almost every college student I meet today, as well as the high-performing twentysomethings employed by SAP—and my own two sons—want to make a positive difference in the world. And they are ready to work hard to do so.

The individuals I see at Howard University are no different. Their professionalism and hunger are palpable. Every one of the two hundred people in the auditorium, from freshman to faculty, is dressed in professional attire. Suits and ties. Skirts and blazers. Well coiffed and attentive, the students are sitting up straight, tablets and notepads ready. *These young people are wearing the jacket!*

I begin my talk by telling the story of the deli. I end with a few words about what SAP is trying to accomplish today. The audience seems to pay equal attention to each topic, as if searching for clues. At the end, I tell them the secret to success is not all that complicated: "You've got to want it more." When I invite questions, almost every hand shoots up. One young woman says she plans on becoming a CEO one day and asks for my advice. *How she owns her ambition!* "You must be proud of whatever organization you choose to work for," I offer, "then pour yourself into it completely, and do not let anyone else but you shape your future." She makes fantastic eye contact, and I return her resolute gaze. "I can tell from your determination that you will be what you aspire to be. I have no doubt."

After more questions, and some parting words, the students line up in the front of the auditorium to speak with me, one-on-one.

Just when I think the experience cannot get any sweeter, a young woman in a buttoned-up navy blue suit, white blouse, and pearls is standing in front of me. "Hi, I'm from Amityville, Long Island." Amazing, yet not really.

No one's past ever disappears, nor should it. My memories of vacuuming up flood waters, delivering newspapers, hauling dirt, clearing tables, waxing floors, serving customers, and climbing stairs on hot Manhattan days with a copy machine strapped to my back are never far from my own mind. My history keeps me rooted, even as I strive.

Of course, I do not know this young woman's history, but I do know that her story is just beginning.

The two of us pose for a photo. Later that day, I send it out with a tweet:

> Two kids from Amityville, Long Island,
> living our winning dreams.

The end . . . for now.

ACKNOWLEDGMENTS

THE DECISION TO start sharing my story began with a desire to inspire others to embrace their own "winner's dream" with resolve and passion. As more people suggested I write a book, I did so with the intention of giving readers a front-row seat to my experiences as I lived them. The book was also an opportunity to recognize the many people who helped shape my own winner's dream.

Since my earliest years, I've been surrounded by believers. I am forever grateful for their support throughout my life, as well as for helping me share my story now.

Most significantly, my family. My mother, Kathleen, remains the soul and inspiration of my life. Without her bright light and winner's dream from the beginning, none of this would be possible. Mom, I will never forget . . . To my dad, Bill: You are my father, my coach, my friend, and I thank you for everything you continue to do for our family, and for being the best dad there is.

My highest aspiration has been to be a good husband and father, and that remains my passion. To my wife, Julie: From the moment we met and through each year together, your presence and love makes my winner's dream possible. You are the heart and soul of our family, and an incredible mother. Marrying you was the single best decision of all. I am beyond grateful for your partnership in life, as well as with this book. We lived so much of the story together, and in reviewing the manuscript you were able to see the big picture while refining the smallest details. Your wise counsel enhanced every page of *Winners Dream*. I love you, Julie.

To my incredible sons, Michael and John, my greatest accomplishment and most meaningful legacy: I could not be more proud of each of you. Your determination, your talents, and your achievements are made more impressive by your generosity, kindness to others, and your respect for humanity. I feel so blessed to share in your lives, and I look forward to *your* winners' dreams unfolding—on your terms.

To my brother, Kevin: From childhood to today, you have always been so much more than a sibling—you are my friend, my confidant, and always my best man. You have the biggest heart of anyone I know, and my respect for you is immense. Gennifer, you are a sister and a soul mate. When Mom was sick you were her North Star, and your tireless care for her through thick and thin meant so much to Mommy and to all of us. I deeply admire your inherent goodness and strength of character; they are your essence. You are a hero. Our special bond is forever.

I am also appreciative to my aunts, uncles, and cousins. My uncle Jack introduced me to California and the world beyond the East Coast enclaves where I grew up; Uncle Gene's early influence exposed me to the business world. To my best high school buddy, Eddie Kubacz, who died too young at thirty-four from the effects of lupus disease. For all the great times, especially when you picked up our wedding tab, thank you and God bless you always. In the end, I am who I am because of my family, as well as friends who believed in me. I realize that some people came to believe in me over time as they wondered whether "it was real," which makes what we have today even more significant.

Documenting my life for the book has been a journey unto itself. Looking back to revisit the past helped me look forward, and the process enhanced my ability to lead in the present. My writing collaborator, Joanne Gordon, was a remarkable partner in the book's evolution. She found my voice on the page, and helped me write my story in a manner that allowed me to prioritize the demands of running a global corporation. I could not have possibly imagined a better writer and friend. For SAP as well as for *Winners Dream*, Nick Tzitzon continues to pour his heart and soul into all of our work together, almost as much as I do. And after so many years together, Barbara Rendina is not only an amazing executive assistant, but a trusted confidante. Barb, I am thankful for all you do every day.

To the entire team at CAA, your belief in the power of my story kicked off this journey. In addition to Richard Lovett, Michael Levine, Paul Danforth, Rob Slocum, Zach Nadler, Michelle Kydd Lee, and Jeff Jacobs, I especially want to thank Simon Green, whose enthusiasm and expertise steered the book in the right direction. At Simon & Schuster, my story found a perfect home. Jonathan Karp shared our vision from day one, and throughout the process Ben Loehnen's editorial guidance honed the story for readers while honoring its authenticity. Additional thanks go to Brit Hvide, Lance Fitzgerald, Jackie Seow, Richard Rhorer, Elina Vaysbeyn, Seth Russo, Tim Murphy, Phillip Bashe, Joel Breuklander, and Irene Kheradi for their commitment, creativity, and for helping to bring the book to readers around the world. I am also appreciative to our transcriber, Chris Gorley, for her precision and professionalism; to Heidi Peiper for her diligent fact checking; and to the talented photographer Blake Little and his exceptional crew.

To supplement my own memories for the book, more than fifty people kindly took time to share their own recollections from as far back as my days in Amityville and my earliest years at Xerox. Recalling our times together felt like a joyful family reunion. Each person in *Winners Dream* made the book—and more importantly made my life—richer. I am forever grateful.

Every day at SAP I am honored to work among tens of thousands of talented, committed individuals. Although there are too many to name in this short space, I would especially like to acknowledge Hasso Plattner, for believing in me throughout our global journey together, as well as Jim Hagemann Snabe, for being a fantastic co-CEO and friend. I would also like to thank SAP's executive board—Werner Brandt, Rob Enslin, Bernd Leukert, Gerd Oswald, and Luka Mucic—for their ongoing support. In addition, SAP and the book have benefited from the expertise of Deepak Krishnamurthy, Alex Atzberger, Richard Knowles, Brad Brubaker, Melissa Lea, and Courtney Robinson. A special thank-you to Greg McStravick, who for twenty-five years has been a trusted colleague and dear friend.

In addition to the people acknowledged above, my collaborator, Joanne Gordon, would also like to thank her literary agent, Stuart Krichevsky; her dear friends; and her loving family—David and Virginia Gordon; Susan Newman; and especially her extraordinary son, Theo—for giving her the freedom and support to pursue her own dreams, then as now.

Finally, to readers. Thank you for sharing in my journey. My intent was to connect with you on an emotional level through authentic stories. My humble hope is that my book furthered the pursuit of your own winner's dream. Why? Because your winner's dream is the essence of who you are. It is your power; it is your strength. Your winner's dream represents *your* hunger, *your* inner magic, *your* capacity for empathy and for execution. The purity of your winner's dream is what emboldens you to triumph over thunderbolts and be a crusader on behalf of yourself and those around you. So imagine it, be ever loyal to it, and be forever inspired by it. Ultimately, your winner's dream is *your* journey as you strive to be true to yourself and create a life of authenticity.

My deepest appreciation,
Bill McDermott

INDEX